The New Unionism

Contemporary Issues Series

1   Tariq Ali (ed.): *New Revolutionaries: Left Opposition*
2   A. B. Downing (ed.): *Euthanasia and the Right to Death: The Case for Voluntary Euthanasia*
3   Keith Hindell and Madeleine Simms: *Abortion Law Reformed*
4   Geoffrey Spyer: *Architect and Community: Environmental Design in an Urban Society*
5   R. S. Morton: *Sexual Freedom and Venereal Disease*
6   Ken Coates and Tony Topham: *The New Unionism: The Case for Workers' Control*

Ken Coates and Tony Topham

The New Unionism

THE CASE FOR WORKERS' CONTROL

PETER OWEN · LONDON

ISBN 0 7206 0242 4

PETER OWEN LIMITED
12 Kendrick Mews Kendrick Place London SW7

First British Commonwealth edition 1972
© 1972 Ken Coates and Tony Topham

Printed in Great Britain by
Bristol Typesetting Co Ltd
Barton Manor St Philips Bristol

Foreword

In spite of the best efforts of our publishers, this book was completed almost a year before we were able to see it set in type. In some fields of inquiry, a year is of no consequence. But in this area, a year is a very long time indeed. Writing now in April 1972, there are a number of quite crucial developments which, while they have made it possible for the reader to judge how far the argument contained in these pages stands up against the facts, have also necessitated some brief introductory remarks.

When we completed our manuscript, the collapse of the Upper Clyde Shipbuilding Consortium was a brand-new event, as shocking as the fall of Rolls-Royce, and while there was widespread public concern about the matter, the mutterings about 'working in' were still, from the viewpoint of an outsider, very largely speculative. Everyone knows what in fact happened : the workers not only announced the occupation of their shipyards, but appealed to the whole Labour Movement for support, while they took control of the gates of the yards, admitted the press and television to what must have been the most publicized industrial dispute of modern times, and guaranteed work to all of their colleagues who faced 'dismissal' by the liquidator. The response was electric. The two largest mass demonstrations in Scottish Labour history shook Glasgow, Scotland and the Government. Many thousands of pounds flowed into the Clyde shop stewards' fighting fund, from British trade unions and the world at large. The Labour Party and the TUC resolved upon the nationalization of the shipbuilding industry. For months the struggle continued, until the Government announced the decision to grant substantial financial aid to three of the four yards which it had reprieved from closure, and to look favourably upon a bid from an American corporation to rehabilitate the fourth yard for the construction of oil drilling rigs. Long before this decision, the final results of which are not, at the time of writing, completely clear, the example of UCS had swept through the factories and produced a veritable host of imitators : first at the plant of Plessey's, just mentioned in our text; then at the River Don Steel Plant, where a 'work-in' did much to

5

rescue a major sector of the Sheffield steel industry from the ill-effects of mass redundancies arising out of rationalization projects; then again, in quick succession, in a series of largely successful 'sit-ins' at Allis Chalmers in Mold, Fisher-Bendix in Liverpool and elsewhere; and most recently in an experiment in full self-management at a small leather goods enterprise in Norfolk. If workers have been quick to utilize and develop the new weapon of factory occupations in a variety of responses against arbitrary dismissal, at the same time it has also been deployed with considerable effectiveness in an extended dispute on pay and conditions in the engineering industry, which resulted in the occupation of more than a score of plants as workers were threatened with lockouts when they announced a work-to-rule in support of their claims.

UCS clearly triggered off a substantial response. But its example not only transformed a whole series of industrial disputes : it also provided quite novel examples in a wider field. The idea of a social audit, stocktaking the full social costs of adverse industrial decisions, canvassed in this book, was vividly brought to life by the Scottish TUC, in its inquiry into the social effects of the UCS closures.[1] This inquiry, which summoned a wide range of expert witnesses, was the first of many which will be brought into being by the Labour Movement, as it confronts the anti-social results of a whole series of business activities and decisions.

All these developments have naturally stimulated interest in the central concern of this book, which is the growth of an explicit trade-union demand for workers' control over the major decisions involved in modern industry. Of course, the impulse which pushed forward the wave of factory occupations was the defence of the 'right to work'. The workers concerned were not asserting their right to manage their enterprises for themselves, and they were willing to negotiate about any proposals which could gain their employment security. At the same time, it has been clear to everyone who has cared to examine the situation that the 'right to work' could only be asserted, in the conditions of 1971, *against* the traditional managerial prerogative to hire and fire at will, and even more significantly, *against* the logic of the market, which had

---

[1] Cf. Michael Barratt Brown, *UCS: The Social Audit,* Institute for Workers' Control pamphlet (1971), and Robin Murray, *UCS: The Anatomy of Bankruptcy* (Spokesman Books, 1972).

ordained that certain operations were 'unviable'—which is to say, unprofitable in narrow commercial terms. The significance of the call for a social audit, and of the repeated insistence of the UCS shop stewards on the human priorities they have been defending, is that it poses a radical challenge to the basic assumptions of private capitalism, and to the authorities which administer its institutions.

A similar threat, on a different level, was dramatically issued by the British miners, in their extraordinary strike during the early weeks of 1972.[2] Their strategy of aggressive picketing of power stations precipitated a deluge of letters to the newspapers, pointing out that the coal in those stations had been 'bought and paid for' by the Electricity Generating Board, and was therefore no concern of the miners. The miners, and legions of railwaymen and lorry-drivers, totally disregarded these arguments, although there is good reason to suppose that a few years ago they would have done no such thing. The most sacred institution of modern industrial exploitative society, private property, had become an obstacle to be overcome and routed. Routed it was, with the most important trade-union victory of modern times. It is no accident that on the day after the strike, Mr Joe Gormley, the miners' President, was giving an interview to a socialist weekly in which he was prepared to consider far-reaching changes in the structure of the National Coal Board.

The whole issue of democratic control of the nationalized industries is obviously brought in question by such events. A nationalized shipbuilding industry could scarcely be administered on authoritarian Morrisonian principles, after the lessons of the Upper Clyde. The gross inadequacy of the Coal Board from the miners' viewpoint could not have been more openly revealed than it was in a dispute of unparalleled militancy, unity and, let it be said, bitterness.

While industrial relations were being transformed in the new upsurge of trade-union self-confidence, the Government was carefully working through to reach the final stages of its Industrial Relations reform, designed to contain and roll back trade-union rank-and-file initiative and power. The TUC responded with a qualified refusal to co-operate. The Labour Party in opposition was

[2] For the background to this dispute, see Michael Barratt Brown, *What Really Happened to the Coal Industry?*, Institute for Workers' Control pamphlet (1972).

compelled not merely to reject the whole of this package of institutions and rules, but to seek to elaborate alternative proposals.
The most plausible of these at the time of writing appears to be a
proposal for an Industrial Democracy Act, which, after the repeal
of the whole apparatus of constraint upon the unions, would
attempt to legislate for the widening of trade-union influence and
effective power. As to whether such proposals will be agreed, it
is too early to be certain. They are certainly being canvassed, and
at the very least they will provoke the most general debate that
has yet taken place on the issue of democratic control of work
and of economic life.

Aside from these general considerations, there are a number of
specific points which should be added to the narrative of our text.
Firstly, in our discussion of the structure of the nationalized steel
industry, we have documented the shortcomings (which have been
considerable) of the limited scheme for the appointment of
'worker-directors', who were neither appointed by, nor accountable
to, their supposed constituents.

In March 1972, BSC announced its intention to amend the
worker-director scheme. This decision followed a confidential inquiry, led by Ken Alexander of Strathclyde University and involving
research workers from three other universities. The main revisions
of the scheme, which received the backing of the TUC Steel Committee, are :

(i)   Improvement will aim at 'helping employee directors give
      a shop-floor point of view in divisional boardrooms'.
(ii) Links with unions will be strengthened, and employee
      directors will be given the right to hold union office.
(iii) Individual unions will decide how local membership
      should make nominations—which will then be short-listed
      by the Steel Committee and Corporation together. BSC's
      Chairman will still make the final appointments.
(iv) Employee directors will concentrate on those works which
      fall in their 'designated areas', whilst still taking an interest
      in division matters as a whole.[3]

These changes, which are modest, reflect the great weight of
criticism levelled at the original scheme, from within the steel
unions, and by commentary from outside the industry. The

[3] Details are from *Steel News*, BSC's newspaper (2nd March, 1972).

Alexander inquiry will, we hope, be published in full, since it contains a detailed analysis of workers' attitudes, particularly on the fundamental question of the accountability of workers' representatives to their constituents.

Secondly, in documenting the complex growth of modern technologies and the new industrial concentrations which implement these, we have drawn attention to the plans, which were under consideration at the time we wrote, to create a new productive centre around the scheduled new London Airport at Foulness.

More recently, the Government has announced preliminary plans for the development of the Foulness complex. It appears from these that heavy industry (including steel production) will be excluded from the site. At about the same time (later in 1971), it was revealed that the earlier European project for a merger between the German steel firm of Hoesch, and Hoogovens of Holland, was to go ahead after all. A central company owned 50-50, will be set up near the German-Dutch border. German trade unions withdrew their earlier objections to the merger when the two firms accepted that the joint company would be subject to a workers' participation formula.

None of this affects our general point, that the Foulness project highlights the urgent need for trade-union unity in the face of multi-national 'planning' of conglomerate investment schemes. It does, however, leave further question-marks surrounding the future of British Steel and its work-force.

Thirdly, our somewhat pessimistic concern with the affairs of the National Union of General and Municipal Workers, whose leaders have certainly been the rearguard of the old orthodoxies within the TUC, has presented one side of the balance-sheet which was very plain at the time we wrote. Today, the other side is becoming more and more apparent, as a veritable upsurge of rank-and-file concern has made itself felt within the union. Not only has the public commitment of its main spokesman, Lord Cooper, to consider registering his organization under the terms of the Industrial Relations Act, been overruled by the pressures of his membership and of his colleagues in the TUC : but in a whole series of militant actions, both at UCS, in the engineering sit-ins in Lancashire, and elsewhere, rank-and-file NUGMW members have revealed an audacity and flair which speak sharply against the notion that bureaucratic control of their union retains its former total authority.

Of course, there is not a section or indeed a chapter of this book which would not benefit from expansion in the light of the experiences of the last few months. All this emphasizes the truth that our task has always been one which has involved us, all the time, above all in learning from the workpeople about whom we are writing. They are demanding teachers, and they have not yet given us the benefit of a fraction of their wisdom. We confidently expect to be taught much more in the near future.

KEN COATES AND TONY TOPHAM

Contents

CHAPTER   PAGE

   Acknowledgments   12

Part One: New Times, New Needs

1 The New Unionism   15
2 Some History   18
3 The Present Crisis   30
4 Some Definitions   39

Part Two: The Struggle for Workers' Control

5   Preconditions for Advance   63
6   Shop-Floor Controls   71
7   Control Over the Companies   86
8   The Social Audit   96
9   Workers' Control at the Industry Level   109
10 Trade-Union Strategy in the Public Sector   138
11 Trade Unions and Free Communications   148
12 Trade-Union Structure : Impediment or Stimulus?   155
13 A Political Arm for the Unions   179

Part Three: Participation

14 The Responses of Authority, and Some Answers   191

Part Four: Self-Management

15 Towards Self-Management   217

   Bibliography   237

   Index   241

Acknowledgments

Above all we wish to acknowledge, with grateful thanks, the un-tiring guidance of Michael Barratt Brown, many of whose ideas and insights are quite shamelessly incorporated into this book, often without adequate attribution. The truth is, he has taught us so much that we can never be quite sure when we are in his debt.

With the same sense of obligation, we need to place on record our very great debt to all the members of the Institute for Workers' Control, whether trade-union activists, academics or professional workers: without their comradeship and expertise, freely and generously granted, we would have made far more mistakes than those we have, doubtless, made here. To Bill Jones and Ernie Roberts we owe a special word of thanks, because their patience and dogged persistence against very large odds have not only put them in the front line in their organizations, but have made them very wise counsels as well as courageous examples.

We also want to thank, with no less warmth, our wives and families and those colleagues who sustained us through the work of preparing and writing this book, together with Michael Levien for his exceptionally painstaking concern with the details of its publication.

K.C. and T.T

Part One

New Times, New Needs

Chapter 1

The New Unionism

The Labour Movement, like all other institutions of contemporary society, is in the midst of a great crisis, in which a moody flux of ideas and actions stirs, seethes, and at times bubbles over. Old and hitherto unquestioned traditions come to be the object of fierce controversy, while new methods of work and adaptations to conditions begin to produce quite novel reactions and attitudes. Basic assumptions which were universal yesterday seem suddenly to be quite absurd. While the crisis of British society is very much a result of contradictions within its structure, above all within the economy of a one-time imperial metropolis relegated to the status of a middle-rank power, the crisis of trade unionism does more than simply reflect the overall difficulties of the body politic in which it is situated. Trade unions, like *all* other organizations, are at least partly motivated by the external and internal social pressures which are brought to bear upon them : in part, they react to circumstances which they did not determine and over which they have had no control. But trade unions are also like *some* other organizations in that they come to form goals of their own, which influence not only their own behaviour, but also that of those upon whom they act. There have, in the past, been many changes in the circumstances of trade unionism which have not fundamentally altered trade-union ideals and aspirations. Yet, from time to time, throughout recent English history, there have been major upheavals in which the Labour Movement has succeeded in reshaping its own model of the world. William Blake pointed to the distortions that occur if you 'see with, not thro', the eye'. The same immediate constellation of facts can mean very different things to people whose imaginations work at different levels. The imaginations of working people, their ideas of what they hold in potential, their notions of what they have it in themselves to be, can only develop fully when they are able to create organizations in which they can see effective means for changing their conditions. How-

ever, such organizations have always up to now been met by and
contained within the very world which they have sought to transform, and this has recurrently dashed the hopes of succeeding
generations of their members. As hope has been eroded, so bureaucracy has swollen out to fill the space left behind. Bureaucracy in
the Labour Movement is not primarily a matter of the division of
routine labour, or of caste : privileged (or at any rate powerful)
elites do emerge as the process unwinds, but they emerge for a
reason. That reason, which may be, at the immediate level, any one
of a hundred material pressures, begins to impose itself in a situation in which expectation is cheapened, in which hopes are dulled,
and in which the goal of human brotherhood is obscured by a mass
of practical concerns.

Today, we seem to be on the brink of a new resurgence of trade-
union idealism, of concern with far more than the day-to-day
defence of gains made. Due to its very structure, society seems
less and less capable of releasing the scope of the people caught
within it : even at the crudest material level, the contradiction
appears openly and unashamedly, for while each firm is concerned
to discourage greed in *its own* employees, since it needs to buy
labour as cheaply as is consistent with the quality of its products, in
order to maximize its returns, it is at the same time hell-bent upon
inciting greed in every *other* firm's employees, in order to be able
to dispose of what it has manufactured. So we get multi-million-
pound advertising campaigns, some of which are blatantly trivial,
but all of which are insistent to the highest degree; while from time
to time we are encouraged to listen to sermons about the virtues
of thrift and self-sacrifice.

Even aside from its crises, this society is awakening needs and
desires far faster than it can slake them. But the crises are there,
and they serve to aggravate the difficulties. Clever and well-
educated working men (who today number millions) find all this
more and more intolerable, and they are increasingly ready to
reject it as the model for humane social organization. At the same
time they are, every day, made sharply aware of the unreason-
ing and oppressive authoritarianism which is necessary to administer
it. So the need for new goals, or revised versions of old, largely forgotten ones, is becoming more and more real, more and more
imperative. Of course, in George Woodcock's rather academic
jargon, in the trade-union movement 'structure is a function of

purpose'. New goals imply changed organizational forms, the development of new methods of work. The argument which has been awakening among active trade unionists during the past years has not yet produced a new consensus among the established organizations of Labour. Old ways of thinking and organizing still maintain their hold, and there is still some uncertainty about what the unions of the late 'seventies will look like, never mind about how society itself will appear by 1984. What is not in doubt is that things will not stay as they are.

When we speak of 'the new unionism' we are trying to define the kind of trade unionism which we want to see prevailing during the next five years or so. We think that the seeds of this trade unionism are presently germinating, and we are optimistic that they will thrive and ripen. Of course, the peculiar English climate may prove too much for this hope. If trade unionism does not evolve in the direction of larger social ambitions, demanding the pursuit of wider goals, there is no evidence at all that it will be allowed to linger on in its present state, defensively adapting itself to conditions which no longer correspond in the slightest degree to those with which it was designed to contend.

Chapter 2

Some History

The label 'the new unionism' applies already to one particular historical event, and we are, not unnaturally, aware of the parallel which this suggests with our own times. There is some controversy among historians as to the exact significance of the chain of events which began with the match-girls' strike of 1888 and culminated in the Great Dock Strike of 1889. The 'new' unions may not have been so novel as their organizers believed, and their development may have been more convoluted and less consistent than was supposed, or at any rate claimed, by the Webbs in their *History of Trade Unionism*. This does not in the least affect our argument, because what was undeniably 'new' in the 1889 upsurge has something very clearly in common with those things which we think are 'new' in our own situation today. That the 1880s are a world away from our time, and that the future is not necessarily written in the past, we do not for a second wish to deny.

Three years before he came into prominence as one of the key leaders of the London Dock Strike, Tom Mann wrote a pamphlet entitled *What a Compulsory Eight Hour Working Day Means to the Workers*. It contained this passionate appeal:

> To Trade Unionists, I desire to make a special appeal. How long, *how long* will you be content with the present half-hearted policy of your unions? I readily grant that good work has been done in the past by the unions, but in Heaven's name, what good purpose are they serving now? All of them have large numbers out of employment even when their trade is busy. None of the important societies have any policy other than of endeavouring to keep wages from falling. The true unionist's policy of *aggression* seems entirely lost sight of; in fact the average unionist of today is a man with a fossilised intellect, either hopelessly apathetic, or supporting a policy that plays directly into the hands of the capitalist exploiter.[1]

[1] Dona Torr, *Tom Mann and His Times,* Vol. 1 (Lawrence & Wishart, 1952), pp. 214–18.

Words like these give some impression of the commitment which was to trigger off the explosion of trade-union organization among the unskilled workers. For all the later qualifications which have been written around it by specialists in trade-union history, the Webbs summed it up very clearly :

The great dock strike of 1889 was the culmination of an attempt to organize the unskilled workers which had begun in London two or three years before. The privations suffered by the un-employed labourers during the years of depression of trade, and the new spirit of hopefulness due to the Socialist propaganda, had led to efforts being made to bring the vast hordes of un-skilled workmen in the metropolis into some kind of organization. At first this movement made very little progress. In July 1888, however, the harsh treatment suffered by the women employed in making lucifer matches roused the burning indignation of Mrs Besant, then editing *The Link*, a little weekly newspaper. . . . A fiery article had the unexpected result of causing the match-girls' revolt; and 672 of them came out on strike. Without funds, without organization, the struggle seemed hopeless. But . . . public opinion was aroused in a manner never before witnessed . . . and after a fortnight's obstinacy the employers were com-pelled, by sheer pressure of public opinion, to make some con-cessions to their workers.

The match-girls' victory turned a new leaf in Trade Union annals. Hitherto success had been in almost exact proportion to the workers' strength. It was a new experience for the weak to succeed because of their very weakness, by means of the interven-tion of the public. The lesson was not lost on other classes of workers. The London gas-stokers were being organized by Burns, Mann, and Tillett, aided by William Thorne, himself a gas-worker, and a man of sterling integrity and capacity. The Gas-Workers and General Labourers' Union, established in May 1889, quickly enrolled many thousands of members who in the first days of August simultaneously demanded a reduction of their hours of labour from twelve to eight per day. After an interval of acute suspense . . . the eight-hour day, to the general surprise of the men no less than the public, was conceded without a struggle, and was even accompanied by a slight increase of the week's wages.

The success of such unorganised and unskilled workers as the Match-makers and the Gas-Stokers led to renewed efforts to bring the great army of Dock labourers into the ranks of trade unionism. For two years past prominent London Socialists had journeyed to the dock gates in the early hours of the morning to preach organised revolt to the crowds of casuals struggling for work. Meanwhile Benjamin Tillett was spending his strength in the apparently hopeless task of constituting the Tea-workers and General Labourers' Union. The membership of this society fluctuated between 300 and 2,500 members; it had practically no funds; and its very existence seemed precarious. Suddenly the organization received a new impulse. An insignificant dispute on the 12th of August, 1889 . . . brought on an impulsive strike of the labourers at the South-West India Dock. The men demanded sixpence an hour, the abolition of sub-contract and piecework, extra pay for overtime, and a minimum engagement of four hours. Tillett called to his aid his friends Tom Mann and John Burns, and appealed to the whole body of dock labourers to take up the fight. The strike spread rapidly to all the docks north of the Thames. Within three days ten thousand labourers had, with one accord, left the precarious and ill-paid work to get which they had, morning after morning, fought at the dock gates . . . and in the course of the next week practically all the river-side labour had joined the strike. Under the magnetic influence of John Burns, who suddenly became famous as a labour leader on both sides of the globe, the traffic of the world's greatest port was, for over four weeks, completely paralysed. An electric spark of sympathy with the poor dockers fired the enthusiasm of all classes of the community. Public disapproval hindered the docks' companies from obtaining, even for their unskilled labour, sufficient blacklegs to take the strikers' place. A public subscription of £48,736 allowed . . . an elaborate system of strike-pay, which not only maintained the honest docker, but also bribed every East End loafer to withhold his labour; and finally the concentrated pressure of editors, clergymen, shareholders, ship-owners, and merchants, enabled Cardinal Manning and Sydney (afterwards Lord) Buxton, as self-appointed mediators, to compel the Dock Directors to concede practically the whole of the men's demands. . . .

The immediate result of the dockers' success was the formation of a large number of Trade Unions among the unskilled labourers. Branches of the Dock, Wharf and Riverside Labourers' Union (into which Tillett's little society was now transformed) were established at all the principal ports. A rival society of dockers, established at Liverpool, enrolled thousands of members at Glasgow and Belfast. The unskilled labourers in Newcastle joined the Tyneside and National Labour Union, which soon extended to all the neighbouring towns. The Gas-Workers' Union enrolled tens of thousands of labourers of all kinds in the provincial cities. Organisation began again among the farm labourers. The National Union of Agricultural Labourers, which had sunk to a few thousand scattered members, suddenly rose in 1890 to over 14,000. . . . Within a year after the dockers' victory probably over 200,000 workers had been added to the Trade Union ranks, recruited from sections of the labour world formerly abandoned as incapable of organisation. All these societies were marked by low contributions and comprehensive membership. They were, at the outset, essentially, if not exclusively devoted to trade protection, and were largely political in their aims. Their characteristic spirit is aptly expressed by the resolution of the Congress of the General Railway Workers' Union on the 19th of November 1890 : 'That the Union shall remain a fighting one, and shall not be encumbered with any sick or accident fund.' 'We have at present,' reports the General Secretary of the National Union of Gas-Workers and General Labourers in November 1889, 'one of the strongest labour Unions in England. It is true we have only one benefit attached, and that is strike pay. I do not believe in having sick-pay, out-of-work pay, and a number of other pays. . . . The whole aim and intention of this Union is to reduce the hours of labour and reduce Sunday work.'

A wave of Trade Unionism, comparable in extent with those of 1833-34 and 1873-74, was now spreading into every corner of British industry.[2]

A (for the most part) cogent series of objections to the Webbs' interpretation of these events can be found in Chapter 2 of Clegg, Fox and Thompson's definitive *History of Trade Unions*.[3] Clegg has argued that the Webbs, who were out of sympathy with the leaders of the old craft unions, failed to appreciate the grass-roots advances made by their organizations and overestimated the consistency and dynamism of the new forces. Will Thorne (who was, it is said, taught to read by Eleanor, the daughter of Karl Marx), the outspoken opponent of 'sick pay, out-of-work pay' and so on quoted by the Webbs, was by no means able to speak for all his colleagues in the new organizations : both the Seamen's Union and the National Amalgamated Union of Labour paid accident and funeral benefits from the moment of their inauguration.[4] Yet this does not for one moment detract from the point that the friendly

[2] Sidney and Beatrice Webb, *History of Trade Unionism* (1912), Workers' Education Association Edition, pp. 388-92.
[3] Vol. 1 (Oxford: Clarendon Press, 1964).
[4] Ibid., pp. 94 *et seq.*

society component in the new unions was, in the heat of their
formation, distinctly secondary to their combative and militant
role. The great growth of membership recorded by the Webbs,
was, as the modern critics document in detail, distinctly set back
when the employers began an organized counter-attack in subsequent years. But virgin territory had by then been occupied by
trade-union organization, and it was never wholly surrendered
again, even if its defence was sometimes difficult. The tactics
of the great upsurge of 1889 were certainly modified in subsequent
battles, but it was the original strategy which ensured that there
were gains in the first place to maintain or advance.

The new unions picketed aggressively, a circumstance that owed
much to the fact that they suffered more from the incursions of
blackleg labour than did the established craftsmen's unions, since
their professional skill-barrier was so much lower than it would
normally be in the craft sectors. They were heavily professionalized,
spending large sums on organizers' salaries, but it is clear that
this fact, too, arose from the nature of their task, which was to
service a less educated and more shifting population than that represented by the old unions. The new unions were intensely political
in the broad sense, even though not all their leaders were socialists :
all of them understood political action as a far more pressing
necessity than had the old Lib-Lab trade-union leaders, and all
construed it within different terms, bringing it closer to the ground
and seeking to make its impact immediate and direct.

The instinctive political genius of the agitators who came together into the leadership of the Great Dock Strike can be plainly
seen in the skilful use which they were able to make of the newspapers. Mass-circulation daily newspapers were a new force in the
late 'eighties : the development of rotary presses, newsprint manufacture from wood-pulp, the first fallout of the Education Act,
and the existence of an extended railway network combined to
make possible an unprecedented growth of the press.[5] Printing
orders for daily journals could rise from thousands to hundreds of
thousands. In the 'fifties all the major national daily newspapers
had circulations of well under 10,000. By the 'eighties the time was
ripe for the forerunners of the modern newspapers. Such radical
breakouts as *Reynold's Newspaper,* which was itself to play an

[5] See Raymond Williams, *The Long Revolution* (Chatto & Windus, 1961),
Pt II Chap. 3.

important role in the Dock Strike, had long established that Sunday journalism, at any rate, could be relatively big business. It was joined in 1888 by the *Star*, the first modern (evening) daily newspaper. 'Everything about it was brisk, bright and human. Its largest article was only half a column,' writes Francis Williams.[6] It was a radical journal, aiming directly at the newly literate strata of the working and lower-middle classes, and ready to agitate on a wide range of questions in order to build its circulation. It employed the young George Bernard Shaw as its music critic, who peppered his reports about concerts with socialist agitation : 'What we want is not music for the people, but bread for the people, rest for the people, hope for them, enjoyment, equal respect and consideration, life and aspiration, instead of drudgery and despair. When we get that I imagine the people will make tolerable music for themselves, even if all Beethoven's scores perish in the interim.'[7]

It was sufficiently sympathetic to the workers' cause to prompt Engels to write to Lafargue in Paris insisting that he organize the bombardment of its office with letters, in order to counteract the lies of a rival socialist faction which had won over the *Star* correspondent with 'absinthe and vermouth'.[8] Of the public subscription of £48,736 for the Dock Strike, reported by the Webbs, only some £16,000 was subscribed in Great Britain. Trade-union bodies gave £4,200, but the appeals of the *Star* brought in a total of £6,700, by far the largest single British contribution.[9] If the *Star* could play so large a part in funding the struggle, its role in overall public relations can hardly be overstated. The dockers' victory, like the earlier triumph of the match-girls, was the first social victory of the emerging mass-media. They were soon to be called to order and set to work, in disciplined formation, for the other side.

If the impact of the new unions was dramatic, their subsequent deployment was severely practical and profoundly political. Such bodies as the Gas-Workers' Union rapidly began a serious labour of grass-roots campaigning and organization, contesting a whole

[6] *Dangerous Estate* (Arrow Books, 1959), pp. 114 *et seq.*
[7] *London Music as Heard by Corno di Bassetto* (Constable, 1937), p. 133.
[8] *Engels-Lafargue Correspondence*, Vol. II (Moscow: Foreign Languages Publishing House, 1960), p. 240.
[9] See the balance-sheet reproduced in Ann Stafford's *A Match to Fire the Thames* (Hodder & Stoughton, 1961). The bulk of the funding was of course subscribed by the colonies, notably Australia. Some large part of this was collected in response to the appeal of *Reynold's Newspaper*.

series of local elections, through which means they secured representation on local authorities with substantial controls over the industry
in which they worked. It is scarcely an exaggeration to say that the
work begun in 1889 was to culminate in the formation of the
Labour Party itself, and not only because of the growth of local
socialist activity which it produced. At the heart of the agitation
which mobilized the gas-workers, the dockers and the rest was the
crusade for shorter working hours, which was understood in a very
much deeper sense than simple social amelioration.

Tom Mann, who had published his first tract on the issue of
shorter hours, described in his *Memoirs,* exactly how, as a boy, he
came to appreciate the shorter working week, and what it meant
to him :

> We settled in Birmingham, and I became apprenticed to a tool-
> making firm. This was in 1870, the year the Elementary Edu-
> cation Act was passed. Its operation was too late to be helpful
> to me, as I was already in my fifteenth year, when it became
> law, and had been at work five years. By degrees it dawned on
> me that I had missed something in the educational line . . . the
> only school I could attend was Sunday School, to which I went
> regularly, and I became a regular churchgoer as well. . . . The
> working hours at the factory were sixty a week . . . but fre-
> quently we were called upon to work overtime, usually two hours
> of an evening, thus leaving at eight o'clock instead of six
> o'clock, and as we started punctually at six in the morning, it
> made a long day of it.
>
> At this time I knew nothing at all about trade unionism, but
> occasionally one or other of the men would be pointed out to
> me as 'belonging to the Society'. I had no clear idea as to what
> this signified, until, when I was sixteen, I became conscious of
> some kind of activity amongst the men, particularly the 'Society
> men', which neither I nor my boy workmates could make much
> of. As the weeks passed, we overheard mention of the Beehive,
> the trade union paper, which, however, I have no recollection
> of having seen at that time. Then we heard of meetings being
> held. We youngsters had not so far been counted of sufficient
> importance to be consulted, or even informed, till we learned
> that the men were negotiating with the firm about the Nine-
> Hour Day. The next bit of news was indeed exciting. We learned
> that every person in the firm, men and boys, was summoned to a
> meeting. This was the first meeting of the kind I had ever
> attended. The proceedings did not last long. The business
> consisted of a report from the committee that had been negotiat-

ing with the firm for the nine-hour day, or fifty-four hour week, instead of the ten-hour day and the sixty-hour week. It was proposed that all should continue to start at six in the morning, and leave at five in the evening instead of six; also that there must be 'penalization of overtime'. This, I gathered, meant that the men would refuse to work overtime unless there was more than the ordinary time rate for it. All the proposals being endorsed, negotiations were continued and completed, the firm granting the conditions. How truly pleased I was I need not trouble to add, and how thoroughly all enjoyed the dinner held to celebrate the event required no further comment! I did not know at the time that there was a general move throughout the country establishing the nine-hour day in all engineering works; but so it was, and I had good reason to be glad of it.[10]

The earlier victory of the ten-hour movement had been hailed by Karl Marx as 'the first great victory of the political economy of labour over the political economy of capital'. In a very real sense this was true, but the immediate result was, for Tom Mann, an explosion of frontiers of a slightly different character to that hoped for by Marx :

The reduction of working hours to nine a day, coupled with the stoppage of overtime, had a very important bearing on my life. The firm having agreed to pay extra for overtime, very astutely gave orders immediately for a considerable extension of the factory, sufficient to accommodate an additional hundred men and boys. This was exactly what the men had aimed at, and I believe all were delighted at the diminution of overtime. For myself, I very rarely worked any overtime after this during the additional five years I remained there to complete my apprenticeship.

Fortunately for those of my age, others who had sorely felt the need of education, had already—in co-operation with influential persons—taken action to establish evening classes in the town. Thus, at the Midland Institute, at the Severn Street Institute, and elsewhere, classes on many subjects were available at very reasonable rates. Three evenings a week for five years I attended classes in connection with the Science and Art Department, South Kensington. In addition I attended a Bible class one evening a week, and found it very helpful. Also I went on one evening a week to the meeting of a temperance society of which I was a member. Every Sunday evening, along with a

[10] The Fitzroy Edition (MacGibbon & Kee, 1967), pp. 4–5.

young religious enthusiast, I attended a church or religious service of some kind, and became familiar with all varieties, not only of forms of worship and doctrine, but also of preachers and their styles. This left one evening only out of seven for ordinary purposes during the winter months.[11]

Within a few years Tom Mann had been converted to socialism and was interpreting the new gospel through his own very direct experience.

The campaign for shorter hours, which began as a bargaining demand, rapidly became a crusading political issue. 'A *legal* eight-hour' day became the slogan of the industrial agitators as well as Sidney Webb. Cunninghame-Graham tried to persuade the House of Commons to consider such a measure, and the Fabians published, as one of their earliest tracts, an Eight-hour Bill, which sold widely. Mann interrupted the deliberations of the Royal Commission on Labour, to which he was appointed, to consider proposals for an eight-hour day 'by trade and local option'. From hundreds of soap-boxes, stump orators preached the message. The first May Day demonstration in London, arranged (on a motion moved by Mann) by the London Trades Council, made it the central issue. Nothing could have been more neatly calculated to prise apart the tradi-tional loyalties of working-class supporters of the old political parties. Neither Tory nor Liberal could normally be expected to enthuse about wholesale reductions in hours, so that the pattern of conflicting interests, so frequently obscured in the nature of the political process in Britain, became, for growing numbers of young literate workers, plainly apparent. The reverses suffered in the counter-offensive of the employers' associations against the unions, and the ultimate indignity of the Taff Vale judgment at the turn of the century, might have taken a much more damaging toll of the workers' organizations, had it not been for the undercurrent of aggressive optimism which was generated in the eight-hour campaign. Simple in the extreme, the call for a shorter working week was more than a tactical demand : its effects were to produce all the elements of a strategic realignment of forces.

At the beginning of this upsurge Friedrich Engels was quite con-vinced that it spelt out a new departure for the English Socialist Movement. He saw in the ability of the socialists to reach down

[11] Ibid., pp. 5–6.

and organize that stratum of the working class 'which is only just above the *lumpen-proletariat*' a total novelty, which would transform the unions and overcome the innate conservatism of the craft-based sections. The very instability of the dock labour force was, in this assessment, an advantage, since it guaranteed the continual stable leadership of the socialist organizers of the upheaval. Things would never be the same again, he thought.

Nor were they. But they were seldom, if ever, as different again. The process by which the established order contained the revolt and restabilized the shifting ground upon which it rested, still needs extended analysis by the Labour Movement. The neutralization of the impact of the new unions took a long time, but was accomplished. As the Labour Party grew, it was the descendants of the gas-workers and the dock labourers who were able to provide solid support for a new elite of 'reforming' politicians, none of whom had the very slightest commitment to the kind of fundamental change to which Tom Mann devoted his whole life, or Will Thorne the best years of his youth. Engels's faith in the socialist leadership of the late 'eighties was misplaced : but there were social movements at work in this process of greater historical significance than the accumulated mistakes, or stupidity, or perfidy, of a handful of socialist innovators.

The sociology of the working class at the time of the outburst of the new unionism still, of course, comprehended a very extensive labour aristocracy, which had created the craft unions, alongside a huge underclass of grossly deprived people. Booth's survey, *Labour and Life of the People*, found one-third of the metropolitan population living in poverty, many concentrated in the dock area. By 1900 Rowntree had confirmed, by use of far more advanced sociological apparatus, a similar poverty statistic for York. The labour aristocracy thrived on until the First World War, and Eric Hobsbawm has itemized its decline from that time onwards under four headings.[12] In the first place, the basic industries of the nineteenth century collapsed, creating the depressed areas of the inter-war regime. Secondly, skill differentials were consistently eroded by changes in wage systems until the 1950s. Thirdly, mass-production techniques brought about the rise of a vast army of semi-skilled machine operators, while the numbers of unskilled labourers in such sectors of industry declined steeply : while,

[12] *Labouring Men* (Weidenfeld & Nicolson, 1968), pp. 300 *et seq.*

lastly, in some industries skilled men were 'declassed' by mechaniz-ation, and in most live industries the growth of technical and supervisory white-collar occupations reduced still further the lingering advantages of skill. Hobsbawm notes that these changes have frequently been accompanied by a political movement to the left by ex-craft unions, such as, for instance, the Boilermakers' and the Engineers' Unions. Yet, during the major part of this century, the great General Unions, under the heavily centralized leadership of Bevin, Deakin, Williamson and now Lord Cooper, have re-mained overwhelmingly faithful to the perspectives of a distinctly conservative Labour Party.

The basic alternative to this orthodoxy was again defined by Tom Mann, in the great syndicalist upheaval of which he became the spokesman in the years prior to 1914; in the amalgama-tion movement which began to regroup and consolidate trade-union forces; and in the post-war development of the 'minority move-ment' around the slogan of workers' control. In 1926 this phase of trade-union history was terminated, and Beatrice Webb wrote in her diary that the defeat of the General Strike was 'the death-gasp of that pernicious doctrine of "Workers' Control" . . . intro-duced by Tom Mann and the guild socialists'.

Just as Mann had discovered, in the late 1880s, in the shorter hours' campaign, a crucial lever for prising apart the great mass of working people from the received opinions of the social and cultural system in which they worked, so, before 1926, he had pioneered the first modern attack on the fundamental indignities of capitalism and industrial authoritarianism. The slavery of wage-workers may be more severe in poverty, or it may be mitigated by affluence, but it remains, in a fundamental sense, a very real slavery. To assume that high-wage levels, even if they were less imaginary than those dreamed up by the publicists who so loudly discuss the 'problems of affluence', could ever compensate for this basic unfreedom, is to assume that men are capable of putting aside their manhood and trampling upon their own spiritual potential. There is plenty of evidence that individual persons are indeed capable of this : but there is no evidence at all that such a condition can ever be acceptable to a whole society, to entire strata of its population.

If Tom Mann was prepared, as an apprentice agitator, to fight for the free time in which to learn to be a fuller human being, and if, as an older trade-union leader, he became an advocate of freedom in work itself, and a partisan of society in which industry would help people to realize their own personalities, to become what they have it in themselves to be : so, in the same way, the Labour Movement as a whole has recurrently extended its horizons, in order to look beyond the next meal or the additional paid holiday to the need for a new style of social living.

Yet from time to time the horizons have also been restricted. If things were not as Beatrice Webb predicted, after the General Strike, then at any rate the call for an emancipatory trade unionism lay dormant for many years after 1926. Men who were forced to preoccupy themselves with solutions to mass unemployment, to socially induced poverty, became all too content, during long years of privation and persecution, to narrow their vision and lower their aims. Forced to think small and see dark, the Labour Movement evolved, through the late 'thirties, the style of response which still cramps so many of its key leaders. In the political field, in particular, a succession of moral devaluations have reduced the idea of socialism to an abstraction as remote as the Holy Ghost— comforting in its absence, but distinctly subversive should it ever come near to materializing as a present fact.

But those days are over. The new unionism of the 1970s will involve new sectors of the work-force, and will consolidate the grip of trade unions on the technically advanced industries and services. It will endeavour to cater at the same time for the new poor, for the renewed army of unemployed, for the forgotten 10 per cent of Britain's population. But above all, it will either replicate the upsurge of 1889 in the crucial respect that it will re-establish the goal of a new social order, as an immediate, practical concern : or it will fail in all respects, and in the process result in a terrible setback for all the people it has come to represent.

Chapter 3

The Present Crisis

Largely as a result of the failure of the 1964-70 Labour governments the old complacency is cracking up. Today, a combination of new developments makes it unlikely that the unquestioned hegemony of the established order can ever be fully restored in any framework of consent. Firstly, the British economy faces acute structural crisis which, in the immediate future, can only get worse. The advanced world economy has, ever since the Second World War, been going through a new industrial revolution, based upon the militarily stimulated technologies of electronics, light alloys, plastics and artificial fibres. In this development Britain has been seriously outpaced, not only by the USA and Europe, but also by Japan. Caught in a contradictory role as a world banker and colonial policeman on the one hand, and an industrial power on the other, a succession of British governments have failed completely to find an adequate response to this situation. They have proved quite unable to juggle adeptly enough to keep all the necessary balls in the air. Their principal rivals have not merely secured faster growth-rates, and with them increments of competitive power : they have also secured, from the point of view of capital, a healthier 'mix' within those growth-rates, based on the introduction of the new techniques and machines which have augmented the net productive power of their economies. In Britain, a belated 'rationalization' drive under the Wilson Government produced a massive merger-boom, but it did not solve the problem of large-scale under-investment by the application of a wide scale of new plant and techniques, so much as it fudged the issue by making more intensive use of existing plant, much of which was already ailing; and at the same time increasing the numbers of unemployed and non-employed people in the overall economy.

The advocates of concentration of scale in the economy normally argue that it is a stabilizing factor. Sometimes it is, though *what* it stabilizes is a question worth asking. But in the case of Great

Britain, there is evidence that the merger-boom is having the opposite effect to that of stabilization of the economic structure.

> The Board of Trade estimated in 1969 that nearly 40% of the mergers falling within the statutory scope of the Monopolies Commission since 1965 created or strengthened a 'technical monopoly' (that is, one-third or more of the market share in the hands of a single firm). Over 80% of mergers were with other companies in the same product fields. Nevertheless, this does not create a stable monopolized system. Instead it produces simultaneously enough elements of monopoly power to require a greatly strengthened system of public accountability. . . . At the same time it *also* produces *violent competitive pressures*, often highly destructive of capital and of existing jobs and job expectations; in other words, a system in which each giant firm is having to run very hard (in research, in innovation, in cost reduction, in the exploitation of marketing techniques) to maintain its long-run security. Thus the typical company of this era is a multi-plant, multi-product company, and increasingly one that operates multi-nationally. . . . We are not looking at a stabilized, monopolized pattern of production and trade. The giant multi-product company may well exert some degree of monopoly power in relation to some parts of its product range; but in many other products, in other national markets . . . it is likely to have to face more or less intense competitive pressure.[1]

All this adds up, in Hughes's expression, to a 'highly dynamic and unstable system'. Even before the merger-boom, all post-war capitalist governments have depended upon enormous levels of direct State intervention, investment and spending, in order to stabilize and develop their economies. This new concentration makes such intervention all the more necessary. But the pressure to cut back on State spending, strong from the earliest diagnoses of the 'English disease', and now raised to new levels under the Heath administration, can only undermine still further the stability of an unstable edifice. And, all the time, as more and more of the giant companies go transnational, their devices for avoiding the credit and tax controls of national governments will create an even more pronounced disruption of the balance.[2]

Yet the expectations of advance in the population of Britain are

[1] John Hughes, 'Giant Firms and the British Trade Unions' Response', *Trade Union Register* 1970 (Merlin Press), pp. 64–5.
[2] See Robin Murray, 'The Internationalisation of Capital', *The Spokesman*, No. 11 (April 1971), 17–39.

conditioned in the world-wide division of labour among the advanced nations. Orthodox predictions emphasize this : it is, today, anticipated that the number of cars produced will go on doubling in each decade; that the working population will continue to shrink with the raising of the school-leaving age and the lowering of the pensionable age; that the number of students undergoing courses in higher education will double by 1980; that service trades will continue to expand whilst extractive industries will decline; and so on. Many of these anticipations are, indeed, necesssary, if Britain is to remain in the economic race with its main present-day competitors. But whether she will be able to keep running, or collapse in exhausted convulsions, is a far more open question.

In just over fifty years the industrial structure of Britain has changed radically. From almost 80 per cent in 1911, manual workers now comprise slightly more than 65 per cent of the employed population. Self-employment has declined considerably, and the number of employers of labour is constantly diminishing. (Taking both groups together as a proportion of the whole population, they have declined from 6.8 per cent to 4.2 per cent). But the clerical, supervisory, professional and managerial sectors have continued to multiply, from 13.4 per cent to 29.6 per cent.[3]

Whatever extrapolations are made of these trends, it is absolutely clear that the 'tertiary sector' of the economy will continue to grow, that intermediary white-collar strata will grow very fast, and that manual workers will decline in numbers. It is also perfectly plain that the concentration of capital will continue irreversibly, and that the continued narrowing of, at any rate, the power elite, will proceed visibly year by year.

The very rapid growth of such trade unions as the technicians' and supervisors' ASTMS, coupled with the annexation of such growth points as DATA, the Draughtsmen's Union, by the AEU, and the persistent development of the Clerical and Supervisory Group within the TGWU (which represents an intelligent immediate strategy by the great General Unions) still lags far behind the growing challenge which these employment sectors are offering the unions. The development of the technology of numerically controlled machines can only result in a diminution of the num-

[3] Michael Barratt Brown, 'Some Thoughts Preparatory to a New Politico-Economic Strategy', Institute for Workers' Control *Monthly Digest*, No. 13 (1969).

bers of workpeople employed in operating them, and a hundred similar developments will erode the old manual working class while enlarging the new technically formed proletariat.

All of these trends argue the need for a fresh outburst of new unionism. To them must be added other equally important facts. The maldistribution of income has been becoming more and more acute throughout the past decade and a half, and the numbers of people in relative poverty have been steadily increasing. There is some evidence that the absolute extremes of poverty itself have also been somewhat aggravated during the same period. A small minority of the poor are organized in unions.[4] A much larger number can be organized, and more still can benefit from such positive initiatives as the TGWU's recent campaign on pensions.

At the same time, the growth of the student population coincides with both the diminution of classic professional opportunities and the sharp crisis of academic values, in which the slow-incubating but doggedly persistent 'functionalism' of much modern higher education comes ever more obviously into conflict with the liberal, universalist pretensions of the old university system. Student protest grows out of these stimuli to reach over to a radical rejection of the whole society which generates them. If unions have in general been slow to appreciate these events, already the ASTMS is recruiting members in universities, and there is little doubt that, over the years, a bridge will be built between the more rational student dissenters and the wider trade-union movement.

Within all these profound social movements, and potentially linking them all, there is an ever-present feeling of alienation, suffusing wider and wider areas of industry and society. On a simple level it takes the form of the factory workers' greeting, 'Roll on Friday!' With every development of technology, however, it becomes more insistently apparent and uncontainable. As power slips further and further away to the top of the industrial pyramid, so resentment precipitates in solid chunks to the bottom. In September 1968 the Department of Employment and Productivity carried out a survey into the extent of absenteeism from work. They found that 15 per cent of male workers drew less than their normal full-time pay. The reasons for absence include sickness, injury, late starting or early finishing, and 'truancy'. Together they

[4] See Ken Coates and Richard Silburn, *Poverty: The Forgotten Englishmen* (Penguin Books, 1970).

B

Percentage of total number (column 1) losing pay, by reason:

	Total number in sample (Basis A)	Number losing pay	All reasons	Short time, etc.
SALES	1,590	96	6.0	0.1
Shop saleswoman and sales assistant	1,316	83	6.3	0.2
SERVICE	2,336	254	10.9	0.2
Cleaner, charwoman	498	63	12.7	0.0
Chef/cook	272	16	5.9	0.0
Hairdresser—ladies	174	10	5.7	0.0
Kitchenhand	379	53	14.0	0.6
Waitress	176	18	10.2	0.0
DRIVER DOCKER AND OTHER TRANSPORT	139	36	25.9	0.0
OTHER	5,861	1,765	30.1	0.8
Forewoman or supervisor	191	13	6.8	0.0
Assembler—semi-skilled	409	134	32.8	0.0
Assembler—unskilled	227	75	33.0	0.4
Inspector, viewer, examiner—semi-skilled	221	67	30.3	0.5
Machine operator-machinist (not sewing or woodworking)—semi-skilled	369	125	33.9	1.1
Machine minder (not sewing or woodworking)	100	37	37.0	0.0
Packer, bottler, canner	554	158	30.7	1.6
Sewing machinist—skilled	327	192	34.7	0.5
Sewing machinist—semi-skilled	347	104	31.8	1.2
Textile worker	751	87	25.1	0.9
Labourer	515	232	30.9	0.4
TOTAL: ALL MANUAL FEMALES	10,052	2,168	21.6	0.6

SOURCE: Department of Employment and Productivity quoted by Elspeth Ganguin in 'Worker Walk-Out of Boring Jobs', *Financial Times* (14th October, 1969).

Certified	Sickness Uncertified	Voluntary absence	Late arrival or early finish	Holidays or other approved absence	Miscellaneous
1.6	0.9	1.8	0.2	1.1	0.3
1.6	1.0	2.1	0.2	1.1	0.2
2.3	1.0	2.8	2.5	1.5	0.8
2.2	2.0	2.2	3.2	2.2	1.0
1.1	0.4	2.9	0.4	0.4	0.7
1.7	0.6	0.0	1.1	1.7	0.6
4.0	1.1	3.4	2.1	2.4	1.3
1.1	0.6	4.5	3.4	0.0	0.6
7.9	2.9	7.2	5.8	2.9	1.4
3.0	3.7	8.1	12.1	2.9	0.9
1.6	0.5	1.6	1.6	1.6	1.0
3.2	4.4	9.3	12.7	3.7	0.5
3.1	2.6	12.8	11.0	2.2	3.1
1.4	2.7	8.1	14.5	3.6	0.5
3.5	4.6	7.0	16.5	2.2	0.8
1.0	6.0	9.0	14.0	5.0	8.0
3.5	3.3	9.7	8.5	2.9	1.7
2.3	4.2	9.7	16.1	2.9	0.9
5.5	4.9	8.3	12.2	2.1	0.3
1.4	4.0	9.2	6.1	2.9	0.9
4.1	4.1	7.3	13.0	2.4	0.7
2.6	2.6	5.8	7.8	2.2	0.9

point to a very real dissatisfaction. The highest concentration of absentees who lost pay was among production fitters, 31.3 per cent of whom stayed off work. Two-thirds of those workers had not produced sick-notes. Platers, riveters and miners all came high up the list. Very low down came policemen, caretakers, postmen and firemen. One-quarter of the semi-skilled workers in engineering assembly stayed off, for at least some of the relevant times, compared with only 3.8 per cent of the foremen. Reporting this survey, the *Financial Times* drew special attention to the results of the inquiry among women workers : 'It does seem significant that while the proportion of machine minders and sewing machinists and assemblers who lost pay for various reasons is very high, the proportion of supervisors, cooks, or hairdressers is much lower. Among the unskilled assemblers, for instance, the reasons were largely in the voluntary absence, late arrival or early finish category. And the same applied in the machine minder and sewing machinist sectors.' (See statistical table, pp. 34-5.)

Dr Beric Wright has claimed that, throughout Western Europe, sickness and nervous debility in industry have been expanding in proportion to the scope afforded for their treatment and compensation. He has also shown that the percentage of absences among directors tells a totally different story from that indicated by manual workers. Directors keep on working. His explanation for this is that the challenge of responsibility produces its own response, and it is difficult to fault this judgment.[5] Of course, absenteeism is imperfectly measurable. Sabotage, and other more drastic direct symptoms of frustration, can only be assessed at all by guesswork. Even more difficult to evaluate is the underlying terrain of attitudes and responses in which such open and direct reactions find their roots. One is bound to offer impressionistic evidence about such matters. But the impressions are very powerful. A. D. Lane, a lecturer in sociology at Liverpool University, has graphically expressed his own reactions as a machine minder :

When the sociologist asks me what I like most about this job I say : security. I give security top rating. Partly because I know this is intelligible to 'them' but mainly because I know it is useless to expect work demanding involvement. Because I know

[5] See Ken Coates, 'Wage Slaves', *Essays on Industrial Democracy* (Spokesman Books, 1971).

that it is an unattainable ideal to expect work that would use my actual or potential skills. Yet, although I say 'The days of the craftsmen have gone', I still stubbornly resist the productive forces and relations that make me a thing. I do not ultimately accept defeat. From time to time, a complex of circumstances gives a transparency to my situation. My resistance, always latent, becomes overt. Over grievances apparently trivial I revolt. I 'go slow'. I work to rule. I sit down. I walk out without warning.

I don't like tea machines : the tea is lousy. I don't like it when the machine breaks down : I am thirsty. I don't like an oil mist over the machine shop : it makes me sweat and stink of swarf and oil. I don't like mistakes in my pay packet : it means a protracted wait at the wages office after knock-off time. If I were a 'reasonable' man I would accept that these irritants, superficially seen as minor, are subject to remedy in the fulness of time. But for me these apparent trivia are symbolic of my oppression. . . .

'Human relations' and 'man management' types can manipulate all they like : they leave me unmoved or at most contemptuous. The assumption underpinning their theory is that harmony prevails—or ought to. They choose to ignore, or to lend no credence to, the idea that I am in fundamental conflict with their system.[6]

Feelings like this are more general than most outsiders to industry may imagine. And they are being more and more articulately expressed, as the school system, with all its manifold inadequacies, still awakens hopes, and creates skills, in young people who will, in this system of production, never be realized to the merest fraction of their potential.[7] If the production worker feels his impotence in this way, increasingly the new working class of technicians and professionally qualified employees is producing people who react similarly. The radicalism of the major growth-unions in the white-collar sector, DATA and the ASTMS, reflects this mood, even though it finds political expressions which by no means correlate with the mass of membership opinion in the organizations concerned. What Clive Jenkins expresses accurately is the underlying assumptions and frustrations of his membership rather than its precise reactions from day to day, to such issues as the Common Market or the Budget. But he will be readily forgiven many liberties with the block vote, while he continues to keep his

[6] 'The Machine Minders', *New Society* (30th January, 1969).
[7] See the two-volume Pelican, *Work* (Vol. 1, 1968; Vol. 2, 1969), ed. Ronald Fraser.

finger on that vital pulse. Subterranean though this generalized frustration is, in the normal course of events, it can still erupt. And when it does, the new mass media, although they can be, theoretically, as tightly controlled as Northcliffe's newspapers were, are still, in practice, liable to see and record it all happening. The directness of television has already, in the United States, done for Black Power what the *Star* did for the London dockers, and it is not by any means certain that this is the last good deed (however inadvertent) of the cameras. And within the media themselves, including the newspapers which have, for more than half a century, served the given regime, the same convulsions which afflict industry at large are having their effect. Already severely alienated, newsmen and journalists are beginning, in hopefully large numbers, to be disaffected.

Where does all this frustration and difficulty lead us? Brute sociological facts seldom prove anything with complete certainty: economic trends may fulfil the gloomiest prophecies, without ever revealing the kingdom of heaven at the other side of their all too accurately foreseen apocalypse. Political prophets are better at woe than they are at redemption. Yet all this can be soberly understood, and it remains true that the accumulated discontents of the British political economy *demand* a new style of response by the organizations of Labour. Such a response will ask a working man or woman, as did the eight-hour campaign, what a man's life is for. It will hold out human horizons beyond the sums of production statistics. It will challenge the power of one man over another, in order to develop the social capacity of all men within nature. It will call for the establishment of democratic forms everywhere in industry. It will close its ranks against inequality, poverty, deprivation: but it will also wage implacable war against subordination, manipulation, and all authority that is not freely and spontaneously required by those over whom it is exercised.

If it comes in time, such a response will restructure all the established institutions of the Labour Movement, just as did its forerunners. It will stand more than a good chance of going beyond that, to reshape society as a whole. But there is no predetermined or preordained certainty that it *will* come in time, and if it fails to materialize, the British workman's future is a bleak one.

Chapter 4

Some Definitions

When the first effects of the upsurge of working-class political influence were felt by the Liberal and Conservative parliamentary parties towards the end of the nineteenth century, and governments began those reforms which led towards the 'welfare state', Sir William Harcourt, a Liberal politician of the period, made a famous remark : 'We are all socialists now.'[1] By this he simply meant that the political parties which were seriously interested in electoral success were bound to make certain concessions to the working class, involving greater State intervention to protect workers from the worst insecurities of the wages system. At the same time, capitalists themselves were turning away from the strict doctrine of *laissez-faire*, which had taught that governments should not intervene in the economy. Capitalism in Britain therefore began to recruit the State to act on *its* behalf—demanding tariffs, for example, to protect it from the competition of newer industrial nations such as Germany and the United States. These departures from pure 'free enterprise' liberalism were often interpreted by orthodox politicians as a move in the direction of socialism, which, for some people, had come to mean State control of industry. Yet alongside the alarm of anti-socialist politicians (which found popular expression in the attitude of prosperous Edwardians to 'licking stamps' in order to comply with Lloyd George's first National Insurance scheme) there was also, contained in that phrase 'We are all socialists now', a note of quiet complacency. 'Socialism', after all, could be tamed, diluted, and adapted until it became a device for reforming and improving capitalism. Even conservatives need feel no alarm about the arrival of such a flexible philosophy in their midst.

There is a similar situation today, in respect of one of the most

---

[1] Harcourt was responsible, as Chancellor of the Exchequer, for the introduction of death duties in 1894, a measure which was itself regarded as a dangerous example of 'creeping socialism'.

central tenets of socialism, that of industrial democracy. The term is so general, all-embracing and has such wide appeal that politicians and philosophers of all shades of opinion prefer to pay lip-service to it, rather than to oppose it outright. Very few could be found, for example, in the Conservative Party or the Confederation of British Industry, who would launch a campaign for industrial autocracy, however autocratic their actual working practices may be. On the contrary, many in those institutions are to be heard today uttering benevolent words about the rights of workers to 'a say' in the management of industry. In other words, 'We are all industrial democrats now'! In this situation, it is vital that we attempt the task of giving precision and definition to our use of words and phrases in this field. Obviously, Harcourt did not wish to classify himself as a disciple of Karl Marx. Equally, it is clearly not the intention of Harcourt's present-day descendants to identify themselves with the Institute for Workers' Control when they speak of industrial democracy. As with 'socialism', it all depends on what you mean by the words. In this chapter we shall discuss several different interpretations, starting with the notion of trade-union opposition, and going through joint consultation, workers' participation and workers' control, to workers' self-management.

Trade Unions as Opposition

There is a theory, developed by Professor Hugh Clegg[2] and Anthony Crosland,[3] which holds that there is no need to search for industrial democracy, since it already exists in modern capitalist Britain, and in all countries with similar institutions. It is, according to its own main author, a 'creed of democracy achieved, of trade unionism which has arrived'.[4] But it is also, he admits, 'pessimistic and traditional' and rests on 'liberal thought which preceded the rise of Socialism'.[5]

According to Clegg, the essence of democracy is the right of opposition to governments. Dictators nearly always suppress opposition parties; the mark of democracies is their toleration and indeed

[2] H. A. Clegg, *A New Approach to Industrial Democracy* (Blackwell, 1960).
[3] C. A. R. Crosland, *The Conservative Enemy* (Jonathan Cape, 1962), particularly Chap. 14.
[4] Clegg, op. cit., p. 29.
[5] Ibid.

their encouragement of opposition. Although coalition governments may be formed in times of crisis, the normal situation in parliamentary democracies is a government composed of one or more parties, which is faced by an opposition of one or more parties. This, says Clegg, *is* democracy. He then uses the parliamentary situation as a model for industry. He says that wherever trade unions exist, which are independent of employers and managers, they fulfil a role comparable to the opposition party in parliament, whilst the management is the equivalent of a governing party. Provided that trade unions do not share responsibility with management, and maintain a vigorous opposition to it, we shall have industrial democracy. Nothing more is required, and since the situation which Clegg desires appears to exist in Britain and other advanced capitalist countries, we have, according to his theory, already 'achieved' democracy in industry. It also follows from his argument that the ownership of industry is quite irrelevant to the question of democracy. For, clearly, independent trade unionism may exist in nations in which the economy is mainly composed of private industry, while it is possible, on the other hand, to have State-owned industrial collectives in which trade unions exist only as a shadow of the workers' organizations with which we are familiar in capitalist Britain. If Clegg's argument were to be proved, what a remarkable triumph for conservatism, capitalism and the whole *status quo* of our social and political system! And indeed Clegg does claim that his theory justifies our social and industrial arrangements in their entirety : 'The new theories . . . argue that the political and industrial institutions of the stable democracies already approach the best that can be realized.'[6] One is reminded, somewhat oddly no doubt, of the Duke of Wellington, who, defending the parliamentary system of his day (which included widespread corruption, and which limited the right to vote to a tiny and wealthy minority) against the 1832 campaign for parliamentary reform and a democratic franchise, said that the British constitution was 'the most perfect institution ever devised by man'. No one would deny, of course, that it was quite a useful arrangement for the Duke. 'Perfect for whom?' is the obvious response to such a claim.

It is useful to put Clegg's argument under the microscope, for such an exercise will reveal not only the false assumptions behind

[6] Ibid.

his analogies, but also assist us to clarify our minds about the term
'industrial democracy'. When we have completed the analysis, we
shall be better placed to begin our own definition of what is meant
by this phrase.

The analogy which Clegg draws between Parliament and industry
is false. In his scheme the government party is the equivalent of
the employer, and the opposition party is the counterpart of the
trade union. But whatever one thinks of their merits or vices, both
parties in Parliament arrive there by the same process of election,
whereas the two 'parties' in industry arrive in their 'seats' by very
different methods. The 'government' in industry is in the hands of
men who are not subject to any process of election. Inherited wealth
remains the single most influential factor in determining the composition of industrial government; education, skills and expertise are
also influential to a greater or lesser degree, but in a class society,
there is no equality of opportunity in the obtaining of these qualifications. The trade-union 'opposition party', on the other hand,
represents a mass voluntary movement, of working- and what is
sometimes called lower-middle-class people. The representatives of
that movement who actually express the opposition are active at
many levels, from shop steward to general secretary. Their policies
and actions are to a greater or lesser degree (depending on the level
of internal union democracy) governed by the views of the members of their organizations. The contrast between the sources of
power of the two 'parties' could not be more complete. On the
other hand, there is a single, uniform process (one man, one vote)
by which politicians of all parties find their way into Parliament.
(Of course if we were to probe deeper, we should have to examine
the ways in which wealth and social class exercise a powerful
influence on the make-up of the House of Commons, to say nothing
of the House of Lords and the higher ranks of the Civil Service
and the Armed Forces, all of which are part of the State with which
Clegg is so content. There is the further vital question of the
degree to which wealth and property operate behind the scenes to
influence the decisions of the Government, quite regardless of the
formal powers of parliamentary majorities.) Clegg's analogy really
does betray him rather badly; if he took it seriously, he would find
himself arguing for the election of management, so that it really
could be compared with a political party. He is, of course, opposed
to any such extension of his theory.

Similarly, if he regards trade unions as an opposition party, he ought to expect them to behave like one. In other words, trade unions should be straining every nerve to overthrow the existing 'government' of industry and replace it with their own representatives! No opposition party in politics would accept that its constitutional duty is to remain in permanent opposition. But again, Clegg would be dismayed by such an interpretation of his analogy. He insists that trade unions should remain forever independent of management—a permanent opposition. We shall ourselves argue later that it would indeed be wrong for *trade unions* as organizations to become entangled with management decisions. That is because they fulfil an essential and permanently necessary defensive function on behalf of their members. But where does this leave *trade unionists*? The right to oppose management and employers is not, we can now see, the same thing as the right to self-government, which is enjoyed in our kind of society by a small minority, within which the degree of managerial authority is sharply pyramided towards the top levels, where enormous powers accumulate. This right is enjoyed without elections, or any procedures to ensure the accountability of the managers to the managed. Only a complacent intelligence could arrive at the conclusion that this system represents, in Clegg's own words, 'democracy achieved'.

Clegg arrives at this position by assuming that the right of opposition is both the necessary and the sufficient condition for democracy. It is perfectly true that the right of opposition is necessary to democracy, but by itself it certainly does not guarantee it. Other elementary conditions for democracy are the right to elect those who exercise decision-making powers and to remove them from office without unnecessary delay. There is much more to it than that, as we shall see, but the right to participate in the choice of government, as well as to work for its replacement, is a basic requirement. Indeed, an opposition which is confined permanently to a negative role, is no more than a fig-leaf covering the absence of true democracy. The mere right to oppose, protected by a government which will never surrender office or have to face an electorate is a very precarious freedom. It amounts to a right to 'say what you like, provided you *do* as you are told'.

So much, then, for the central point of the 'opposition' theory. There are two other matters arising from it, which must be cleared up before we move on, one concerning the actual functions of trade unions in our society, and the other concerned with the question of ownership.

It is confusing to consider trade unions merely as an opposition. Certainly they represent—in their traditional form in capitalist countries—a force which is independent of management and employer. But, unlike opposition parties in Parliament, they are constantly making agreements with the other side, for which (they are equally constantly told) they must accept joint responsibility with the employer, and which they are required by convention to enforce amongst their members. In other words, trade unions occupy a permanently contradictory position. They are an opposition to that system in which men and women are hired by others for a money payment. But they are also a part of the system, helping to regulate and determine the rules and terms on which it will be carried forward. Moreover, in both these functions, as representatives and as regulators, they are normally restricted to a very narrow part of the total economic process. They may regulate and represent, on questions of wages and working conditions. All the rest—the process of production, location of industry, investment, expansion, contraction, distribution of the product, safety, health, welfare, education, technology, etc.—is 'managerial prerogative'. There may be minor encroachments of trade-union influence in some of these fields, and we shall argue later that an important strategy for advancing democracy in industry consists in applying trade-union methods to questions hitherto closed to the unions. But in essence, trade-union influence is normally confined to the terms on which human beings sell their labour power.

This does not necessarily mean that the trade unions are acting against the interests of their members in fulfilling this dual, narrow function. Indeed it is the basis on which our very minimum of democracy rests, for without it no solid institution or social force stands between us and outright autocracy (dictatorship), in both industry and government. That is why we feel justified in pointing out that the authors of the 'opposition' theory of democracy have been astonishingly inconsistent. Both Clegg and Crosland have lent their considerable influence to support the politics of incomes policy which, in recent years, has seriously undermined the role of trade unions as an independent opposition. Trade unions have seen their independence threatened by attempts to incorporate them in the

administering and policing of wage-restraint policies, or in collaboration with employers to raise productivity. They have seen their
power to oppose threatened by legal limitations or the promise of
them.[7]

We pointed out just now that trade-union influence has traditionally been exerted on only a narrow part of the industrial front.
The attempt to extend that front, so that unions bargain over a
whole range of new issues (financial policies of companies, the right
to hire and fire, safety, etc.), which is developing at present, is a welcome extension of democratic influence in industry. However, the
trade unions have for many years, and most particularly in Britain,
assumed a further and even wider role. They have provided the basis
on which the working class has entered into parliamentary democracy, to achieve overall social and economic reforms. This is an
aspect of trade-union work which hardly fits into Clegg's theory at
all, since he does not feel the need to explore the connection
between industry and government. Trade unions enter politics
not simply to provide an opposition for the sake of appearances,
but because they wish to change the power relations which exist
in society; and industry is the most important influence in society.
It is not an island on which men have willingly and without
extreme distortions of their political beliefs accepted different rules
from those which are applied in society at large. The Labour
Movement which arose in the first instance to assert democratic
principles right across the board, has in fact suffered from the
effects of such a distortion. Its original concept of democracy
was indivisible; it has been crippled and thwarted by the acceptance of a situation in which men are supposed to act as citizens
when they find themselves 'at home', and as 'hands' when they find
themselves 'at work'. Clegg's theory mirrors this schizophrenia and
perpetuates it.

If we are right about all this, then ownership becomes once
again a crucial issue. Clegg argues that since democracy is simply
opposition, it does not matter who owns your factory; you can have

[7] Professor Clegg lent his weight and influence to government wage
restraint and the incorporation of the unions, by serving as a member of the
Prices and Incomes Board, and by his contributions to the findings of the
Donovan Royal Commission on Trade Unions' and Employers' Associations.
Anthony Crosland was of course, as a member of Harold Wilson's cabinet,
in a position of direct responsibility for incomes policy and restraint on trade
unions in the period 1964–70.

an effective trade unionism regardless of ownership. In fact he does not use this point to argue for neutrality between private and social ownership; he definitely prefers private ownership. For he argues that the experience of communist-governed societies proves that State ownership becomes State tyranny, and that independent trade unions have been destroyed in such circumstances. This argument makes a powerful appeal, based as it is on the experience of Russia and other countries where revolutionary transformation of property and industry into State monopoly has been followed by authoritarian and anti-democratic government. It is this experience (which is not the experience of 'communism' of course, but of its reverses under Stalinism) that has dominated and distorted socialist thinking for the past forty years, and which seems so powerfully to reinforce the conservative doctrine which Clegg has adopted. The defenders of State tyrannies which masquerade as 'socialist democracies' share the responsibility, with their anti-communist counterparts, for the lack of progress towards socialism and democracy in the Western countries since the 1930s. There are Cleggs in Russia and the other Eastern European countries who argue as partially as he does in defence of their own *status quo*. They maintain that since private ownership has been abolished, then by definition industrial democracy prevails. Our reply to them is similar to our answer to Clegg. Social ownership (like opposition) is necessary but not sufficient of itself to guarantee industrial democracy. Without the abolition of private ownership, industry remains dominated by a small, unaccountable, very powerful, very wealthy elite, whose influence in industry and governments is the influence of an owning class, and is profoundly undemocratic. But without both independent trade unions and democracy, in industry and government, the establishment of socialist ownership does not lead towards industrial democracy either. It is noteworthy that wherever demands for industrial democracy have appeared in communist countries (during the Hungarian revolution of 1956, and in similar revolts in Poland, and more recently in Czechoslovakia), or where it has been practised (as in Yugoslavia), it does not take the form advocated by Clegg, but aims rather to establish social self-management. We shall return to this matter later.

Joint Consultation

It is significant that Professor Clegg's pessimism about industrial democracy, on which he built his 'new approach' in 1960, arose in part because of his disillusionment with the practice of joint consultation, of which he had been an enthusiastic supporter in earlier post-war days.[8] Public ownership of the basic industries, combined with the statutory requirement that the nationalized boards should establish consultative machinery, had been the basis of Labour's policy in the 1945-50 period. Consultation was seen by some at that time as a step on the road to full industrial democracy, and by others as a convenient device to placate and head off more far-reaching demands for workers' control.

Joint consultation was first given government blessing after the First World War and at that time it was undoubtedly adopted as a concessionary method to contain the influence of the workers' control movement which dominated trade unions and labour politics. It was in this setting that the proposals of the Whitley Committee for joint consultation were advanced.[9] Briefly, they recommended that industry and the State should voluntarily adopt the practice of the most advanced private employers and set up joint management-employee committees where workers could be consulted on a range of welfare and production matters. The idea was taken up in government establishments and by the Civil Service unions, and in State employment such committees go by the name of 'Whitley Councils' to this day. In private industry the most lasting effect of the Whitley recommendations was not in the field of consultation, but in establishing industry-level negotiating machinery on wages and conditions, the Joint Industrial Councils. But there was also, both during and immediately after the 1914-18 war, a spate of activity in which joint production, or joint consultation committees, were set up in private industry. The initiative came chiefly from the employers, though trade unionists often took up the idea with more or less enthusiasm. Following the collapse of the post-war boom in 1920-1, however, the number and significance of these committees fell away very sharply. The

[8] H. A. Clegg, *Industrial Democracy and Nationalisation* (Blackwell, 1951).
[9] The Whitley Committee on Relations Between Employers and Employed issued five reports between 1917 and 1918.

pressure of workers for greater power in industry which had carried the workers' control movement so far between 1910 and 1922, declined drastically as the unemployment queues undermined the bargaining powers of workers.

After the defeat of the General Strike a policy of close co-operation between unions and employers was followed by trade-union leaders and by prominent industrialists such as Sir Alfred Mond. The practice of American 'company unionism' was given a stimulus by the first wave of 'New Deal' legislation in the USA, which required employers to bargain collectively with their workers. In order to avoid recognizing *bona fide* trade unions, many American companies set up anti-union organizations in their own factories, in which they went through the pretence of bargaining and consultation.[10] Similar practices were adopted by British companies; ICI in particular established its well-known Works Council scheme in the 'thirties as a method of diverting workers' activities into company controlled consultation, and away from genuine trade unionism.

During the Second World War, there was a widespread rediscovery of the method of joint consultation. Supported by the shop stewards' Engineering National Council, and by the Communist Party, which had considerable influence on the shop floor, Joint Production Committees became almost universal in engineering and munitions factories. These committees, on which works managers, engineers and foremen sat alongside shop stewards, often discussed the whole range of production problems as well as the traditional issues of welfare, canteens and toilet facilities. Employers were frequently enthusiastic about this development, since they found that in their keenness for maximum war production the shop stewards were often prepared to support and indeed advocate every kind of breach in traditional trade-union rules and controls, and even to participate in the administration of shop-floor discipline. The growth of these committees did not therefore serve to raise the political questions of control and authority in industry, as had happened in the First World War. With a few exceptions, shop stewards and unions alike combined to strengthen orthodox managerial power rather than to contest it. Of course, in the process, stewards approached closer to the point of managerial

[10] Henry Pelling, *American Labor* (University of Chicago Press, 1960), p. 160.

authority, and acquired knowledge and experience in areas of decision-making which were normally denied to them. But the artificial situation in which stewards were prepared to endorse the purposes of management—higher output, longer hours, dilution, tight discipline, and suspension of custom and practice—came to an end after the war.

After the war, Joint Production Committees declined in favour and influence, and the less exacting practice of joint consultation was officially sponsored, especially in the nationalized industries. But by the early 1950s the advocates of consultation had to concede that there was widespread disillusion amongst workers concerning its effectiveness. When the next and present wave of demands for workers' control developed, it was met, not with the offer of consultation, but with a variety of concessions labelled workers' 'participation'.

The word 'consultation' tells us all we need to know about its practice. Workers are to be 'consulted' about managerial decisions: '. . . the function of a Joint Works Council or Production Committee is clearly advisory and not executive—except in so far as the Board may specifically confer executive authority for a particular purpose or occasion, and accept responsibility for the outcome'.[11] Or consider this revealing piece of worldly wisdom from the pen of a disciple of the Clegg-Crosland school:

> There is no greater morale booster for a worker than the feeling that he too is consulted on policy questions and plays his part in influencing managerial decisions. Of course, in any form of democracy there is an element of humbug. Our rulers never, in fact, allow us as much power as they pretend to. The sovereign people can only be permitted to exercise its power on certain limited occasions and within certain defined limits— otherwise the operations of government would be paralysed. Nevertheless the illusion of power is good for us, besides imposing important restraints on our rulers.
>
> This applies to industrial democracy, where the element of make-believe must of necessity be greater than in political democracies.[12]

Of course, trade unionists may attempt to use joint consultation to extend their influence and knowledge of a company's affairs,

[11] G. S. Walpole, *Management and Men* (Jonathan Cape, 1944), p. 43.
[12] M. Shanks, *The Stagnant Society* (Penguin Books, 1967), p. 160.

as the Shop Stewards' Handbook of the TGWU advised its members to do.[13] Generations of trade unionists have had to work consultative machinery, and sometimes managed to turn it to their advantage, despite the intentions of its designers. But the weight of evidence which accumulated during the 1950s told of workers who had become weary, frustrated and sceptical, as their participation on committees became more and more limited to such trivialities as the strength of the canteen tea. (The frequency with which this particular example is used to show the futility of joint consultation suggests that, even in this minor matter, the long years of consultation left the canteen brew as pale and unstimulating as the committees whose solemn proceedings were supposed to put some body into it!)

Reactions to this feeling took several forms. In 1953 the TUC, alarmed at the situation, especially in the nationalized industries where consultation is obligatory, recommended an educational drive to persuade workers to drop their 'out-of-date' demands for executive authority and reconcile themselves to consultative advisory functions only.[14] The Labour Party's left wing demanded that joint consultation should be made 'effective'. They sought to breathe life into the dead words with which the Labour Government of 1945-50 had promised workers a new 'status' in the nationalized industries.[15] Some, like Clegg, retreated, as we have seen, from the quest for *any* sort of new status, real or imaginary, and attempted to give dignity and theoretical justification to the existing status of workers. Others again, like the Derbyshire miners, aimed to capture joint consultation for their own purposes, discarding illusion but not the committee structures which, they argued, could be transformed by an injection of genuine militancy.[16] Trade unions such as the TGWU began to demand that the artificial dividing line between subjects which were considered 'suitable' for negotiation and those on which only consultation was allowed, should be broken down, so that bargaining took place across a much wider field.

[13] Transport and General Workers' Union *Shop Stewards' Handbook* 1964, pp. 48–9.
[14] Trades Union Congress, *Interim Report on Public Ownership* 1953, paras 112–15.
[15] *Keeping Left, New Statesman* pamphlet (1950), pp. 30–1.
[16] Derbyshire Area, National Union of Mineworkers, *A Plan for the Miners* (1964), pp. 22–5.

In general terms, there emerged during the 1960s two diverging strands of opinion and policy. One challenged the whole tradition of the wasted years since the 1920s, and aimed to build a new movement for workers' control, and the other searched for new formulae to give the appearance of democracy without too much of the reality, through forms of workers' participation.

Participation

During the French student movement and widespread workers' occupation of factories in France in 1968, General de Gaulle made grandiose but extremely vague promises to reform industry and society so as to allow workers and students greater 'participation' in affairs.[17] A poster from the student movement appeared shortly afterwards on the walls of Parisian buildings. It read simply:

I participate
You participate
He participates
We participate
You participate
They profit!

We have called this chapter 'Some Definitions'. In fact it is extremely hard to define participation precisely. In our chapter on the question we hope the issues are clarified (see Chap. 14). Meanwhile, we must simply assert that there is participation and 'participation'. A whole variety of devices and pieces of machinery have been proposed or implemented, in many countries, whose sole object is to obtain the consent of workers to the continuation and strengthening of the profit-making system. In that sense, participation is the historical successor to joint consultation. At the same time, workers themselves have sometimes demanded participation, in ways which show that they are interested in obtaining more power and control in industry, rather than seeking to collaborate in corporate schemes for their own castration. Ernie Roberts, the Assistant General Secretary of the AUEW, has cautioned us about the danger of dogmatic pronouncements based

[17] For a thoroughly researched and informative account of the French factory occupations, see Andrée Hoyles, 'The Occupation of Factories in France: May 1968', *Trade Union Register* 1969 (Merlin Press), pp. 243–99.

merely on a dislike of certain words : 'Participation or control? Well, I don't like to see the juxtaposition of these two phrases because I don't want the movement again to develop into a discussion on the basis of semantics, as to what one word means and what the other word means. It really means *precisely what the workers that use it mean*, and that is determined by what they are demanding.'[18]

That is well said, and it points to the fact that participation is best studied by attention to practical examples.

Joint consultation itself is an example of workers' participation. History suggests that the Paris poster is entirely apt as a description of *that* practice. To explore the wider context of the term, we may discuss the example of the steel employee-directors' scheme in more detail. In 1965-6 a movement arose amongst the steelworkers in Britain for major steps towards democracy in the about-to-be-nationalized steel industry. It started in the workers' control conferences, and later became the official programme of the National Joint Craftsmen's Co-ordinating Committee of craft unions in the industry. The Minister of Power, Richard Marsh, at first resisted the idea, but then made certain concessions. The scheme which was finally put into practice provided for the appointment of three employees to each of the Area Boards set up under the nationalization act. These employees (1) hold only a minority of the seats on the Area Boards, (2) are required to resign from any union office such as shop steward, which they may hold, during their period on the Board, (3) are required to accept corporate responsibility for the decisions of the Boards, and (4) are appointed by the National Steel Corporation from names submitted by the Steel Unions' Committee of the TUC. They can therefore in no way be considered as representatives of the workers in the industry, since they are neither elected by them, nor are they accountable to them. They are nevertheless expected to 'carry the can' for the Boards' decisions. They are placed in minority positions, and so cannot expect to influence the decisions for which they are held responsible. Moreover, the Area Boards under the present constitution of the National Steel Corporation enjoy little or no authority anyway. Hugh Clegg himself told a story about the

18 Ernie Roberts, 'Trade Unions and Workers' Control', *Workers' Control: Report of the 5th National Conference Held at Coventry, June 10th–11th, 1967,* ed. Tony Topham (Centre for Socialist Education, 1967), p. 58.

employee directors which illustrates this latter point, on the television discussion programme 'Management in the Seventies'.[19]
Apparently one of the employee directors had the nerve to say, at
a board meeting : 'We were appointed to participate in the making
of decisions. When are we going to start making decisions here?'
To which an orthodox managerial director replied : 'Oh! we're not
actually expected to make *decisions* on the Area Boards!'

The kind of device embodied in the steel directorships is obviously
aimed at incorporating workers into situations where they have
'responsibility without power'. As such, it was given an enthusiastic
welcome by an editorial article written for *The Director* (the
Journal of the Institute of Directors) in March 1967 : 'The idea of
getting workers on to the boards of directors is now beginning to
develop a notable head of steam. . . . The Government want the
unions to share in the responsibility for the working of a major
industry. More important, they want the unions to share the
responsibility for some of the expected unpopular decisions.'

It should be noted that amongst the unpopular decisions facing
the steel industry is a projected run-down of the labour force by
up to 100,000 workers by the mid-'seventies!

We may conclude that the steel director scheme is too crude
to take in any but the most innocent worker or trade union. It is
little more than a modification of the practice, common in
nationalized industries, of appointing one or two superannuated
trade-union general secretaries to the Boards, a practice which
has obviously had no effect in increasing the influence of the shop
floor on the decisions of those Boards. There are suggestions that a
modification to the Companies Act will, in the future, permit the
practice adopted in steel to be applied 'on a voluntary basis'
throughout private industry. Despite the words of *The Director,*
there is very little 'head of steam' behind this idea in the trade-
union movement. This does not mean the unions should ignore such
schemes. Whenever they are promoted, a real opportunity occurs
for workers to raise demands for genuine representation, and thereby
to increase understanding of the whole issue of industrial democracy. This has been well demonstrated in both the steel and
more recently the docks industry cases, which we shall discuss
later.

More serious issues concerning participation are raised by the

[19] BBC 1, 22nd February, 1970

growth of productivity bargaining and plant bargaining generally. We shall have more to say about this (see Chaps 6, 7 and 8), but we may make some general points at this stage. In the spate of literature, discussion and policy-making which has accompanied the spread of productivity bargaining, as well as in the general aftermath of the Donovan Commission on Trade Unions, there has been no shortage of plans to 'involve' the shop stewards in elaborate patterns of participation at the plant or company level. Employers have very little chance of imposing productivity deals by decree, and they have learned the value of protracted negotiation and even intimate discussion with shop stewards. Associated with these new bargaining methods are recent concessions which have been made in a few instances to shop steward or trade-union demands for the opening of the books. This concession may be given a general stimulus, in a diluted form no doubt, in the emerging Industrial Relations Act, and its accompanying 'Code of Practice'. In many plants, joint productivity committees have been set up to oversee the implementation of an agreement after it has been signed. Joint committees of managers and stewards have been created in some plants to determine the pattern of job evaluation schemes. And so on. Certain general tests may be applied by the shop stewards and unions, in deciding whether or not to become involved in this kind of activity. Firstly, are we accepting new patterns of negotiation at the expense of previous positions of strength which we have built up? Are our representatives on the new types of committee held strictly accountable to the shop floor? Are reporting-back procedures adequate to ensure accountability? Are we accepting 'responsibilities without powers'? Are we being placed in a position where management can hold us responsible for 'unpopular decisions'? Are management using us as sounding-boards to obtain information about the situation on the shop floor? Are they using us as messenger boys to carry their communications to the shop floor? Are we in danger of becoming part of management's supervision network? How much information is management really giving us, and how much are they still concealing? These tests need to be rigorously applied, and regular reviews of the situation are necessary, since in some recent cases even experienced trade unionists have found themselves subjected to brain-washing techniques of participation. Ultimately, the best safeguard against management-contrived schemes lies in the independent working out of shop-floor and trade-union strategies based on a firmer concept than that of participation—in other words, based on the idea of workers' control.

Workers' Control

The term 'workers' control' has the advantage of being clear-cut, when compared with 'participation'. 'Workers' control' emphasizes that the purpose of the policy and strategy should be to establish control, by workers, over the hitherto unfettered decisions of the ruling party in industry, namely the employers and their managers. In this sense (which is not to be confused with the full industrial democracy possible in a socialized society, where 'self-management' is the more appropriate term) the germs of workers' control exist, in greater or lesser degree, wherever strong independent trade-union and shop-floor powers act to restrain employers in the exercise of their so-called 'prerogatives'. When shop stewards operate their own overtime roster, or when they regulate, however informally, the speed of work, or when shop-floor strength and action prevent the carrying out of an arbitrary dismissal, there workers' control is being exercised. In this sense workers' control always exists in a conflict situation. This is something which many honest people find hard to accept, even when they are perfectly ready to recognize that bargaining about wages and conditions is an expression of conflicting interests between employers and workers. Managerial authority derives from above, from the legal owners of the business, from rights of property, from the law of contract, and from the economic power of the buyer of labour. The authority of the workers and their representatives, however, originates from below, from the collective will of groups of workers. When they assert that will to obtain a wage rise, they are in conflict with management's authority. Similarly when they exercise that will to control overtime, speed of work, discipline, tea-breaks, or a hundred and one other things, they are in conflict with the established power. The movement to extend the control of workers over arbitrary authority, and over their working environment, is a movement for 'workers control'. Seen in this light, workers' control is not something which is either established or not: it varies in degree and scope according to the circumstances of particular times and places, industries and occupations. Thus the dock-workers have established more workers' control than the shop assistants. The explanation for the differences between these two occupations clearly rests on differences in relative militancy, solidarity and bargaining power. The reverse situation applies to the different employers. When a shop manager sacks a shop assistant on the spot, for lateness, and gets away with it without arousing protest from the rest of his staff, he is obviously in possession of more authority—arbitrary authority—than the docks employer whose power in such a case only extends to imposing temporary suspension. Between these two cases we may cite that of an engineering works manager, who tries to exert his legal power to fire a late arriver, only to find himself with a damaging strike on his hands which compels him, because of the state of his order-book, to reinstate the sacked man. It is hardly necessary to say that the new legislation on industrial relations is carefully, indeed wickedly, designed to put an end to all such encroachments of managerial authority.

Of course, workers' control of the kind described here is unevenly developed by different groups, and is at the best only a partial and limited form of democratic restraint against authoritarianism. We do not advocate contentment with such a haphazard situation. We are saying only that this is where we start from. We do not start from 'pie in the sky', or from anything abstract or remote; we start from the living experience of workers. We begin to understand with something like amazement, as we look at the obstacles and the past defeats, that, in spite of the legal relationship which says that workers are 'hired hands' with no powers to intervene in the making of most decisions, in spite of the insecurity of the wage-worker, in spite of the great legal and economic powers of employers, men continue to assert their right to control their immediate situation at work. This firmly based, though often unrecognized, instinct, is the basis from which we can assert the higher and wider demands for full workers' control. But we should always remember that, until the question of ownership is solved—that is, so long as employer authority is still a separate thing based on property rights—workers' control will continue to be asserted as a countervailing element in a *dual* power, existing alongside and contesting the established power of capital and its agents.

This does not mean that at all times, and in all places, industrial life is lived in an acute state of tension. Sometimes the issue lies dormant for generations, the distribution of power in favour of employers being largely accepted. At other times, however, employers resent even the minor controls which workers have established through custom, practice, trade-union representation, and, in some respects, through the law. Employers then launch campaigns to re-establish managerial control and to change the law; these are at first resisted by workers, and may then be met with counter-demands for more workers' control. It is in these circumstances, when workers are beginning to formulate their own positive demands, that a conscious movement for workers' control springs up, in place of limited and separate tugs-of-war, factory by factory and industry by industry. Such a movement may take several forms, as we shall see in the next chapter. It may result in new and far-reaching reforms of institutions or laws. It may take the form of direct action, the setting up of workers' councils, or the occupation of factories. It may take altogether more modest forms, such as the framing of new rules regarding trade-union rights, or the setting up of workers' representation in or alongside the existing decision-making centres of industrial power. It may be temporary, with the employers re-establishing their authority after more or less prolonged political or industrial struggle. It may leave a residue of gain, in the form of permanent new restrictions over the exercise of employer prerogatives. Or it may usher in a process of total transformation of society, in which every institution, from Parliament to property, is subjected to a system of accountable democracy. Such a transformation would involve sections of society who are not usually described as 'workers'. In this sense only, 'workers' control' is perhaps not the perfect term with which to describe the kind of movement we have in mind. Teachers, students, journalists, technicians, professional people, artists, writers, musicians, workers in the mass media of television and radio, civil servants, health-workers and scientists must and will all be involved in the process of asserting democratic control over their environment and institutions, if the whole of society is to engage in the total process of democratization. But in imagining the beauty of such a development, we should remember that it all begins with, and falls back upon, the day-to-day claim to control which arises out of the simplest forms of trade-union activity.

Self-Management

We have seen that workers' control encompasses a wide variety of situations, ranging from familiar shop-floor practices to a total challenge for control of industry and society. But when we have overcome the power of property, and when industry is fully socialized, how then shall we interpret industrial democracy? If the authority of capital and private ownership has been finally removed, with what will it be replaced? Very often, democratic socialists have replied by saying: 'Why, with workers' control of course.' We do not mean to be pedantic, or to descend to a merely semantic argument, but for the sake of clarity we would suggest that the term 'self-management' is best employed to describe the democratic administration of socialized industry. In such a situation there is no property-owning class against which workers must establish control. There is rather an economy—machinery, plant, equipment, transport facilities, and all of society's lifeless hardware—which needs to be administered, renewed, developed and directed towards social purposes.

In order that this administration be democratic, it will be necessary to create, out of the experience and understanding built from the preceding movement for workers' control, a system of self-managing, accountable and elected councils, reaching outward and upward from plant and school, factory and hospital, depot, mine and mill to the central administrative and planning bodies of the whole society. This is what the Yugoslav system set out to achieve in the 'fifties. Although the reality of their industrial democracy is now threatened by the increasing concessions which the Yugoslavs have made to the power of commercial market forces (see Chap. 15, pp. 224-30), they had the correct instinct when they named their method 'workers' self-management'.

Following this usage, it seems sensible for us to speak of 'workers' control' to indicate the aggressive encroachment of Trade Unions on management powers in a capitalist framework, and of 'workers' self-management' to indicate attempts to administer a socialized economy democratically. While insisting that there is most unlikely to be a simple institutional continuity between the two conditions, it seems quite clear that workers' control can be a most valuable school for self-management, and that the notion

of self-management can be an important stimulus to the demand
for control. Between the two, however it may be accomplished,
lies the political transformation of the social structure.[20]

[20] Ken Coates, 'Democracy and Workers' Control', *Towards Socialism*
(Fontana Books [and in *New Left Review*], 1965), p. 293.

Part Two

The Struggle for Workers' Control

Chapter 5

Preconditions for Advance

We are now prepared to answer some practical questions. We have established some key features of the society and industrial system in which we live in present-day capitalist Britain. We have outlined something of the tradition of workers' control which exists in the British Labour Movement; we know that the roots go deep and that we can draw on them for some of our guidelines. We believe that, whilst the independence of the trade unions must be preserved at all costs, they should not rest content with a merely oppositional role in industry. Of course, we are conscious of the dangers present in the development of positive, aggressive policies, since we have already warned that demands for industrial democracy may easily become entangled with schemes to disarm the workers' organizations. We have argued that the goal of the unions should be nothing short of a socialized, democratically planned system of self-management. We must recognize, however, that, in order to achieve such a society, the unions have no way of avoiding conflict with existing authority based on private ownership and on the rights of property, and must inevitably co-exist with it in unsatisfactory compromise meanwhile. Unless workers are prepared to assert the demand for workers' control over and *against* the undemocratic powers of management and employers as they exist today, they ought not to flirt with the rhetoric of democracy, since it can only cheat them if they do.

We have already agreed with Hugh Clegg's proposition that trade-union independence from State control is a basic prerequisite for industrial democracy, although we profoundly disagree with his contention that this independence is a sufficient condition for it. Repeated attacks by successive Labour and Conservative governments upon trade-union independence, from Labour's one-sided incomes policy up to its White Paper *In Place of Strife* of 1969, through to the Industrial Relations legislation of Mr Heath's government in 1971, constitute, even on Clegg's terms, a fundamental assault upon industrial democracy, actual or potential. It is an illusion that the State or its judiciary exists to promote industrial democracy or the evolution of socialist social relations; on the contrary, the whole basis of law in Great Britain is the sanctity of private property, which, while it to some extent upheld the freedom of the citizen in an economy of small artisan producers, has the effect, in an economy of mass-production, of conscripting the State as an instrument for the domination of one class over another. The Conservative Government's attempt to reduce the legal status of labour to that of a commodity, which is bought and sold according to a strict and enforceable law of contract, represents only the most extreme version of a political economy in which private capital remains the dominant power in society. Such a view collides with the concept of a free human personality, growing to the fullest limits of its potential in a society of equals, which goal is central to our approach to trade unionism.

It is not necessary to this argument to enter into detailed examination of the ways in which the Industrial Relations Act undermines trade-union independence, or to trace the precise course taken over the years by the shifting legal status accorded to, or won by, the unions. The broad outlines are clear enough. In the 1871 Trade Union Act, the unions won a minimum legal status which protected their funds against the worst depredations of criminal and civil law. They were henceforth able to function as such, although immunity from the law of criminal conspiracy, and from civil actions for breach of contract of employment, was withheld until 1875 and 1906. However, they were enabled to register merely by 'complying with the [very minimal] provisions of this Act with respect to registry' and provided their rules were not in an ordinary way unlawful. Any seven or more members of a union could take the step to register in this way.

The definition of 'trade union', which was settled in 1871, provided a very extensive cover for workpeople's reactions to their situation. As summarized by Citrine, it reads :

The expression 'trade union' for the purposes of the Trade Union Acts, 1871 to 1940, means any combination, *whether temporary or permanent* [our italics], the principal objects of which are under its constitution, the regulation of the relation between workmen and masters, or between workmen and workmen or between masters and masters, or the imposing on restrictive conditions on the conduct of any trade or business . . . whether such combination would or would not, if the Trade Union Act, 1871, had not been passed, have been deemed to be an unlawful combination by reason of some one or more of its purposes being in restraint of trade.[1]

The stipulation that 'temporary' combinations may be considered as trade unions has to be read in the light of the reference to their 'constitution' : but it effectively prevents legal discrimination between 'official' and 'unofficial' bodies, provided both have objects which qualify them. If this definition did not apply, then strikes of 'unorganized' groups—which is to say, informally or spontaneously organized groups—would be discriminated against. Since most new developments in the formation of unions have begun, historically, in strike outbreaks, subsequently evolving into 'permanent' organizations, this provision is of great importance. In 1875 the right to picket peacefully in pursuance of a trade dispute was, arguably, granted by the Conspiracy and Protection of Property Act. In 1906 the Trades Disputes Act sought to remove the worst excesses of the law on civil conspiracy as applied to a trade dispute, whilst the term 'trade dispute' was widely defined to mean 'any dispute between employers and workmen, or between workmen and workmen, which is connected with the employment or non-employment, or the terms of the employment, or with the conditions of labour, of any person, and the expression "workmen" means all persons employed in trade or industry, whether or not in the employment of the employer with whom a trade dispute arises'.

These statutes still represent probably the most liberal and widely applicable definition of trade-union rights achievable under a capitalist system of property relations. They have of course been subject to numerous reinterpretations during subsequent years, both in statutes such as the Trades Dispute Act 1927, which was repealed by the Attlee administration, and by judges of Courts of Appeal and the House of Lords, as for example in the notorious Rookes *v.* Barnard case which required another legislative intervention by the Wilson government. The judiciary seems seldom to miss any opportunity to narrow the definition of what constitutes a lawful strike.

[1] *Trade Union Law* (Stevens, 1960).

C

The new proposals and enactments of the 1971 legislation launch
a frontal attack on earlier legislation in all major respects. The
registration of trade unions with a new State Registrar is made
an essential condition for the enjoyment of a privileged legal
status by trade unions. Non-registered unions, or indeed 'two or
more persons' acting together in pursuit of any normal trade-union
functions outside this framework will be liable to a whole series
of civil actions through the new system of Industrial Tribunals and
the Industrial Relations Court. This is bad enough, but the conditions laid down for a successful application for registered union
status are so stringent that they constitute a serious invasion, by
State agencies, of the internal government and democracy of trade
unions. The TUC has correctly described the imposition of the
need for registered status as being akin to requiring a 'state licence
to operate' as a trade union. Apart from the several retrogressive
specific requirements concerning trade-union rules which the new
Registrar must enforce, he is also given undefined and sweeping
powers to impose 'any other requirements . . . as a condition of
registration'.

A collective agreement between employers and trade unions is, in
any just view of the matter, regarded as a social compromise which
provides a temporary resolution of conflicting interests. Under the
new legislation, such temporary accords may be confined within
a framework of legal enforceability which will give them an altogether harmful permanence. Any breach of such agreement which
may occur, through an outbreak of strike action, or any other
forms of non-co-operation with the purposes or instructions of the
employer, will render trade unions (even registered ones, in many
circumstances) and/or groups of workers—particularly 'unofficial'
shop-floor leaders—liable to financial penalties. This can only
imply that in countless situations which, in the tense environment
of modern industry, arise every day, there is now introduced a
serious element of unfreedom, of forced labour.

The list of 'unfair industrial practices' in the new law is a very
extended one, each of which carries with it the threat of financial
penalties, and ultimately, in those cases in which workers defy
court orders to desist or to pay compensation, the possibility of
imprisonment. Moreover, the possibility is that this law encroaches
upon freedom of speech in a very wide and undefined sense.
Clauses 85 to 87 of the original Bill provide not only that anyone

(other than a registered union) who calls for strike action, or other forms of industrial action, which breach contracts, or anyone (whether directly involved or not) procuring or financing such acts, shall be liable to damages. The solicitor-general in the Heath government conceded, during exchanges in the House of Commons, that these provisions might mean that newspaper articles, or comments made on television, would come within the scope of liability. Mr Jack Jones, General Secretary of the TGWU, has consistently warned trade unionists that the passage of this law will introduce an era of industrial espionage, as employers must require informers on the shop floor if they are to identify the initiators of industrial action so that proceedings may be taken against them.

This book is not designed as a text on trade-union law, and the above summary is no substitute for the far deeper analysis of the new situation arising from the law which is urgently necessary. Everything which we say in this and subsequent chapters is now inevitably coloured by the attitude which is being adopted, not only in Britain but throughout the capitalist world, towards trade unionism : this can rightly be designated as corporatist, involving what has hitherto been regarded as a totally unpermissible degree of State regulation of workers' organizations. In such a context it is necessary to preface any discussion of workers' control strategies by asserting the minimum conditions which trade unionists require in order to fulfil their basic role as a defensive opposition to managerial and State domination of their lives, and without which the advancement of alternative positive goals, if it is not to be severely restricted, must be carried on within a new framework—outside the established formal systems of 'industrial relations' and even, in some cases, outside the law.

These minimum conditions, then, include :

(a) The right to organize without State intervention in, or employer domination over, the process of trade-union rule-making and recruitment.

(b) The right to bargain freely and, where required, continuously.

(c) The right to withdraw labour and to take other forms of collective industrial action, which right must be defined as a civic freedom, inherent in all members of the collective, not limited to certain organizations or institutions, or to certain circumstances.

Without these rights trade-union independence is nullified, and the function of the unions is subverted, from the purposes intended by the members who formed them, to those of external authority.

Since, in the present state of law, ownership and control, industry is governed by a small hierarchy, a wealthy elite which is accountable almost solely to the owners of industry, the immediate purpose of the movement for workers' control is to enforce accountability upon industrial management. Management should be accountable both downwards, to the workers in industry, and socially, 'across the board' to the community, for the consequences of its actions. What kind of powers do workers require to achieve this end? What areas of decision-making need be subject to workers' control? And what methods should be used to establish, maintain and widen such control?

The powers which workers need may be summed up in four words: power to obtain *information*, to establish *supervision* over management activity, to impose a *veto* on arbitrary decisions and to obtain *representation* for workers to carry out these functions. The areas of decision-making to which these powers should apply include literally the whole field of industrial activity. Wages and working conditions have long been generally accepted as legitimate trade-union territory, but even here a considerable and permanent struggle continues which, even when pursued with the greatest vigour by unions, only succeeds in preserving the *status quo* with great difficulty. New systems of wage payment, new methods of determining wage structures, the control of overtime, and the fundamental questions of equal pay and of a minimum wage are all, at present, occasions for sharp contest relating to the control of industry. Beyond them lie the wider questions: the right to hire and fire, the control of redundancies, the enforcement of industrial safety, the speed and manning of work, the location of industry, investment decisions, industrial health and welfare, the decisions about product mix, rationalization, trade-union and workers' education, and so on. Suffusing all these specific issues are these questions: Who controls the economy? Who determines the economic policies of governments, in whose interests, and to what ends? Workers have approached these widest questions through the industrial and political organizations which they have created; hence a key aspect of the workers' control movement concerns democracy within the trade unions and the working-class political parties. To all these issues we shall return in detail later in this section of our argument.

What methods should be applied to achieve the powers required in the territories outlined above? Historians of the Labour Movement have sometimes suggested that there is a 'pendulum swing' at work over long periods of time. Sometimes, it is said, the unions have favoured purely industrial activity, and shunned politics, whilst at others the working class has pursued political action and neglected trade unionism. It is not necessary for our purposes to discuss the validity of this view of history. Our own opinion would be that the working class achieves its maximum effect when it walks on both its legs; in other words when it uses both political and trade-union industrial methods to achieve its aims. Thus the objectives which we listed in the previous paragraph may and should be pursued through :

1 Pushing the frontiers of trade-union bargaining beyond the field of wages and conditions into all the areas listed above.

2 Campaigning, where appropriate, for changes in the law, for the extension of nationalization with workers' control, and for legislation standardizing basic conditions, such as the minimum wage, or equal pay, or the thirty-five-hour working week.

3 The establishment of the workers' own areas of unilateral rule-making and control, on the shop floor; or, in other words, the deliberate extension and refinement of what is often called 'custom and practice'.

4 The creation and control of political organizations committed to advancing workers' control programmes.

5 The fostering of trade-union education, which assists towards the understanding of industrial democracy in an independent way, removed from employers' ideas of the limits which should be imposed on 'shop-steward training'.

There is a further method, which has been favoured at certain points in history, and which is still applied in some few instances. That is the method of direct establishment of self-management in co-operative factories; particular islands of democracy set down, as it were, in the general sea of capitalist authoritarianism. The whole co-op tradition belongs to this method, and although retail co-operation has an important place in the modern distribution industry, it has not, up to now, proved possible even there to create effective workers' democracy. The Peace Factories and the Scott-

Bader Commonwealth[2] are other examples of direct factory democracy. These experiments are interesting, and may teach us useful lessons in the construction of rules and constitutions for the future democratic industry at which we aim. But their experience is limited. Time and again in history the workers, or some section of them, have sought to break completely with the system, by 'contracting out' of it. The trouble with this is that the system *outside* the ideal factories goes on as before, and because of its scale and its financial and technical resources, the outside capitalist world remains much more 'efficient' in purely market terms than the utopian islands of democracy. If the market determines that expensive machines shall be manned for three-shift working in the predominant private sector, the idealists in the producer co-operatives will have to follow suit or go bust. The financial resources of society are under the control of the businessmen and the banks, and the Labour Movement has always found it quite impracticable to accumulate sufficient finance to set up an effective alternative, rival system, alongside and within the capitalist system. This is why such experimental factories have been so limited in size and influence, and why they have often been dependent for their creation and survival upon wealthy benefactors or philanthropists. And so we would argue that whilst such factories have a certain value as laboratories, and as witnesses to men's aspirations towards better things, we should not expect that industrial society as a whole can be transformed into a social democracy simply by multiplying such experiments. The citadels of arbitrary industrial power must be stormed directly, not bypassed piecemeal.

Having looked at aims and methods in general terms, it is now necessary to enter into greater detail. We shall discuss in turn shop-floor practice at plant level, formal bargaining in the plant, the strategy in relation to large companies, the demand for information and the conducting of workers' inquiries into companies and industries, the development of workers' control plans at the level of single industries, and the problem of democracy in trade unions and Labour parties.

[2] The Scott-Bader Commonwealth is a small, independent company which manufactures chemicals at its Wollaston factory. It is governed by a fully democratic constitution in which all employees participate on a basis of formal equality. A somewhat pious account of it is to be found in Fred H. Blum, *Work and Community* (Routledge & Kegan Paul, 1968).

Chapter 6

Shop-Floor Controls

Informal, unwritten rules and practices have existed amongst work groups from the beginning of human time. The pace and pressures of modern industrial life, together with increasingly remote and technocratic control of the processes of production, make such protective (or, to those who do not like them, 'restrictive') practices more necessary to workers than ever they have been. There is, for example, the almost universal code of conduct which lays down that workers should not individually race to set back-breaking speeds of work, which might be used to drive less healthy or less adaptable and 'willing' workers to intolerable levels of strain. There are other 'rules' of a similar character, which prescribe that workers should protect each other from the attention of supervisors, should not 'squeal' about fellow-workers who may breach company regulations, and so on. There are informal but effective social sanctions which are applied to people who break the unwritten codes. At another level, there are industrial groups and occupations which establish rules to control recruitment and entry into the job, and these may be either informal or actually written into trade-union rule-books. Rules governing apprenticeship ratios, trades-men's qualifications, closed-shop or union-shop enforcement, the regulation of piece-rate determination, manning scales, the conditions under which overtime will be worked, are yet further examples : although at this level, we enter territory which may be subject not to unilateral rules made by the workers but to negotiated and jointly regulated agreements in which the employer is involved.

Provided there is solidarity, and that the state of the market for his product makes the employer reluctant to embark upon mass-discipline or dismissals, these unilateral controls require very little formal union organization. We may take the following example from the car industry. A worker describing the men's resistance to speed-up explains :

On an assembly line the men were scheduled to produce 96 engines, although they had only the men to produce 90. Management brought pressure to bear, the lines started to go faster. Production leapt to 106 an hour, until this increase was noticed by one of the workers, whereupon he stopped the line. The charge-hand remonstrated : 'What's wrong? Why has the line stopped?' The man told him : 'The speed. We're making up to 110 per hour.' 'Up to the office,' said the charge-hand (prelude to suspension and sack). As they walked towards the office the charge-hand noticed that the whole section (minus a few ACs* and company men) were following. 'All right, forget it,' he said. 'Back to work.'[1]

Developing out of this kind of situation, and based on it, come the controls which are more formally exercised on behalf of the workers by their representatives, the shop stewards. Allan Flanders describes how the management at Fawley Oil Refinery came to realize, in the late 1950s, that the shop stewards had established control over a considerable number of shop-floor decisions, particularly through their control of overtime working : 'They [the managers] all cared, or came to care, about what they regarded as an abdication of responsibility on the part of management in labour relations. This had taken the form of allowing things to drift so that, by default, the initiative had passed increasingly into the hands of the shop stewards.'[2]

Similar positions of bargaining strength have been built in post-war years, by stewards in several important industries, notably engineering, through their regular opportunities to renegotiate piece-work payments. 'Incentive schemes determine pay in a way that cuts across managerial authority to assess the real level of work. Any able shop steward could run rings round the attempt to measure work by rigid schemes such as were involved in the present financial incentive pattern.'[3]

The existence of shop-steward committees extending outside individual plants (the so-called 'Combine Committees'), in industries

---

* Arse-creepers.
[1] B. J., 'I Work at Fords', *Solidarity*, Vol. 2, No. 9 (1962).
[2] Flanders, *The Fawley Productivity Agreements* (Faber & Faber, 1964), pp. 101–2.
[3] A. D. Newman, Glacier Institute of Management, reported in *The Guardian* (10th June, 1964).

such as motors, has led to the extension of shop-floor control over wage structures also. 'The knowledge of the higher piece-rates or earnings in some plants acts as an inducement to those stewards in the plants with lower piece-rates or earnings to catch up. Thus, although the individual incentive-rates in various plants were not centrally controlled by management and permitted variations in average earnings between plants, the unofficial Combine Committee created pressure to equalize earnings upwards in all plants in all regions.'[4]

This type of activity has been typical of well-organized plants and industries under full employment. It was the growth of shop-steward control and bargaining influence during the 'fifties, at a time when national union bargaining was achieving only very modest gains for workers, that finally attracted the attention of governments, and was one of the chief motives behind the drive for incomes policy, the 'reform' of collective bargaining and trade unionism, productivity deals and the like, with which we are so familiar today. We might conclude that if workers successfully develop a certain level of informal unilateral control, then they will face a counter-challenge in the form of management initiatives in local bargaining. Trade unions too have responded to the challenge of the shop floor's self-reliant activities, though not always in a uniform way. Some unions, such as the TGWU and the AUEW at the present time, have placed themselves on the side of this growth of workers' control and campaigned for its extension. Others, however, like the electricians' and plumbers' EETU/PTU, have sought to conclude agreements with employers, and to tighten their internal rules, in ways which assist managements' drive to define and limit the role of the steward in local bargaining.

Bargaining at the Plant Level

It is clear after the experience of the years 1966-70 that the shop stewards and the work groups at plant level have not been left in peace to enjoy their local, fragmented and partial controls. These have been the years of direct wage restraint, operated through compulsory incomes policy. During those years the strategy of

[4] Shirley Lerner and Judith Marquand, 'Regional Variations in Earnings, Demand for Labour and Shop Stewards' Combine Committees, in the British Engineering Industry', *Manchester School*, Vol XXXI, No. 3 (September 1963), 280.

productivity bargaining was developed by the Government, the Prices and Incomes Board, and employers, in an attempt to 'buy out' the controls and informal rules which we have been describing, and to re-establish stricter managerial control. There is no space to discuss this strategy in detail in this book, and it has been documented already in a number of available studies.[5] We may attempt simply a summary of the main tactical devices in this strategy.

The shift from piece-work methods of payment to measured day-work comes high on any list of factors included in productivity bargains. Managements which introduce this change are seeking to remove an important area of bargaining from the regular and systematic attention of the shop stewards. Instead of involving themselves in frequent negotiations over piece-rates, the stewards are to preside, at a distance, over a wage system which is fixed for long periods of time. Moreover, the content and pace of the work under measured day-work may be subject to elaborate and pseudo-scientific methods of assessment which are predominantly under managerial control, instead of being the subject of negotiation and 'mutual agreement'. The switch to the new system of payment may also be accompanied by job evaluation, which may lead to loss of steward and union control over the wage structure, and towards a unilateral determination of this by management. The elimination of overtime, which is often an objective in productivity deals, although advantageous for the workers in terms of increased leisure, may remove an important base on which shop-steward control was built, as happened at Fawley. Rules concerning manning, demarcation of jobs, the role of supervision, and similar matters, may be traded away in return for cash compensation in productivity deals. The imposition of penalties for breach of agreement, or for 'unsatisfactory levels of work' may be attempted. Specific clauses giving a wide and sweeping definition to 'management prerogatives' have been included in many deals. Unions have accepted clauses which limit the arguments which they may use to pursue future wage claims. And so on.

We are not inviting our readers to idealize the situation of the fragmented, partial, informal controls of the 1950s, or to conclude

---

[5] Tony Topham, 'Productivity Bargaining', *Trade Union Register* 1969. Also Ray Collins, 'Trends in Productivity Bargaining', *Trade Union Register* 1970, and 'Productivity Bargaining after Aubrey Jones', Institute for Workers' Control *Bulletin*, Vol. 2, No. 8 (1971).

that any involvement in sophisticated bargaining *inevitably* leads to the undermining of control. After all, the piece-work system, which in recent years has given the workers 'mutual control' over speed of work and payments, was originally regarded (and quite rightly so regarded in the earlier years of the century) as a management device to increase the exploitation of labour. There is no reason to suppose that today's workers are less skilled in developing ways to turn the new devices eventually to their advantage, and if they are compelled to work them, they will undoubtedly evolve such stratagems. And there is little to be said for a trade-union response which simply *defends* demarcation, overtime and piece-work for their own sakes, as though they were the last word in industrial satisfaction for the workers. Clearly they are not. But a recognition and understanding of the purposes of employers and governments in their pursuit of the new techniques is a vital beginning to any campaign to *advance* positively workers' control.

Where management presents an outright claim to unilateral authority in the new type of formal plant agreement or productivity bargain, it should be recognized for what it is, and resisted. This can be done by insistence on the principle of mutuality. For example, management may present a draft agreement with the following clauses : '(a) Work study techniques will be used to establish work standards and man assignments which will ensure an even distribution of work, (b) The allocation of work will be explained by management to the operators concerned and their representatives.' The union side might in these circumstances meet the threat to their control implied here, by amending the second clause to read : '(b) The allocation of work will be subject to mutual agreement between the management and the operators and their representatives.' This would not only ensure that *negotiation* must occur about the allocation of work, but also take care of the threat to control implied in clause (a), since management may be left to carry out work study to its heart's content, provided that the *results* are subject to mutual agreement.

More difficult decisions are involved where management not only does not insist on its own unilateral privilege, but actively invites the participation of stewards in the carrying out of work study exercises, job evaluation schemes, and generally in the re-allocation and replanning of work. The response which is most likely to lead to loss of worker control in these situations is a straight acceptance of management proposals. There is very little, if any, evidence that management has ever come forward with proposals which by design and in their results promote the independent control of workers over them! Where management proposes a system of *mutual* agreement, we may hazard a shrewd guess that they are faced with an existing situation in which the workers have already established *unilateral* control over the territory in question! Where management proposes vague consultative or participatory formulas, it is probable that the existing situation is one in which either straightforward mutual agreement prevails, or in which there is a strong degree of apathy and indifference towards production problems on the part of the workers. Whatever the particular proposals may be (for a 'consultative committee', for a 'productivity committee', or for a 'job evaluation committee'), management is inevitably calculating on obtaining *either* more *authority* than it presently enjoys, *or* on securing greater active *consent* by the workers to the changes which it wishes to introduce.

After a thorough examination of management's proposals for a more formal bargaining relationship, the stewards may simply conclude that it would be wise to reject them. The context in which the proposals have been presented may make this difficult, however, since there may be gains to be made by bargaining, and in any case the very opening up of the question of control presents the stewards with the opportunity for a positive strategy rather than mere rejection. If, after examining the alternative responses discussed in the next few paragraphs, the stewards and local union bodies *do* decide on a straight rejection, the necessity for a detailed, careful presentation of their case to their members, to safeguard themselves from being isolated by management's appealing offers, should be very heavily underlined.

If the stewards decide against either the straight acceptance or rejection of the management's productivity and participation proposals, they have two further alternatives open to them. One is to enter into bargaining in order to *amend* the proposals, the other to table their own *alternative* draft and to insist that this be the basis of negotiations. In either case, the preparation of amendments or of the workers' alternative scheme must be preceded by careful and extensive discussion throughout the plant and in all the appropriate local union organizations. We suggested, in a previous chapter, a series of checks and questions which should be asked about any scheme of closer 'involvement' at plant level. The answers to these questions should, in any given situation, indicate the ways in which it is necessary to amend management proposals for participation.

Shop stewards have faced, in recent years, some extremely subtle appeals to their self-esteem and sense of status, by managements who realize that the persuasive approach through participation may yield better results than the big stick. Discussing the negotiations leading up to a productivity deal, one of the present authors wrote some time ago: 'Some deals take a year or more to negotiate, with management-steward meetings occurring several times a week, interspersed with week-end conferences in club-like surroundings.'[6] Management enter into such negotiations armed with a new self-confidence which is based often on their own thorough preparations:

> Management has been trained in many industries to take time and care in the preparation of a deal. Before they ever invite the participation of stewards and unions, they have spent perhaps months in behind-the-scenes discussion among themselves, fixing their goals, planning their strategy, reorganizing the 'management team'. In the process they acquire a stronger ambition for full managerial control. As a result, stewards and unions start the bargaining in an inferior position, unprepared, and on the defensive. Even the best and most militant unionists are at a disadvantage in this situation.[7]

To guard against this danger, the stewards and unions should reverse the whole relationship, and ideally aim to initiate bargaining themselves, around a series of proposals which they themselves have drafted. In other words, instead of a productivity bargain we should then have 'control bargains'. It should be possible to apply, at plant level, many of the general ideas which are discussed in this book, or which have been advocated by the TGWU[8] and the Labour Party.[9] The demands for the opening of the books, and for the *extension* of trade-union and workers' control, need to be

[6] Topham, op. cit.
[7] Ibid.
[8] See Harry Urwin, *Plant and Productivity Bargaining* (TGWU, 1970), and *Plant Level Bargaining*, TGWU Education and Research pamphlet (1970).
[9] *Industrial Democracy: Working Party Report*, Labour Party 1967, especially pp. 50–4.

given concrete location and precision by the bargainers. This has been partially achieved in a few instances, through the process of amending management drafts. For example, in Peterborough, the TGWU district officer succeeded in including the following clause as part of a procedural agreement : 'The union will have the right to inspect the Company's books and accounts to assist negotiations for a speedy settlement of any Dispute.'[10]

The TGWU has more recently published *general* advice to its membership, which embodies a considerable part of the strategy discussed here, albeit with some modification. In his 20-page pamphlet, *Plant and Productivity Bargaining* (see *n.* 8 above), Harry Urwin, the union's Assistant General Secretary, stresses that the history of collective bargaining is one of conflict between 'authoritarian management on the one hand, and the aim of working people to control their own working environment', but that national level bargaining has had the effect of removing this issue from the formal agenda of trade-union aims. The growth of shop-stewards' organizations is symptomatic of the workers' aspirations towards control, whilst the modern emphasis of companies and of the (Donovan) Royal Commission on Trade Unions upon plant and company bargaining has been taken up by many unions, with the consequence that they now enter officially into a process which the stewards originally developed.

In his advice to negotiators involved in plant and productivity bargaining Harry Urwin consistently emphasizes the need to preserve, or to establish in new areas, the principle of mutuality. He applies this to payment by result systems, work study and the timing of jobs, and to job evaluation. He stresses that the purpose of management in substituting measured day-work for payments by results is the reimposition of 'stronger managerial control'. Drawing on the practice of the United Automobile Workers' Union in America, he points out that even where management is successful in introducing m.d.w., it is possible and vital that the workers' side establishes mutuality of control over performance standards and manning assignments. Mr Urwin's advice on this point has been triumphantly applied by his union in the making of an agreement to introduce day-work wages in place of piece-work at the Cowley Body Plant of Austin-Morris, a section of the British Leyland

[10] An agreement between the TGWU and Brown & Wrights (road haulage company), of King's Lynn (September 1969).

Motor Company. This 1971 agreement is a model of simplicity and precision in the establishment of all the union's principles contained in the Urwin pamphlet.

Clause 1 establishes that 'all direct workers covered by this Agreement shall be paid a flat hourly rate for all hours worked'. Clause 2 affirms that workers will accept the *use* of work study, but that work standards and manning proposals which management derive from such studies shall be subject to Clause 3, which states that 'man-assignments shall be mutually agreed' and that 'standard performance i.e. effort, shall be mutually agreed'. Futhermore, any modification of these quantities shall be subject to agreement. These controls are associated in the American automobile industry with a Procedure Agreement which is exhausted at plant level, that leaves the way open for industrial action without breach of contract. The result has been that strikes over manning and performance in US plants are comparable in number with disputes about prices which occur in piece-work establishments.

Productivity bargaining itself is defined by Harry Urwin as 'the right of trade unionists to bargain continuously at the place of work for bonuses and other additional payments as their share of the rewards for higher output and improved efficiency' and he insists, moreover, that it should not be regarded as 'a replacement for wage bargaining on comparability, cost of living, profitability, etc.'. The whole effect of the pamphlet's message, then, is to re-establish the nature of bargaining as a *conflict,* and to undermine the notions which many workpeople have, that consensus solutions of 'problems' are possible and that processes of work study, job evaluation and the like have a scientific nature. The union's view of productivity bargaining is contrasted with that of 'some managements' who aim 'to bring about a major change in the payment system designed to give management an authoritarian control over wages and performance standards'. Coming as it does from the union which has for several years been an active pioneer and promoter of productivity bargaining, this is a very significant response to its experiences in the field.

Even more remarkable perhaps is the TGWU's pamphlet, *Plant Level Bargaining* (see *n.* 8 above). This takes the form of a list of 'points to consider when making or examining proposals' and includes trenchant comments on job evaluation, disputes procedures, trade-union facilities, line speeds, fatigue, workers' participation, control, speed-ups, production standards, rating, Rucker plans, etc. etc. It seems a great pity that some of the pamphlet's most penetrating analyses, and the firmest advice to stewards about the nature of the game they are involved in, should have been watered down in a second edition issued by the union after the original work had produced a howl of protest from the press and employers. For those not fortunate enough to have studied the earlier edition, the following extracts indicate the alterations which have been made.

On page 6 of the first edition, we read that, amongst other things, the union's objective in productivity bargaining is that 'the difference between capital and labour for the distribution of the benefits of increased productivity are clearly understood by all members'. This becomes, in the amended version, 'the difference between workers and employers'. The words 'care must be taken not to let members be persuaded by the employer that their interests are the same as those of the owners', which appear on page 11 of the first edition, have simply been omitted from the second. The statement on page 16 of the original edition, that 'indeed management sometimes propose changes with the objective of making trade union solidarity, militancy, vigilance and shop steward and rank-and-file communication more difficult to maintain', has now been rephrased to read 'management sometimes propose changes with the objective of restricting trade union activity at the place of work'. The second edition omits altogether the reference to employers who may be anxious 'to get the union to do their dirty work' that appears on page 17 of the first. Page 25 contained originally a most profound comment on the slogan 'a fair day's pay for a fair day's work', which read: 'This paternalistic concept is the very opposite of all the union's objectives. There can never be anything fair about a master and servant relationship. All that any agreement ever achieves is a "temporarily acceptable day's pay for a temporarily acceptable day's work". Both are always re-negotiable.' The first two sentences have been replaced in the second version by a distinctly less courageous statement: 'This generalized slogan can confuse the practical situation at work.'

However, the great value of the pamphlet survives these amendments and we may still read (page 6) that the union aims to see that 'every agreement should involve an extension of negotiating rights and trade union controls and facilities', and that 'dispute procedure should be such as to enable disagreements to be mutually settled without delay and in the work-place where they arise'.

The whole question of *procedural agreements* is likely to occupy a central place in plant-level trade unionism in the near future. The engineering unions have been negotiating nationally with the Engineering Employers' Federation for the revision of the 1922 York Memorandum.[11] A vital demand which they have advanced is for the inclusion of a *status quo* provision in engineering procedure. At the time the present volume goes to press, the old 1922 provisions still stand. They require workers to operate any changed methods, or to accept any management decisions, for the time being, however strongly they may object to it, whilst they put their complaint 'through procedure'. It so happens, of course, that engineering procedure is extremely long-winded, and a grievance may take several months to complete its journey through all the stages. Meanwhile, the management decision stands. The unions are now demanding that, pending agreement, no *proposed* management change may be implemented if it gives rise to objections from the shop floor. That is, the *status quo* must apply during negotiations. This has significant implications for workers' control at plant level, for it implies that the workers would have the right to veto the unilateral and arbitrary decisions of management over a wide range of issues—dismissals, redundancies, discipline, alterations in speed and content of work, manning arrangements, etc. The *status quo* demand, which received the backing of the TUC in 1969,[12] is a crucial practical way of strengthening plant-level workers' control, and goes a long way towards disentangling shop stewards and unions caught up in the meshes of post-productivity bargaining 'participation'.[13]

Building on these examples, shop stewards and rank-and-file members should be able to formulate policies and programmes which begin to break down managerial secrecy (*information*) and to create powers of *representation, veto,* and *supervision* over

[11] Cf. M. F. Somerton, 'The Procedural Agreement in the Engineering Industry', *Trade Union Register* 1970.
[12] The TUC argued, in *Programme for Action* (June 1969), that management decisions about work speeds, manning, dismissals and redundancy should be subject to *status quo*.
[13] For a survey of recent national and company agreements containing *status quo* provisions, see *Income Data Study: Status Quo* (Incomes Data Services Ltd, April 1971).

management decisions. In order to safeguard gains made in this way, the active trade unionists need to work hard to improve the democratic relations between themselves, the members they represent, and the unions to which they belong. Reporting back procedures, and the right of members to call their delegates and representatives to account, and to dismiss them if necessary, are all vital insurances against the dangers of shop-steward incorporation into management's ethos. The other crucial requirement for advance is that trade unions gear themselves to service the shop-floor initiatives effectively. The whole strategy suggested here requires a big expansion of trade-union education, and of research and accountancy services available to trade unionists, and accountable to them. If the plant bargainers are really to make a challenge for access to information on, and powers of veto and supervision over, the employers' investment plans, they need to acquire self-confidence in handling a whole new range of ideas and facts. All the experience of adult education confirms that workers are of course perfectly capable of acquiring this self-confidence if they obtain the opportunities to do so.

But plant bargaining, and plant-level controls over procedure, *are not enough*. They are the base on which we should build much wider frames of reference. If we do not look beyond our own plants, our view will inevitably be a narrow one. On the crucial question of employment opportunities and redundancies, the trade-union side in plant bargaining must take a wider view than that dictated by the immediate short-term interests of the workers in the plant who will be retained in work. Even when 'no redundancy' promises are made, the goal of modern management is *saving on labour costs*, and this may be achieved in the context of improved productivity by natural wastage, retirement and turnover. The result is, of course, that job opportunities for new entrants into industry are reduced, and unemployment rises. It is very difficult to see this perspective from the plant; if, however, a District Committee of a union, or a Trades Council, did some arithmetic and added together the loss of job opportunities from labour-saving agreements made in the major plants in their locality, the point would quickly be appreciated. We shall return to it when we discuss the question of the 'social audit' later on. At this stage, we may simply repeat the negative lesson : plant bargaining is not enough.

Two recent developments, both connected with the current

assault upon workers' rights and negotiating strengths, have ensured that unions cannot confine themselves to factory bargaining. The Industrial Relations Act renders illegal a large part of the normal weaponry used by workers and their stewards to enforce plant-level controls. The characteristic strike of the 1950s and 1960s was the short, sharp, unofficial stoppage, at plant level, designed to protect or to enlarge the area of shop-floor control. How are these initiatives to be maintained and expanded to include the wider objectives, which unions such as the TGWU are now embracing, without the development of new techniques of struggle? What is required is co-ordinated solidarity which dissuades any employer who is tempted to use the new laws to curb and isolate the militants.

The second development, which calls in question a purely plant strategy, is of course unemployment itself. Here, it is already possible to record that unions are reacting by recognizing the danger of plant/productivity bargaining in an economy of a million unemployed. The TGWU nationally, and the TUC, both expressed strong doubts in early 1971 about the wisdom of continuing to co-operate in productivity agreements which contained any threat of present or future redundancy. The TGWU Midlands Regional Committee, in March 1971, taking its lead from these sentiments, prohibited further negotiations on any productivity deal in its area which involved any likelihood of reduced demand for labour.

Finally, we ought to draw attention to one area of work-place organization in which control agitations are urgently needed and can attract the support of every employee.

Industrial safety and health are areas of managerial authority which have given rise to a variety of demands for extended workers' control at shop-floor level. During the 'sixties the number of factory accidents officially recorded rose by 100 per cent, from 150,000 per annum to over 300,000. Working days lost through these accidents, as trade unionists regularly point out, amount to between four and five times the number lost through strike action.

The question of safety touches the very lives of workers, yet the disposal of machinery, plant, transport, methods of production and the provision of safety equipment are all matters of almost complete managerial prerogative. Orthodox opinion represents the history of employers' attitudes in this context as a steady progression away from the early period of *laissez-faire* capitalism, during which workers were butchered in mines and factories, towards a humanitarian system founded on adequate legal provision (the Factories Acts) and supported by the spread of enlightenment amongst management. It is true that, thanks largely to agitation by trade unions, the worst type of direct inhumanity which produced the slaughter of the miners, railwaymen and factory workers in the nineteenth century has diminished. Even so, there are still some industries, such as building and deep-sea fishing, where direct brutality still prevails in work on a scale which is truly staggering.

Right across industry, and within its most advanced sectors, work has become progressively *more* dangerous within the past few years. Undoubtedly this trend is associated with the intensification of work which follows from productivity bargaining, demanning, and redeployment of workers into new and unfamiliar jobs. In response to trade-union pressures, the former Labour Government introduced a measure (the Employed Persons Health and Safety Bill) on this subject in February 1970. The result of the General Election of June prevented its reaching the Statute Book, but it seems probable that an incoming Labour administration will return to this unfinished work, and even that the Heath administration may make minor concessions.

Labour's Bill proposed that trade unions which were recognized for negotiating purposes should have the right to appoint safety representatives from among the workers in factories and other places of work which employed ten or more people, and that in places employing more than 100 people there should be joint safety committees consisting of the workers' safety representatives and management. The functions of the representatives would include 'conducting inspections in the factory in the interests of the safety and health of those working there'. The employer would be required to give reasonable facilities to the workers' representatives, including access to the scene of accidents and dangerous occurrences. Documents kept by management, as required by the Factories Act 1961, should be made available for inspection by the representatives, who would themselves maintain a register of reports of their inspections, in which to record circumstances prejudicial to the safety and health of the work-force.

These were modest and indeed ambiguous proposals, when compared with the kind of demands being made at that time, on behalf of trade unionists, by spokesmen such as Jack Jones. He had written in 1968 of the need for workers' safety representatives to be 'given real powers, "real teeth" '[14] and in the following year, at his union's Biennial Delegate Conference, he proposed that 'there should be unilateral workers' control over safety'.

The criteria by which any legislation on this subject should be judged are embedded in the general themes of the present volume, and from them certain precise propositions can be derived.

1 Workers' safety representatives should not be placed in positions where they must accept responsibility without power.

2 They should be drawn from existing structures of shop-floor trade unionism, and should be elected by, and accountable to, the workers in the section which they will cover.

3 The employers' legal responsibility for the provision of safe working conditions should not be diminished by the presence of workers' safety representatives.

4 Workers' representatives should not be held jointly responsible for disciplinary measures arising out of breaches of mutually agreed safety rules, unless they have powers of joint control over the administration of discipline itself.

5 There seems to be no good reason why workers should be required to give notice to the employer of their intention to carry out an inspection. The only effect of such a provision would be to enable employers to cover up on defects which they had neglected.

6 It would be necessary, in any effective safety legislation, to provide workers' representatives with access to accounts, and authority to order company expenditure on safety equipment. (Many workers who have served on consultative safety committees could confirm that their suggestions for improved methods of working are often met with rejection from management on the grounds of cost.)

7 The authority to prohibit the operation of unsafe machinery or other dangerous methods of work should be vested directly in the workers' representatives.

[14] *Industrial Safety: Joint Control is the Answer*, Institute for Workers' Control *Bulletin*, Vol. 1, No. 1 (1968).

Chapter 7

Control Over the Companies

The multi-plant company has of course been with us for a long time. Since the turn of this century, when firms in cement, chemicals and cotton led the movement to form cartels and trusts, to be followed during the 'twenties and 'thirties by outbreaks of rationalization and mergers in steel, shipbuilding and again chemicals, an increasing proportion of British workers have found themselves employed by companies with several centres of manufacture. But the spate of mergers and take-overs experienced in the past ten years has transformed the industrial landscape and created an entirely new situation.

In the decade between 1949 and 1958, £1,060 million was expended by UK companies on take-overs, a figure which represented 9.5 per cent of their funds. The comparable figure for the *single year* of 1969 was over £6,000 million, representing more than 16 per cent of their funds.[1] During the 'sixties, forty-five of the top 120 UK companies lost their independent existence through the process of merger and take-over. They included :

Number of Companies

9 S. Co. of W., United Steel, Stewart & Lloyd, Dorman Long, John Summers, Colvilles, Consett Iron, S. Durham Steel, Lancashire Steel all disappeared into the nationalized British Steel Corporation.

4—Lancashire Cotton, British Nylon Spinners, Fine Spinners and Doublers, Goodlass, Wall & Lead were taken over by Courtaulds.

3—G.E.C. (including A.E.I. and Elliott Automation) and English Electric merged to form G.E.C.-E.E.

1—Coates (J. & P.) Paton and Baldwins merged to form Coates, Patons.

2—Leyland and British Motor Holdings (including Pressed Steel) merged to form British Leyland.

[1] Michael Barratt Brown, 'The Two Halves of a Decade', Table VIII: UK Company Take-overs, *Trade Union Register* 1970, p. 322.

3—Bass, Mitchell & Butlers, Charrington & United Breweries merged.

2—Ind Coope, Alsopps, Taylor Walker & Walker Cain formed Allied Breweries.

1—British Aluminium was bought by Tube Investments.

1 Watney Combe Reid and Mann, Crossmans & Paulin became Watney Manns.

1—British Printing Corporation was formed from Amalgamated Press, the Daily Mirror and Odhams Press.

1—Hawker Siddeley bought de Havilland Holdings.

1—English Sewing Cotton and Calico Printers merged to become English Calico.

1—John Dickinson merged with E. S. & A. Robinson.

1—Bristol Aeroplane was taken over by British Aircraft Corp.

1—Reed Paper took over Wallpaper Manufacturers.

1—Lewis Investment Trust was acquired by Sears Holdings.

1—National Provincial and Westminster Banks merged.

2—Barclays and Martins Banks merged.

1—American Tobacco bought Gallahers.

1—Chrysler bought Rootes.

1—Tate & Lyle bought United Molasses.

1—Reyrolle took over C. A. Parsons.

2—Borax and Consolidated Zinc were taken over by Rio Tinto Zinc.

1—Ocean Steamship was formed from Liner Holdings and other shipping companies.

1—Kemsley Newspapers were bought by Lord Thomson.

1—Furness Withy took over Royal Mail Lines.

1—British Commonwealth Shipping took over Union Castle Lines.

45—Total

Source : Michael Barratt Brown, Tables of Statistics, in *Trade Union Register* 1970, p. 323.

A factor of increasing significance is the multi-national nature of many of these companies. In the world's car industry, for example, six companies—General Motors, Ford, Chrysler, Volkswagen, Fiat and British Leyland—control more than 80 per cent of the total world output. In 1968 nearly three million cars from the assembly lines of these firms came from plants located outside the parent company's home country. Both General Motors and Fords produced more than one million cars outside the United States (Vauxhall and Opel in Britain and Germany for General

Motors, and Ford for Britain, Germany and Belgium in particular).
Chrysler produced half a million cars in Europe, through its subsidiaries, Rootes (Britain), Simca (France), and Barreiros (Spain).

We may take one or two examples of British-based multinationals in other industries. The giant General Electric-Associated
Electrical Industries-English Electric Company, which quadrupled
its size through mergers in two years, 1968-9, operates through
120 subsidiary companies in the UK and owns 95 overseas subsidiaries in Europe, Australia, New Zealand, Africa, Asia and the
Americas. In Britain alone it employs 220,000 workers. Dunlop
International Ltd employs 100,000 workers in 120 plants spread
across 26 countries and 5 continents. Sixty per cent of its business
is done outside the UK. These figures refer to Dunlop alone; since
its merger with Pirelli, it has doubled its size and now ranks second
only to Goodyear amongst world rubber manufacturers.

It is clear that in this kind of structure the problems of industrial
democracy and workers' control take on a new dimension. The
international company can play one national group of workers off
against another—as, for example, when the motor companies
continually threaten, during strikes in one country, to shift production to another country. The transnational giant firm has a
literally world-wide choice of sites for development, between which
it can pick and choose according to its assessments of relative
labour costs, and according to the degree of sympathy shown it by
governments, in taxation policy, grants, loans, trade-union laws
and so forth. It is to a large extent beyond the legislative control
of national governments, because it exists in a higher dimension,
in which it can shift its resources almost at will and conceal its
financial and ownership structures. It goes without saying that its
centres of authority are so remote that purely plant-level trade
unionism or workers' control strategies will never come to grips
with them. It stands as the ultimate example of pyramided arbitrary, unaccountable private power in industry and society. And it
makes the general political and social case for workers' control
and social accountability even more relevant and convincing; for
the interests of the giant corporation do not at all apparently or
in reality coincide with the social and economic interests of the
communities within which they operate. When the GEC (or
Dunlop, or Ford) decides to close plant A in country B, and to
expand plant C in country D, it is concerned solely with its own

interests, as measured by its overall financial balances and by its need to strengthen its competitive position in relation to the other, rival monsters in its industry.

The trade-union movement has constantly adapted itself, throughout its history, to the changing technology and industrial structures with which it aims to bargain. Craft, industrial and general unions arose in Britain in turn, to meet particular stages of the Industrial Revolution, in successive attempts to create structures which would match the needs of workers. Similar evolution has taken place in other countries. In the United States, the outmoded craft unionism of the American Federation of Labor was challenged by the more radical and appropriate industrial unions of the Congress of Industrial Organizations. Whatever their names or their origins, the unions which most successfully cope with the phenomenon of the multi-plant company—which is often also a company operating not in one, but several industries—are those which spread their recruitment policies across the board. 'Industrial unionism' was the chosen instrument of an older movement for workers' control in the 1910-22 era. Today the rigid schemes for 'one union, one industry' are more likely to be favoured by governments and employers, who prefer a neat, vertical, orderly structure which is more easy to divide and control, in accordance with their interests. The pace of industrial change, moreover, is so rapid that a union which has all its eggs in the basket of a single industry is vulnerable to that very process of combined decline and innovation which is most easily observed in the fuel and transport industries, and which has left industrial unions like those of the miners and railwaymen stranded in industries which are being tapered away. The effects on the morale, the leadership quality and the militancy of the victims were all too evident in those cases, until recently.

Of course, workers anticipate changes in union structure and control long before the slow-moving processes of trade-union reform catch up with changes in industry. The shop stewards threw up their Combine Committees precisely in order to meet the problem of the multi-plant firm and the inadequacies of national union structures. It is within such committees that workers' control programmes which are appropriate for the large companies can be worked out. But as unions respond to the new needs, programmes and policy-making can be fed back into the large, conglomerate

trade unions themselves, and, provided such unions are democ-
ratized and genuinely service their members with adequate
communications, the whole process of matching the unity of the
large employer with unity on the workers' side can be assisted. We
have more to say on this question at a later stage (see Chapter 12).

But something more is needed if an adequate trade-union strategy
is to emerge to confront the multi-national company. At various
times during the past century, workers have reached out beyond
their national boundaries to form international trade-union and
political links. The craft trade-union leaders of the 1860s, for
example, although in many respects quite conservative in outlook,
collaborated with the socialists of the International Working
Men's Association, to create an organization which would enable
them effectively to combine together with workers from the
European continent. Their purposes included the prevention of
blacklegging across frontiers; employers of the period were apt to
use foreign labour, often transporting it from country to country,
to break strikes. The IWMA (or the First International, as it is
usually called) was effective on several occasions in preventing this
practice. The First International actually formed branches and
recruited members in the principal industrial countries of Europe.
Later examples of international trade-union co-operation took less
direct forms : and today, there are a number of international trade
secretariats which are financed and supported by the separate
trade-union movements of different countries. The secretariats to
which British trade unions are affiliated are usually associated
with the International Confederation of Free Trade Unions. This
body was set up by trade unions in the capitalist sector of the
world as a breakaway from the World Federation of Trade Unions.
Today, the WFTU organizes unions in communist countries,
together with communist-led unions in Western Europe and elsewhere. The ICFTU and some of its trade secretariats have inherited
a certain amount of the anti-communist hysteria of the Cold War
period, and indeed echoes of the witch-hunting politics of the
McCarthy era in the United States can still be heard in some of
its sectors, which have sometimes been infiltrated by governmental
services such as the CIA. Although they are by no means, to put it
mildly, perfect instruments for international workers' collaboration,
in many cases they are undergoing progressive transformations as
more radical unions and their active membership begin the search

for adequate instruments of co-ordination against the giant companies. Thus, the International Transport Workers' Federation was approached recently by the TGWU for assistance to prevent the transfer of container work from the Tilbury base near London, which was in dispute, to Rotterdam and other continental centres.

Individual trade unions in several countries, faced with the problems of the international motor companies, have not waited upon the formalities of the trade secretariats and have commenced the process of working out common policies and strategies to be applied, say, in Ford plants throughout the world. The British TGWU and AEU, for example, broke new ground in 1969 by organizing a policy seminar on the car industry with the leaders of the American United Automobile Workers' Union. In order to achieve full international coverage between Western European and American workers, it will be necessary for the British and Americans to break free of the old divisions between communist and non-communist unions, since the majority of trade unionists in France and Italy, two of the key countries in these regions, are organized into unions with communist affiliations. The threat of the international company is in fact pushing both communist and non-communist unions towards each other, and away from the crippling hostilities of the past. This is a difficult process; it will be greatly assisted as and when workers press their unions to adopt genuinely international attitudes, and to develop appropriate workers' control programmes which stress the common interests and objectives of American, British, German, French and Italian workers. This process will be helped by progressive forces in both camps, and hindered by the old dogmatisms, which in England for instance are represented by the NUGMW and in France by the CGT. We make no apologies, in view of the profound importance of this problem, for citing at this stage an extensive statement by a trade-union leader. It is from the speech made by Hugh Scanlon, President of the AUEW, to the 7th National Conference on Workers' Control held in Sheffield in March 1969. First, an extract dealing with the Ford strike in Britain, which had occurred a month prior to the conference :

There is, of course, the irony of the enormous multi-national corporations attempting to play the role of vociferous public patriots. The saying of Samuel Johnson is very true : 'Patriotism is the last refuge of every scoundrel.' It is true today as it ever was, and if we want immediate evidence of this let us turn to the recent Ford dispute. Faithfully reported in all the mass-news media, we have the press, the radio, the television, and last but by no means least and equally vociferous, Ministers of the Crown, rushing out to say, 'If the workers of Ford's do not stop demanding increases in wages, even increases to bring them parity with other sections of the motor industry, the Ford Company loath as it is, patriotic as it is towards us, will take its production elsewhere, for instance into Belgium.' And this, as we know, was broadcast throughout the country. In addition to which they sought to conduct their industrial negotiations through the medium of the courts. We have to ask why, for I cannot believe that the British industrial management of Ford's, with their industrial know-how, really took such decisions. We have to ask ourselves, were these decisions really taken in Detroit?[2]

This kind of question was given even greater relevance during the 1971 Ford (Britain) national strike for parity with the Midland car workers' rates of pay. On that occasion, Our Ford himself, Henry II, visited Britain at the height of the struggle in March, and was received by the Prime Minister with all the deference due to an international monarch, whilst the British press gave his every word the prominence and respect due to the Almighty Himself. The proceedings of Henry Ford's meeting with the British Cabinet were widely leaked, and it was reported that Robert Carr had assured him that the Industrial Relations legislation would effectively curb the propensity of the unruly workers in his British province to engage in strike action, whilst the Chancellor of the Exchequer stressed the Government's determination to resist 'inflationary wage settlements'. This instructive show of government subservience before the power of the international company was said to be necessary to persuade it not to punish the British nation for the sins of its workers by shifting new investment to Ford Germany, or Ford Belgium.

We must hope that the arrival in Britain—a week after Mr Ford had departed—of Mr Leonard Woodcock, head of the American Auto Workers' Union, and many other international delegates to the conference of Auto Workers' Unions of the world, symbolized

---

[2] Quoted from *Workers' Control and the Transnational Company,* Institute for Workers' Control pamphlet series No. 22 (1970).

the start of effective evolution of at least a countervailing inter-national trade-union strategy to head off the power of Henry Ford to divide and rule his multi-national work-force.

Hugh Scanlon, in his 1969 speech, spoke further of the need for such a countervailing power to match the international flexi-bility of the companies, and he developed this point in relation to his view of industrial democracy.

We not only need international labour solidarity to defend our gains, we also need effective control at every stage over the arbitrary power of top management, and effective involvement in every sphere of decision-making. This necessity also reaches to the very core of what industrial democracy is all about. Now we cannot make a real start towards industrial democracy without eradicating our weaknesses. Many of the real powers of decision-making so far as management are concerned in collective bargaining, are moving away . . . from the plant and company to conglomerate or holding-company level. Unless we develop parallel national and international structures with real authority, and I emphasize this, with real grass-roots on the shop floor, so that consultation can take place with the stewards at every and each level; unless we do these things, workers will find themselves increasingly in a position of weakness before such remote and concentrated management. We must strengthen and complete union power in those sections where it is weakest. This is vital if we are to measure up to the international com-bines. . . . The main and most immediate objective, which is the starting-point for industrial democracy, is to oppose the position where organized labour can only react to management decisions and fight a difficult rearguard action to reduce the magnitude of their impact. It must be recognized that con-ventional collective bargaining systems are not appropriate for dealing with technological changes, particularly when the time required for planning has been reduced from decades to months. It is no longer possible or desirable to wait for the end of a specific contract period to negotiate when management decisions are already and quite arbitrarily in the pipeline. These deci-sions may threaten technological unemployment, obsolescence of skills, disappearance of trades and industries, and geographical displacement of the workers themselves. To protect workers adequately, we must be involved with decisions as they occur. We need an anticipatory function at the planning and implementa-tion stages. This is getting to the kernel of our struggle for effective industrial democracy . . . it is a question which is actively concerning trade unions in more and more industrialized nations. It is not, however, just a trade union question; it has very profound political overtones.[3]

'An anticipatory function at the planning and implementation stages . . .' If we apply our four watchwords to this idea, we can begin to see the emergence of a strategy and a programme : information, representation, veto, supervision. We can illustrate the application of the strategy from a case which did not arise in Britain, but which did involve a British-based international company, Dunlop's. In February 1970 Dunlop's Canadian division announced publicly, with no prior warning or consultation with unions, that it would close its Toronto factory on 1st May, making 600 workers redundant. It argued that international competition— from Europe and Japan—made the factory unprofitable. Dunlop is, as we have shown, a very big slice indeed of 'international competition'. Whilst it was prepared to close the Toronto plant, it was opening a factory in the United States, was busy merging with the widespread Pirelli empire, and actually obtaining a public loan from Canadian authorities to automate another plant in Canada.

The workers in the factory, through their union branch, expressed complete scepticism, therefore, as to the company's reasons for closure. They suspected that the plant was perfectly viable, but was being closed because profits (in a fairly high wage area) did not come up to the level which Dunlop expected from other locations.

The union branch therefore mounted an all-out campaign behind a number of carefully thought out demands. They demanded (1) that the company postpone the closure of the plant, (2) that the time so obtained should be used to carry out a feasibility study, by the Ontario Government, the union and co-opted experts, which would establish the true financial and economic position of the factory, (3) that the company should consider an offer by the workers, to buy the plant from it, using their severance pay (which would amount to 2 million Canadian dollars) if the feasibility study was favourable (the workers proposed in that case to run the plant as a co-operative), and (4) that the Ontario Government should pass a new law which would require companies to justify all

[3] Ibid.

closure decisions in future, and submit to feasibility studies where these were requested by the workers.

The workers in this case obtained massive public support for their campaign; the New Democratic Party (Canada's Labour Party) took up the matter as a major issue, challenging the refusal of the (Tory) Provincial Government to take any action. Two professors of economics lent their professional support to the workers' case. Moreover, the union reached out to mobilize international trade-union opinion in its support. Telegrams and appeals were sent to unions in Britain (the home of the Dunlop headquarters) and to the International Chemical Workers' Secretariat in Geneva. British MPs raised the question of the arbitrary nature of the closure decision in the House of Commons. Contact was made between the Canadian union and the British Dunlop shop stewards. This case is a pioneering example; its failure to prevent the closure should not be taken as a failure of a strategy which is still in infancy. If readers will retrace the argument of this chapter, and apply it to the steps taken by the Canadian workers, they will recognize that there are, within this example, the seeds of many future actions.

Ultimately, what must emerge from the process of internationalizing the trade-union movement, is a programme which is capable, through workers' control, of *anticipating* arbitrary decisions. The Canadian workers were still in the defensive position of *reacting after* the decision was announced. Workers' control should be established internationally over hiring and firing, over labour organization at the level of each plant, but pre-eminently over investment decisions. It is these latter decisions which determine, months and years in advance of the event, which plants will close and which will expand. These decisions are not taken at plant level. The trade-union demand for the opening of the books, and for 'feasibility studies' conducted in advance of decisions, is highly relevant at the international company level.[4]

[4] For further reading on trade-union and socialist analysis and strategy in relation to the international company, see the articles by Stan Newens, George Doughty and John Hughes in *Trade Union Register* 1970; papers by John Tuchfield, Ernest Mandel *et al.* in *Democracy in the Motor Industry* (Institute for Workers' Control, 1970); and Robin Murray, 'The Internationalisation of Capital', *The Spokesman*, No. 11 (April 1970).

Chapter 8

The Social Audit

The demand that company finances be available for inspection
by trade unionists and their representatives and the belief that this
demand has an important part to play in the extension of industrial
democracy, have a long history. In recent years the demand has
reappeared to occupy a central place in the programmes of progressive trade unions, it has been written into *Industrial Democracy:
A Labour Party Report*, adopted by the Labour Party's Annual
Conference in 1969, it is raised with increasing frequency by
workers threatened with redundancies and plant closures, and it
is now being tabled as a needed amendment to plant agreements,
as we have seen. In view of this escalating process, it is not
surprising that governments and employers are now prepared to
offer certain concessions to head off the demand for *information*.

The proposition that the unions should respond to the national
incomes policy with a demand for the opening of the books was
advanced by the workers' control movement as early as 1964. In
its general form, this was a demand for parity of information with
the employers: 'Not merely the officials who administer PAYE,
but the employers themselves, know all there is to know about
wage incomes. Parity requires not that some commission should
review some aspect of rentier income, but that the workers themselves through their own institutions, should come to know as
much about their employers' resources in turn.'[1]

And again:

The unions contain the *only* people who can effectively ensure
that the employers do not cheat on an incomes policy. If the
accounts of every firm are available to the inspection of its
shop stewards, they will pose the constant risk that cheating
will be unmasked, as the workmen's inspectorate check the

[1] Ken Coates, 'Incomes Policy: A Strategy for the Unions', *Socialist
Register* 1965.

books against the facts of its daily industrial experience. This is
not to say that every shop steward is an accountant. But every
steward can call on the resources of his union and professional
advice can be procured . . . [and] the union grapevine provides
an intelligence network which no Government department could
possibly begin to rival.[2]

This demand was taken up and elaborated by the largest trade
unions in the country. Thus Jack Jones of the TGWU argued in
1966 that 'by forcing companies to recognize unions and "opening
the books" to the scrutiny of trade-union representatives, the dam
of industrial apathy can be burst'.[3] In the following year, he
wrote: 'Wider scope can be won for such [plant level] committees by extending the information available to them. Forecasts
of investment and labour requirements, sales policy, unit costs,
etc., are all essential for realistic negotiating and productivity
consultation. The secrecy of management is one of the most harmful restrictive practices and should be treated as such.'[4]

Hugh Scanlon of the AUEW has returned to the question of
information on several occasions. In 1968 he was arguing that
'the Labour Movement cannot rest contented with a tenuous and
limited say merely in the functioning of welfare facilities. This
is particularly true in the present industrial climate of larger and
larger monopolies only really accountable to their own shareholders who may well become a threat to political democracy
itself. In this connection the slogan of "open the books" to allow
accredited workers' representatives to pursue the financial ramifications of these vast combines is a concrete first step towards the
development of social accountability'.[5] He developed this argument in more detail the following year:

> . . . above all, knowledge is power. For the proper understand-
> ing of the functions and problems of any undertaking it is
> necessary in the first instance to have ready access to the relevant
> information. There seems to be an organized conspiracy to shut

[2] Ibid.
[3] *Tribune* (11th February, 1966). Jack Jones was a member of the Labour
Party Executive's study group on industrial democracy and obviously
influenced its findings.
[4] 'Unions Today and Tomorrow', *The Incompatibles* (Penguin Books,
1967), p. 127.
[5] *The Way Forward for Workers' Control*, Institute for Workers' Control
pamphlet series No. 1 (1968; repr. 1971).

D

off the workers from effective knowledge of the firm's operations, financial dealings and plans. This is in the final analysis an organized conspiracy against society itself. One of the key demands of industrial democracy (and I do not apologize for this and say it with emphasis) is *open the books*. This does not mean as it has so much in the past, just the cooked up balance sheets that shop stewards are frequently saddled with in the negotiations they undertake. It means that workers have full and detailed information concerning costing, marketing, and all other essential financial details. There is no reason why in this demand we should be fobbed off with only a minimum of demands.[6]

We have already noticed the case of the Toronto Dunlop workers, who demanded access to financial information in order to conduct a feasibility study of the prospect for their factory as part of their campaign against closure. Other workers threatened with redundancies have made the same demand. For example, the GEC Shop Stewards' Action Committee, in its fight against redundancies in the Liverpool factories of that company insisted: 'We shall continue to press through our trade unions, the TUC and the Labour Party for a full recognition of our case, and for official support for our claims for no redundancy, for the inspection of the company's accounts by ourselves and our unions, and for an inquiry into alternative production plans for our factories, on which the unions should be represented.'[7]

The Labour Party's *Industrial Democracy Report*, referred to above, published in 1967, goes into some detail as to the information which companies should be required to divulge and it is worth quoting their schedule of necessary information:

The headings of importance, so far as disclosure to the trade unions is concerned, include:
(i) *Manpower and Remuneration Questions*
    Labour force; labour turnover; manpower plan and staff development; absenteeism and sickness rates; accident rates and trends; accident prevention plans including training; other training schemes; labour costs per unit of output; pay-

[6] *Workers' Control and the Transnational Company*, Institute for Workers' Control pamphlet series No. 22 (1970).
[7] Open Letter of the GEC Workers' Action Committee, reprinted in *GEC Workers' Take-over*, Institute for Workers' Control pamphlet series No. 17 (1969).

roll details and methods of payment; managerial and directorial emoluments; and qualifications of directors and senior management.

(An employer should, for instance, be obliged to tell his workers of any agreement made with other employers not to employ each other's recent employees.)

(ii) *Control Questions*

Details concerning holding, subsidiary, and associated companies; directors' shareholdings in the company; beneficial control of nominee shareholdings; internal management structures and definition of decision-making responsibilities.

(iii) *Development, Production and Investment Questions*

Proposed changes of a substantial character of work and/or labour requirements; state of the order book and trend of orders gained and lost; research, development, and investment plans; purchasing policies.

(iv) *Cost, Pricing and Profit Questions*

Cost and pricing structures; breakdown by plant or product where applicable; turnover; financing of development.[8]

An even more comprehensive programme of required information has been made by the economist Michael Barratt Brown in a pamphlet published in 1968.[9] We have omitted the details of his notes under each heading, but in summary form they read :

A *Production*
B *Organization and Management*
C *Sales and Marketing*
D *Finance*
E *Employment Policy*
F *Contribution to the Community*

As an example of the detailed questions under each head in this pamphlet, Barratt Brown suggests that the following are relevant to 'Directors and Leading Executives', which is just one subsection of (B) : 'What are they paid? What other emoluments do they receive—car, chauffeur, petrol allowance, private secretary, subsidized meals, free life insurance, insurance for private medical treatment, pension provision, covenants for private schooling of children, subsidized housing, bonus payments, any other extras?'

The leading questions which clearly arise from the campaign

[8] Labour Party *Report* (1967), pp. 52–3.
[9] *Opening the Books,* Institute for Workers' Control pamphlet series No. 4 (1968).

to open the books are: How do we handle the information?
What do we want it for? Who needs the information? Before
dealing with these important points, however, it is necessary to
say a word about recent offers of concessions in this field. The
Conservative Government has said that it will legislate to give
trade unionists the right of access to the same information that
is available to shareholders. This is an offer of precisely nothing,
since the information to which shareholders have access is already
available to the public. The balance sheets and profit-and-loss
accounts, which the Companies Act requires companies to publish,
contain only the most general information, much of it useless, and
some of it misleading. Many professional accountants are extremely
critical of the form in which the published accounts are made up
and would be very loath to make judgments about a company's
position on the basis of such information alone. The trade unionists
require access to very much *more* than is currently available to
the shareholders. The Conservative Party's meaningless gesture on
this matter tells us only that they are very much aware that the tide
of the demand is running strongly and that they ought to sound
'progressive'.

The same conclusion can be drawn from the efforts already
made by some managements to give away a few secrets. Shop
stewards in a stevedoring company in Hull were recently shown
books of accounts in the company's offices and allowed to study them
for an hour. These books demonstrated, with copious quantities of
red ink, the regularity of the company's losses! They were unable
to take the books away for proper study, and they were unable to
bring in a specialist to advise them on the interpretation of the
figures. Again, an engineering company offered to open its books
to trade-union inspection, in return for trade-union acceptance
of a complicated productivity bonus linked to 'added value'. The
shop stewards in that situation were rightly dubious of the offer,
but were prepared to test it by sending in an accountant from their
own research centre. But inquiry revealed that the union did not
employ a qualified person, and were (also rightly) reluctant to
become involved in an extremely complicated managerial manoeuvre with all kinds of possible snares and traps. 'Every governing class in history has tried to clothe the business of government
in mystery, and the clerks who carried on the actual business
have always resorted to magic words and signs to blind the

ignorant. It is not for nothing that the most representative organization of British businessmen is the secret society of Freemasons.'[10]

Fancy formulas for calculating bonuses or the 'sharing' of 'added value', combined with the selective doling out of misinformation, adds to the possibility of confusion amongst workers, and to the danger that some shop stewards may find themselves cosily incorporated into management's ethos and 'mysteries'.

The Prices and Incomes Board spoke with breathtaking cynicism about the need to make apparent concessions in this matter, and recommended that 'more information' should be given to workers, 'in order to win the confidence of the unions' for productivity deals. 'We do *not* suggest, however,' said the Board, 'that *all* relevant information should be made available to trade-union representatives' since 'such facts might give the unions precise information on what the employer could pay before he had any notion of the figure for which they were prepared to settle.' The Board went on to distinguish between those union representatives who would 'respect as confidential' the information they were given, whilst another type would 'conceive it to be his duty to turn all he learns directly to their [the workers'] advantage in negotiations'.[11] Clearly in the case of this kind of approach, the unions must preserve an attitude of total scepticism towards the 'information' that they are offered. And in all the concessions which employers and government are prepared to discuss, there is a common reservation—they wish to preserve for the employer the right to withhold 'information the release of which might be damaging to a company's commercial interests'. This reservation was expressed by the Labour Government, in its promised reform of company law, and has been repeated by the Conservative Party and by numerous spokesmen of the employers. 'An end to commercial secrets,' they cry boldly, only to add more quietly, 'except those that are commercially necessary.'

Clearly the unions require an unambiguous, general and unrestricted access to all commercial secrets. This does not imply that they should turn away all doubtful and phoney offers of partial information, since appetite grows with the eating, and workers

[10] Ibid.
[11] *Productivity Bargaining,* National Board for Prices and Incomes, Report No. 36 (June 1967), Cmnd 3311.

in the typical multi-plant company who are really getting to grips with their employer's financial ramifications will want to probe deeper and deeper. There are certain rules, and certain implications for the unions, which can be derived from this discussion. First, there is the need to preserve scepticism—a healthy attitude of disbelief is essential. Secondly, workers and workers' representatives who obtain access to information should be obliged to report back to their members. There must be no suggestion of a few privileged workers sharing confidentiality with their employers. Thirdly, the unions must be prepared to 'gear up' their specialist services to members, so that union-paid accountants and financial experts are readily available; this is a practical necessity, since we are not all trained accountants, and is also required to prevent the management from simply calling the bluff of the unions. If the management is confident that the unions have no such personnel available, they will readily agree to an exercise in opening the books, trusting to their superior skills to protect them from exposure to sharp practices and concealment of vital information. Fourthly, the unions must reinforce their 'expert' services with a big expansion in the education of their members—education directed to raising understanding not merely of technical matters of accountancy, but more important, of the wider economic, social and political significance of information and decision-making in industry. Finally, the members must ensure that this trend does not result in an 'Americanization' of their unions, in which a new breed of academic or business specialist assumes a dominating role within their organizations. If lawyers, economists and accountants are to be enrolled by the unions, then they must be held strictly accountable to the membership, at grass-roots level. There is, hopefully, no shortage of young, radical minds, who view with dismay the prospect of working for Big Business after their student days are over. The Labour Movement should tap this supply of skilled manpower, and use it for its own independent purposes in unmasking the secrets and mysteries of business. The workers should bear in mind, however, that the backroom experts are helpless to fulfil their role unless they work alongside the shop-floor workers who are the real experts on the practices of their own company. A company accountant may arrange the books—in order, for instance, to claim excessive depreciation charges. The workers themselves, once mobilized for the task, possess the necessary knowledge to say whether a piece of plant or machinery is actually in the condition to justify the book entries.

Let us now return to the question of why we need information, and what we should use it for. We would suggest that the purpose of demanding access to company secrets does not consist in simply obtaining more income for the workers in the particular company. This may well be a strong (and entirely justified) motive, particularly when productivity deals are involved. Companies which have concluded productivity bargains are extremely secretive in many cases about the savings which have resulted. Workers are entitled to know every detail of the consequences of their negotiations for company profits. In many of the big productivity deals of recent years unions have settled for a very meagre share of the total saving achieved. But the long-term interests of the whole working population may be ill-served if the aim of the bargainers is to achieve a higher material prosperity only for the highly mobile, highly flexible, trained and retrained and re-retrained workers who are fortunate enough (in the short run) to work for companies which have rationalized themselves to the last degree. Unless the wider social and economic consequences of company decisions are taken into account, even the 'privileged' sector of the working population will be highly vulnerable. If the dole queue has been doubled in length as a result of all-out labour-management co-operation at the plant and company level, then workers who remain in employment are themselves in a much weaker state to preserve a bargaining position.

It cannot be too strongly stressed that the whole trend of capitalist company policy is towards *labour-saving investment*. That is why we have called this chapter 'The Social Audit' and not simply 'Open the Books'. *The trade-union and Labour Movement needs information in order to make a 'social audit' of the consequences of capitalist decision-making, and to prepare alternative plans based on the social needs of communities.* This sounds terribly complicated, but the basic process is very simple. Let us take as an example the working community of an industrial centre in Britain, Teesside. There, the ICI employs 25,000 workers, and the steel industry a further 25,000. These are the only two *major* employers of labour in the area, and the whole life of that community is consequently heavily dependent upon the decisions taken by the directors of ICI and the British Steel Corporation. Plans are already

in the pipeline for the rationalization of the steel industry, and
throughout the country some 100,000 workers may lose their jobs
in consequence over the next five years. The ICI expressed its
intentions a few years ago of negotiating a productivity agreement
(Manpower Utilization and Payments System) which, having been
applied to some smaller plants, has produced a redundancy or cut-
back in the employed labour force of 18-25 per cent. The precise
effects of the remote decisions of the central boards of the two
industries could not be known to workers *in advance*. And if they
remained solely concerned with their own industries, they might
hope to conclude agreements which provided for severance. payments, and other ameliorations of the worst effects of the schemes
on individuals. But if they were able to assemble all the information
available to the top management of both industries, and feed it
across the industrial boundaries to one another, then they would
be in a situation to weigh the full social effects of any bargains
they might wish to strike. From that step they could go on to
prepare not only a negative protest about the decline in labour
demand which is threatening their community, but also to work
out alternative means of using the resources, both material and
human, which are accumulated in a community like Teesside.

The trade unions representing ICI workers presented an elaborate
and pathfinding claim to the company in 1971, which, in addition
to demands for wage increases, backed up with substantial analysis
of both company and national statistics, included a series of proposals for a 'positive employment programme'.[12] In discussing the
future of the 'Weekly Staff Agreement' (a productivity deal which
superseded the earlier MUPS scheme and which now covers the
majority of ICI workers) the trade-union document (submitted to
the company in April 1971) points out that : '. . . we need to beware
of meeting the "no redundancy" pledge by the arbitrary curtail-
ment of recruitment (particularly of young workers) which may
have damaging social consequences in areas such as the North
East, where ICI is a major employer and the range of alternative
employment is limited. This points to the need for a wider process
of joint review of manpower requirements, with respect being paid
to the social responsibilities of such a large firm'.

The document goes on to propose that joint discussion between

[12] See *A Positive Employment Programme for ICI* (TGWU booklet, April
1971).

the unions and the company should take place on investment programming, which is 'essential if the underlying basis of WSA is not to be undermined by the spectre of growing unemployment in the communities in which our members and their families live'. Furthermore, in a section on environment and pollution, the unions express their anxiety that 'the growth of their real incomes is not to be at the expense of the health of themselves, their families and their communities', and go on to propose the extension of joint management/trade-union committees on safety to include 'the effects of the production process on the whole community, instead of those who happen to be employed within ICI itself. There is nothing idealistic about this—we are thinking of our members' families and their children's children'. The unions propose that they be free to co-opt technical experts from local universities, departments of health and other relevant bodies on to ICI's safety committees, and that a general committee be established nationally by the company and the unions, concerned with the environment, to which both sides would bring technical expertise.

The language and the conceptual framework of these proposals may be heavily influenced by the corporate philosophy which ICI feeds out to its employees and which therefore inevitably at this stage conditions the attitudes of trade unionists in ICI. Yet the demands are important, for we are now in territory beyond the factory gates. We are not thinking simply in terms of plants and the short-term interests of workers within plants; we are thinking socially, and beginning the process of democratic planning. This is a process which must begin with plant-level workers' control of the kind we have discussed above. But it must lead outwards to embrace the widest social and political questions of the transition to socialism.

Capitalist theory argues that the market ensures the best use of resources and that by trying to maximize profits the capitalist is obeying the rule of the market. So the capitalist concentration on the use of resources is on cutting costs. The socialist looks at things quite the other way round. He asks—'What resources are available? How can we act, how plan our economic policies so as to make the best use of resources?' The criticism that condemns capitalism is its failure to use available resources, its waste of resources. That is true of many types of resources, machines, materials and so forth. But the real resource that matters is people. People produce wealth. Also people want to be wanted, want to contribute to the community they live in, want to be active and to be stretched in the deployment of their skills and abilities. As a producer and as a consumer a man or a woman wants to live a full life. So good use of resources . . . is the first of socialist aims and on this planning can help. . . .[13]

The quotation above is from a study of computers, and their potential value to socialism and democracy. Obviously, the investigation of the complex processes of industrial activity, investment, location of industry, employment plans and the like requires the accumulation of large amounts of detailed information. The computer, and allied electronic aids such as *data banks* (devices in which, say, 500 million bits of information may be stored in one square inch of space, and made available at the press of a button) make it potentially possible for ordinary people to handle such information for social and democratic purposes. Equally, of course, this 'information revolution' can give, in the circumstances of a society dominated by small elites of industrial dictators, enormous and uncontrolled power to a few.

Which way things go is the political issue that has to be fought, and this is the issue here and now. Groups of men and women who are politically aware and awake, and seek to stimulate more and more people to shape a collective will, that is aims and policies for the social organism in which they live and work, will need to draw on such information as is currently available. But at the same time, it is necessary to campaign that information relevant to social and economic decision-making should be freely and fully available and also that the most advanced computer techniques be developed so that anyone who wants can obtain the specific information he needs rapidly and have it presented in the clearest and most quickly grasped forms.[14]

But of course the new trade unionism cannot and does not wait for the fruits of its struggle for open books and access to computer techniques before beginning the process of social audit. The ICI claim, already mentioned, contains important references to the social costs of pollution and of labour-saving investments and pro-

[13] Stephen Bodington, 'Socialism, Democracy and the Computer', *Can the Workers Run Industry?* (Sphere Books [and the Institute for Workers' Control], 1968), p. 112.
[14] Bodington, op. cit.

ductivity programmes. The trade-union submission in this case also includes a complaint about 'the inadequacy of the information available for intelligent discussion of our common interests' and claims access to detailed breakdown figures of ICI's employee remuneration and numbers employed, and demands that the returns made by ICI to the Government should be 'sent to us at the same time and in the same form as they are sent to the Department of Employment'. The unions propose further that a joint working party be set up 'with the object of concluding a *General Information Agreement*'.

The documentation which accompanied the trade union's claim for parity of earnings for Ford workers with car workers in other firms, also probes the limits of information which is currently available on profits, productivity and comparative performance of Fords in all its international operations.[15] New standards of social criticism of the behaviour of the large companies are set by the trade-union cases in both these major bargains of 1971. For example, the union documents subject the impact of government taxation policy, on both workers and companies, to close scrutiny, implying thereby that trade-union concern should be widened to include a total critique of the consequences, for income distribution, of the joint operations of governments and employers. These are all positive developments in the policies of the new unions, and in particular of the TGWU, which was responsible for the preparation of the cases presented to both Ford and ICI. In both cases, too, the union received vital assistance from John Hughes's research unit at Ruskin College, an example which should foreshadow a more general tapping of skilled advice, for which we have called earlier in this chapter. Of course this evolution is accompanied by the danger, which bears re-emphasis, that British trade unions will evolve along American lines towards business unionism. The settlement reached after the gigantic efforts of Ford's workers and shop stewards in their nine-week strike of 1971 serves to underline this danger, since it not only falls well short of the parity with other car workers on which the whole documentary case was built, but, far more serious, also embodies American-style contractual features—a guarantee of two strike-free years and a promise not to return for more money until that period has elapsed. As always, our conclusion must be that a purely trade-union strategy, however

---

15 *The Ford Wage Claim* (TGWU booklet, December 1970).

much influenced by the quest for wider horizons and by a determination to attack global targets, is constrained within the limits which the consciousness of its members can reach through a process of bargaining. Just as we concluded that plant bargaining is not enough, so we affirm further that the pursuit of social goals cannot be confined within collective bargaining, but must grow from that origin, outwards towards a political programme.

We have traced a broad path in following this line of argument through to this stage. Let us sum up. The demand for information is a demand for power and democracy. It has arisen in the trade-union movement out of the sheer logic of the pressures under which trade unionists have been labouring for the past six or seven years. They have been pressed to accept wage restraint, but denied knowledge of other forms of income. They have been pressed to accept productivity deals, but denied knowledge of the contribution which their extra output makes to profit incomes, or of the effect of their increased efficiency on employment prospects for their brothers or their sons and daughters. They have been enticed with the prospects of sharing in a 'partnership' to enhance the profits of their own plant, without thought to, or knowledge of, the effects outside the plant. The workers are beginning to respond by demanding more information, first at the plant level. They have been promised something in this direction, but the promises are often intended to divert and deceive. The demand for the opening of the books, once it is unleashed, must and will gather momentum until the essentially *social* nature of production and economy stands revealed. At that moment, the possibility of genuinely communal, democratic planning is opened up. Such planning will increasingly confront and conflict with the arbitrary powers of the giant companies, intensifying the struggle for workers' control. And to service that struggle unions must equip themselves with technical resources and manpower, and also draw on all those resources and all those people in the general community who wish to serve the cause of democracy.

Chapter 9

Workers' Control at the Industry Level

Certain basic economic activities, such as the production of energy, transport, and more recently steel, have become traditionally regarded as suitable for organization under public ownership on an industry (rather than company) basis. This is true also of a number of amenities and services—post and telephones, education, health and hospitals, broadcasting and so on. In the case of the mines, the railways and the post office, the question of public ownership was linked by the unions with demands for workers' representation from very early days in the twentieth century.[1] Yet whilst governments of all complexions have been prepared, *in extremis*, to bring key industries into public ownership, it has remained true under each of them that every attempt by workpeople and unions to insist on directly elected and accountable workers' representation in management has been bitterly resisted.

There is a common reason for the acceptance of public ownership in such industries, a reason which also helps to ensure that the State resists all demands for democratization. It is that the industries concerned have, at the time of nationalization, normally been charged with 'failing the nation'— that is, they have been backward, structurally inefficient and urgently in need of reorganization. This was clearly true of coal and rail transport between the wars and in the immediate post-war period; more recently it has been true of steel and docks. It may well indeed be that all these commercially unsound industries were, at the time of their take-over by the State, failing 'the nation'; of more concern to business was the fact that they were persistently unprofitable. Not only was this the case with the industries themselves, which were predominantly unable to earn profits for their owners, but worse, in such con-

[1] See *Workers' Control*, ed. Ken Coates and Tony Topham, especially § III: 'Industrial Democracy and Nationalisation' (Panther Modern Society, 1970), pp. 247–341; also Branko Pribicevic, *The Shop Stewards' Movement and Workers' Control 1910–22* (Blackwell, 1959).

ditions they were also failing to provide an adequate service to underpin the profit-making of all those other industries which used their products. Since the major customers of the mine-owners and railway companies were other industries (rather than the individual consumer), although the directors of the decrepit sector might put up, as a rearguard action, a political fight for the principles of 'free enterprise', all the other businessmen, and the politicians who represented them, were not altogether unwilling to concede that nationalization might be an answer to the structural problems, provided that the affairs of the widened public sector remained subordinate to the rest of the private interests which depended on them. It would, however, be quite disastrous to this subordination if workers were to obtain a dominant voice in the administration of the newly nationalized industries. As a result they might not only have prevented the carrying out of ruthless schemes for 'rationalization', but also have begun to devise alternative plans, based both on the need to meet social considerations and the possibilities of actually expanding the boundaries of public ownership by effective competition with private industry.

Thus, in the absence of either a successful political struggle or a determined trade-union fight for workers' control, in nationalized industry since the war the boardrooms and the policies of public industries have been dominated by the needs of private interests. Merchant bankers, directors of the big insurance companies and directors of large companies, which have often themselves been major customers of the public sector, have been the most numerous types amongst members of the main nationalized industry boards. Retired officers from the Armed Forces, academics and a diminishing number of former trade-union general secretaries and presidents have occupied the remaining minority seats. More recently, the practice of appointing personalities such as Dr Beeching, who are surrounded with an aura of the supposed genius for organization which they bring with them from high office in the big private companies, has made the resemblance between the nationalized boards and their counterparts in ICI or the oil companies even closer.

We have already spoken of the disillusionment felt by workers in nationalized industries who had been forced to trade in their expectations of a totally new status under public ownership for a purely consultative role in relation to management. The railwaymen appear to have been so demoralized by this, and by the drastic reduction in their numbers, that up to now they have shown no spark of initiative towards a counter-attack : certainly there has been no serious demand for workers' representation in that industry during the current renewal of the workers' control movement. The miners have, here and there, participated in the discussion, but again their terribly vulnerable position has left them with a big heritage of defensive attitudes to overcome. We shall, however, see that there are certain growth-points in their recent programmes and publications. We have already had occasion to refer to the campaign for workers' representation in the steel industry. The following comments are intended to show some of the forms taken by workers' control demands which have been made, or are being made, in a cross-section of industries or sectors of the economy.

Mining

The contribution of the miners to the history of the workers' control movement is second to none. It was in the South Wales coalfield that the syndicalist teachings of Tom Mann found some of their earliest and deepest responses.[2] By the time the First World War ended the miners' unions and the Miners' Federation had been almost completely won over to support for one or other of the many versions of workers' control which flourished at that time. They had experienced some degree of industry-wide management as a result of government intervention during the war, and had begun to think in terms of a socialist programme which embraced the whole industry. Their official demands for nationalization, with 50 per cent workers' representation on the managing bodies, were presented to a government inquiry, the famous Sankey Commission, in 1919. Later, they were driven back from these advanced attitudes by the bitter defensive struggles against wage cuts and unemployment which preoccupied them throughout the 'twenties.

Yet when the Government of 1945-50 came to nationalize the industry, the old aspirations were still present in the consciousness of the mining communities. The Labour Government completely ignored the tradition of workers' control; it established orthodox management authority in the publicly owned pits, and set over

[2] See *The Miners' Next Step* (Reform Committee of the South Wales Miners, 1912).

them a State-appointed Coal Board. The miners' union leadership
at that time did not see fit to embarrass the Government by
campaigning for workers' representation, and instead supported,
for different and incompatible reasons, the Government's blueprint
for bureaucratic management. The miners, after a brief period as
the post-war pace-setters in unofficial militancy and high wages,
became after 1957 the victims of a fuel 'policy' which bent before
the powerful short-term private interests of coal-users (predominantly of course, as we have said, these were other industries
—both public, like the electricity and gas boards, or, at the time,
private, like steel) or of producers of rival fuels, such as oil (and
later natural gas). In response to these pressures, which were expressed both politically, through the lobbies, and commercially,
through the market, the Coal Board and successive governments
endorsed a vast programme of pit closures, regardless of the social
and economic costs which these entailed. Moreover, the Board
and the Union leadership's only 'positive' response to the prolonged
crisis of coal in the 'sixties was to introduce new nationally
determined methods of wage payment (notably, the Power Loading
Agreement), depriving the miners of much of their traditional
bargaining power which had been based on pit-level negotiations
over piece-rates. The new methods of payment were associated with
a prodigious mechanization drive, and gave enhanced authority
to managements to determine work-loads and manning scales. Any
resistance to these measures could easily be met with the warning
that it would reduce the performance of the colliery concerned
below the margin at which it could be allowed to survive. Pits
closed down in hundreds, leaving new derelict areas in which the
old men were retired and the boys went into the army. The logic of
the Board's policy was quite sound, as long as one accepted the
irrational processes of a market economy, in which one fuel was
supposed to compete with others, and in which the owners of oil
companies could more or less dictate the terms of the competition.

The miners' response to these crippling circumstances emerged
(hesitantly, against a background of twenty years of morale-
breaking decline) with the general upsurge of interest in workers'
control. Although nothing approaching the overall conversion of
the miners' union and its rank and file to new radical solutions
has yet occurred, so that the NUM today still has no policies to
match those of the 1910-22 period of its forerunner, the MFGB,

the campaigns that have been launched in the Yorkshire, Derbyshire and other districts of the union during the 'sixties have been
broadly based and carefully related to the real dimensions of the
problem. There has been the Derbyshire miners' strategy of 'taking
up the slack' (in the words of Bert Wynn, one of the most per-
ceptive of miners' leaders since the war) and of seizing new opportunities to turn the formal joint consultation machinery to militant
control purposes.[3] There has been analysis and growing understanding of the adverse implications of the Power Loading Agreement for workers' control. There have been new blueprint
programmes published in the past few years, restating the old
demands for direct workers' representation in the managing bodies
of the Coal Board. And at the widest level there have been
insistent calls for the formulation of a workers' fuel policy, which
would be based on a thorough social-cost analysis of the effects of
the use of various fuels, together with a strategy to protect and advance the interests of workers in every sector of energy supply.
Such a policy would require that miners broke out of their
narrowly 'industrial' thinking and approached the workers in
oil, gas and electricity with proposals for the preparation of joint
policies and co-ordinated action to implement them.[4]

Starting with their own sectional problems, the miners are thus
beginning to reach out to the formulation of genuinely social
policies. At first sight it may appear that the workers in the growth
sector of energy supply (oil, natural gas, electricity) have interests
opposed to those in coal. But the Esso refinery workers at Fawley
have as much interest as the miners in securing access to the
company secrets of their employers. Workers in oil have been
amongst the first to feel the disquieting consequences of productivity and efficiency drives; the workers in coal suffer indirectly
from the competitive urge which forces the oil companies to exploit
their own workers more fully. Both therefore could find common
cause in seeking to subject the policies of oil companies to close
workers' scrutiny and inspection. The miners are discovering that
it is useless to seek control at only one level. Whilst they search for
new counters to the tight managerial controls which are being
imposed at pit level they are also seeking representation at industry

[3] See *A Plan for the Miners* (Derbyshire Area, NUM, 1964).
[4] See *Industrial Democracy and National Fuel Policy,* Institute for Workers'
Control pamphlet series No. 8 (1968).

level, and workers' control policies at the multi-industry level. In pursuing these policies they are saddled with a heavy burden; a union structure which has failed to adapt or respond adequately to this many-sided crisis. Workers' control of the miners' union itself is a necessary hard core of any complete workers' control strategy in the mining industry. We shall return to this question. The adverse experiences of the miners since the 1950s have played an important role in forewarning other sections of the working class in industries which are confronted by similar prospects in the 1970s, notably those employed in the steel industry and the docks.

Steel

The steelworkers are at present one of the most exposed and insecure sections of the whole working population. A recent pamphlet compiled by a Scunthorpe group of steelworkers summed up the multiple threat to their position as follows :

1 The growth in home demand for steel continues to be held back by the very slow growth in the economy as a whole, and by the consequent absence of any growth in capital investment, which always accounts for a large part of steel demand.
2 The competition of Japanese and Continental steel suppliers is already resulting in record steel imports and the latter will become much more serious in the event of British entry into the Common Market.
3 The rationalization of the industry under the British Steel Corporation must soon begin to result in the elimination of some fairly large obsolete plants and the subsequent redundancy of those employed in them.
4 The Conservative Government has announced its intention to 'hive-off' from the nationalized industries their 'peripheral activities' and also to bring private capital into their financing.[5]

The process of long-run decline in the labour force in steel is already well advanced. Between 1964 and 1970 there was a drop of 6 per cent in employment in the industry, which involved about 30,000 men. Some forecasts speak of a further reduction of 60,000 over the next five years, but these were made before the full impact of government policies on the industry had been felt. In April 1971 the British Steel Corporation's demand for a price increase of 16

[5] *The Threat to Steel Workers,* Scunthorpe Group, Institute for Workers' Control pamphlet series No. 23 (1971).

per cent was arbitrarily rejected by the Government and cut back
to one of 8 per cent. At the same time the National Coal Board
announced increases of 16 per cent on the price of the coking coals
which are essential to iron-making, and which will add £18-£20
million to the BSC's fuel bill. The combined effects of these changes
will leave the Corporation with a deficit of £60 million in the next
financial year, and this has precipitated the declaration of 8,000 redundancies in the Scunthorpe and Teesside sections of the industry,
which are additional to the 'planned' reduction of the labour force
in other regions with obsolete steel plant. Scunthorpe and Teesside
were originally two of the very locations where the rationalized
industry aimed to concentrate the expansion of its production! The
industry faces, at one and the same time, unemployment arising
from technological, cyclical and structural causes. There is growing speculation in the business press as to whether Britain should
even try to maintain a big domestic steel industry at all, while the
Government appears not to care about the adverse effects of increased steel imports upon the balance of payments.

The steelworkers' position in the 'league table' of average earnings
has already begun to slip precisely as did that of the miners towards the end of the 1950s, and for the same reasons. As with
the miners, the steelworkers' jobs are often located in regions which
are heavily dependent upon their single industry, where the effect
of unemployment upon their bargaining power is unrelieved. This
means that the impact of the Government's discriminatory pricing
policies, and its apparent acquiescence in the run-down of the
industry, have a direct effect upon the standard of life of steelworkers. The main trade unions in steel were all answered with
a straight rejection to their claim for wage increases during the
early part of 1971, whilst their products were sold at controlled
prices to the car firms whose profits are thus cushioned against the
pressure of rising wages in that industry.

It is an unenviable complex of problems which faces the steelworkers and it requires responses on both the industrial and
political fronts. Industrially, the crisis reinforces the need for
trade-union unity within the work-force, and politically it under-
lines the need for a combined attack upon the exploitation of the
public sector by workers in all nationalized industries as well as
for liaison between the workers in steel-producing and steel-
consuming industries (cars, shipbuilding and engineering, for

instance). Unity between the different sectors of the steel industry's work-force requires that the production workers, the craft maintenance section and the staff workers should break down their traditional divisions and rivalries and create joint policy committees at all levels—from the plant to the National TUC Steel Committee (which already exists, but which is subject only to the most minimal accountability to its constituents in the plants and divisions of the industry). There is no shortage of items for the agendas of such a unified committee structure in the industry. They would include the problem of regaining and extending the area of workers' controls, which has been reduced on the shop floor by the widespread adoption of managerial techniques, such as work study and job evaluation, and eroded by the increased labour mobility and flexibility that have been secured by management through productivity bargaining (which has gone forward in this industry without adequate trade-union attention to the crucial issues of mutuality and 'status quo'). They would include urgent attention to the rising rate of accidents in the industry, the causes of which are identified by at least some steelworkers as being connected with the introduction or extension of those same managerial techniques.[6] And they would include the associated problems : of democratizing the whole trade-union structure in steel, which has for too long been dominated by an inward-looking and often employer-orientated minority of senior production workers; and the need to reach out to make the same politico-industrial links with trade unionism in the rest of the public sector which, we have already suggested, are required by the mineworkers. Finally, they would return to the unresolved problem of the worker-director scheme in the industry, subject it to constant criticism and reappraisal, and revive the original demands of the workers' control movement and the craft unionists in steel, for an adequate system of workers' representation based on the principles of accountability, opening of the books and the right of veto over managerial appointments.[7]

[6] Ibid.
[7] For a summary of the original demands (made by steelworkers) for workers' representation under nationalization, see William Meade, 'Nationalised Steel', report for the Sheffield Steel Group in *Can the Workers Run Industry?*, pp. 147–56. This report also contains a reprint of the official *Documentation of Proposals for Nationalisation*, adopted in 1967 by the National Craftsmen's Co-ordinating Committee for the steel industry, which called for extensive workers' representation.

The Port Transport Industry

The dockers were cited in a previous chapter as an example
of a group of workers who have established more basic controls
over their industrial situation than most. We implied there that
the ability of the docker to prevent arbitrary dismissal of his work-
mates rested upon his traditional militancy and solidarity. This
remains true, of course : but, in addition, the dockers possess a
unique institution with which to reinforce those qualities, namely
the Dock Labour Scheme. Originally set up by the Government
during the Second World War to ensure adequate supplies of
dock labour at that time, it has become, during the post-war
generation, a statutory instrument that confers on the dockers
unusual powers of veto and representation. In every major port a
register of dock-workers is maintained by a local Dock Labour
Board, on which workers' and employers' representatives sit in
equal numbers without any third-party participation. Majority
decisions are required whenever the number of registered workers
is either increased or decreased. The significance of this constitution and authority will not be lost on those who have followed
our general arguments this far.

The other characteristic of the industry, which made it a candidate for nationalization under Mr Wilson's administration (though
not under Mr Heath's), was its obvious backwardness, both technically and in terms of an unrationalized multiplicity of ownership and
control. When the industry was visited by a late technological
revolution, based on the containerization of cargo and other devices
for bulk handling and economies of manual labour, the case for
nationalization and rationalization became an overwhelming one.
(It is a further indication of the obscurantist nature of Mr Heath's
government, if any were needed, that it joyfully abandoned the
Bill for the Reorganization of the Ports, which had been in an
advanced stage before the General Election of June 1970 interrupted its passage). But the existence of a labour force with the
traditional militancy of the dockers, combined with the institutional
experience of workers' control through the Dock Labour Scheme,
ensured that the Labour Government had no easy time of it when
it attempted to put through a bill for nationalization which was
modelled almost entirely on traditional (Coal Board or British Rail)

lines, and which left many loopholes for private shipping and haulage interests to retain or re-establish control after the formal State take-over.

The dockers in the major ports participated in the working out of a full scheme of workers' representation in a nationalized industry, building on the controls already present, and a similar scheme was approved by the Labour Party's National Executive and its Annual Conference during the years of Labour Government. The principal trade union representing the dockers, the TGWU, was also firmly committed to—at the least—a system of *joint* management of the industry under public ownership.[8] The resulting conflict between the Government and the dockers led to a one-day national dock strike for workers' control on 17th March, 1970, and had the General Election not intervened, there is no doubt that further action would have been taken by the dockers, who had begun to appreciate in full measure that workers' control was for them an immediate and a practicable matter. For the implication of the Government's scheme was that a central State board dominated by employer interests would have been in a very strong position to smash the existing scheme of joint control over the hiring and firing of workers. In view of the industry's drive towards containerization and capital-intensive methods generally, the employers had—and still have—an urgent need to be free of the restraints on dismissals under which they must operate at present. For the moment the situation is stalemated, but the dockers can now appreciate that a mere defence of their veto over redundancies is not enough. Whilst the existing dock labour force is protected against the sack, there is a long-run decline in the number of registered dockers as a result of 'natural wastage'. In the past ten years the numbers have fallen from 70,000 to 50,000, and the official estimates provide for further reduction over the years to 25,000 in 1975—a halving of the present strength. It is therefore strongly brought home to the dockers that their apparent security

[8] For details of the campaign to nationalize the ports under workers' control, see *Democracy on the Docks*, Institute for Workers' Control (1971); and for analyses of the industry's situation in recent years, see: Tony Topham, 'The Dockers', *Can the Workers Run Industry?*; Brian Nicholson, 'The First Year of Devlin', *Trade Union Register* 1969; and Tony Topham, 'The Ports Bill, Joint Control and Rationalisation', *Trade Union Register* 1970. The Labour Party's nationalization programme is contained in its *Report of the Port Transport Study Group* (1966).

is based upon precarious foundations, that the impact of technology (and the shifting patterns of the location of the industry, which often takes bulk cargoes and container berths to terminals which are remote from the traditional ports) is affecting both the present size of the dole queue in their own communities and the long-term prospects of employment for their sons and grandsons.

The new unionism of a large, multi-industry organization such as the TGWU is potentially well structured to meet the need arising out of the dockers' situation. That need is the common one we have stressed throughout this study : to widen the horizons of concern, so that the dockers may act in concert with *all* transport workers, many of whom are quite as seriously threatened by the haphazard, market-directed evolution of the container industry as are the dockers themselves. Thus railwaymen, lorry drivers, and merchant seamen can and should find common cause in formulating a workers' alternative national transport policy, demanding co-ordinated public ownership of course, but also insisting upon both the safeguarding of the interests of transport workers and the development of social cost-benefit analysis of the different alternative means of transport. This latter would have to extend to decisions on the location of new ports and terminals, which have far-reaching consequences of a social and economic nature, since they determine the future location of oil processing, iron-ore processing, food preparation and other industries using bulk material imports. In this new situation the docker begins from where he is, with an accumulated and invaluable experience of sectional controls. He should now go out to educate fellow-workers in complementary industries about that experience, whilst in turn learning their problems. Dealing, as do the lorry-men and the seamen, very often with the same employers, and experiencing, as they all do, the subordination of the public sector in their industries (British Road Services, British Rail) to the increasingly international domination of big private transport interests, they have much to learn from each other. The object of this wider unity, however, needs to transcend traditional sectional goals, and embrace nothing less than the social interest of the whole working population in the formation of a grand design for all cargo and passenger transport, which can then, for the first time, be based on true social costs. The combined forces of the transport workers, consciously struggling to extend trade-union veto powers over the market-dominated

transport system, and using at the same time all the political leverage
of which they are capable, would be needed to achieve that
ambitious goal, but nothing less could suffice to overcome the concentration of arbitrary political and economic powers which are now
in the hands of the oil, road haulage and shipping companies.

The Post Office

The postmen constitute a section of workers with a long tradition
of loyal public service, a tradition often abused by their employers,
and never more so than during the 1971 strike for higher wages.
The tragedy of the postal workers' isolation during that episode
can be turned to positive advantage only if the union draws on its
own long involvement with the ideas of industrial democracy, in
order to develop demands for greater workers' control in the Post
Office Corporation. The Postal Workers' Union's support for
workers' control reaches back to the heyday of Guild Socialism. In
1921 the National Guilds League published *Towards a Postal Guild*,
by W. Milne Bailey, which contained a profound attack on the
commodity status of the wage-workers in the Post Office, and a
practical programme for the establishment of an unambiguous
democracy in the government of what was then, of course, a
Department of State. Milne Bailey's tract is often quite contemporary in flavour :

> . . . it will be claimed, the Postal workers are serving the com-
> munity; they labour for the public service. Not so ! That is what
> they want to do, but it is what they cannot do until a Postal
> Guild is realised. The only feeling possible to them at present
> is that they are working for a set of superior officials. Take
> wages. Nominally the public, through Parliament, is supposed to
> control the salaries of State employees and in the past, wages
> have frequently been fixed by Select Committees of the House
> of Commons. The last of these was the Holt Committee in 1912.
> This control is only nominal, however, and a Select Committee
> (composed almost entirely of capitalists) will inevitably adopt
> the usual capitalist method of getting labour for the smallest
> possible wage. It is notorious that in the past, Postal workers
> have been shockingly under-paid.

The UPW has sustained its commitment to workers' control
from the days of Guild Socialism to the present time. Publications
of the union on this theme have included : *The Union of Post*

Office Workers and Workers' Control (1942), *What Does That Mean: Explanations of Terms Used in the UPW Report on Workers' Control* (1943), *The Union of Post Office Workers and the Public Utility Corporation* (1943), *Did We Fight for This? A Challenge to the TUC Conception of Industrial Control* (1945), and *The Business of Workers' Control: the UPW Member's Introduction to Industrial Democracy* (1961). Given this background, it is not surprising that when Mr John Stonehouse, Postmaster General under Harold Wilson, attacked workers' control in the most cynical terms, he was met with firm rebuttal in the pages of the union's *Journal*. Mr Stonehouse had promised a Fabian summer school in August 1968 that he would introduce workers' participation in the management of the Post Office when it was reorganized as a public corporation, but had gone on to declare roundly : 'We must establish the clear distinction between workers' participation and workers' control.' The latter, he felt, was indefensible, since it was 'unfair to the rest of the community' and was, moreover, bound to be inefficient. 'Experience in the co-operative movement,' he said, 'has shown that managerial expertise is a somewhat rare attribute which cannot be developed in every Tom, Dick and Harry. . . .'[9]

This elitist onslaught produced a sharp rejoinder from the UPW *Journal*. On 17th August, 1968, its front-page reply included a reminder to Mr Stonehouse of the origin of his own position : '. . . workers, he believes, would be inclined to take decisions not on the objective facts, but in terms of the "subjective self-interest" they represent. Which, is, of course, rather a sweeping condemnation of the manner in which the Postmaster General thinks working people would act up to their responsibilities . . . even though many of us, of course, are working people embodied in the Labour Party which has thrown up, by a democratic process, leaders such as the present Postmaster General ! . . . This is a challenge which the Union of Post Office Workers cannot let pass.'

Mr Stonehouse's promises of participation came to nothing. Early in 1971 the postmen struck spontaneously, and held public demonstrations against the arbitrary dismissal of Lord Hall from the chairmanship of the Post Office Corporation. They certainly had no constitutional voice, either on his removal or on the subsequent appointment of Mr Rylands, who had by then served

[9] Report in *The Times* (5th August, 1968).

the Government's wage-control policies so well in the interim. After their recent extreme reminder of the 'feel' of the condition of wage slavery, we may well look forward to a renewal of the demand for workers' control from the postmen.

Aircraft

The industries we have so far considered in this chapter have certain features in common. They are either extractive industries or providers of basic infra-structural services to industry (communications and fuels), or manufacturers of basic products whose customers are in other industries (steel). That is to say, they all exist primarily to serve industry, rather than serving mainly the consumer market directly: although, of course, some of their commercial products (domestic fuel, for example) may enter that market. Moreover, all of them have been, to a greater or lesser extent, nationalized or partially nationalized in order to overcome deep-seated organizational weaknesses and commercial failure.

When we turn to the aircraft industry we are considering an apparently different phenomenon—an industry which exists in the vanguard of technological innovation, marketing a finished commodity in one of the fastest growing sectors of the world economy. (For every passenger who flew in 1950, there are 100 passengers flying today, and estimates suggest that there will be 500 by 1985. Air freight is expected to rise from 10,000 million ton-miles in 1970 to 60,000 million in 1985.) Yet the British aircraft industry has in fact staggered from crisis to crisis in recent years, heavily dependent throughout upon government contracts and subsidies, and experiencing all the kaleidoscopic transformations of the merger/take-over game. Finally, Rolls-Royce, which through this process had become the largest firm of its kind in Europe and had acquired a total monopoly of aero-engine manufacture in Britain, became, in 1971, the latest loss-maker to qualify for rescue-by-nationalization.

Probably no industry outside aircraft production demonstrates more fully the deep interlocking connections between banking and finance, industrial capital and the State. Probably none, except the car industry, illustrates the social nature of the production process so fully and transparently as does aircraft. (Like the

motor industry, it is ultimately concerned with the assembly of
parts, and has therefore gathered around itself a vast
periphery of components companies, which are mutually inter-
dependent, as indeed are the air-frame and aero-engine makers.)
It is not, therefore, surprising that the aircraft workers have
produced some of the most clear-sighted analyses of their situation and have supported advanced demands for nationalization
with workers' control.[10] Their case has, of course, been established
on socialist lines : they seek the nationalization of profits along with
effective workers' control and social and public accountability of
the industry's programme and finances. They have analysed in
detail the composition of the boards of the three main companies
—Rolls-Royce, Hawker Siddeley, and the British Aircraft Corporation—and have shown the comprehensive interlocking of merchant
banking, insurance companies, engineering, nuclear energy, steel,
electronics, radio, computers, oil, rubber, glass, armaments, shipbuilding and other interests on those bodies. They have illustrated,
in the words of an official report (Plowden Report) on the industry
that 'the present situation is dominated by the increasing depen-
dence of the industry on Government decisions in both the military
and civil fields. The military programme has for many years been
determined and paid for by the Government. The scope for
independent initiatives and action on the part of industrial
management is small' and 'it would seem that the average degree
of Government support in recent years has been somewhere
between 30 and 45-50 per cent. It has probably been higher
still'.[11] They have demonstrated that between 1945 and 1969 the
British taxpayer has subsidized the industry to the extent of over
£3,000 million on military aircraft and missiles, and has further
contributed some £130 million towards the cost of civil aircraft
developments between 1945 and 1965—and this does not include
the Government's share of the colossal Concorde project. They
have absorbed the lessons of the scandals arising from the excess
profits made by Hawker Siddeley and Bristol Siddeley on government contracts during the 'sixties, and have demanded the opening

[10] See *The Aircraft Industry and Workers' Control*, Bristol Siddeley Engines
Shop Stewards' Combine Committee (March 1969). The pamphlet is the
result of nearly three years' study and research by a working party
established from the Stewards' Committee, and includes a Foreword by
Harry Urwin, Assistant General Secretary of the TGWU.
[11] Quote in *The Aircraft Industry and Workers' Control*, p. 8.

of the books of the aircraft companies. Out of this analysis, the aircraft workers have produced a programme for nationalization of the whole industry, which includes the requirements that:

1 There should be a single nationalized aircraft company, governed by a board on which the workers' elected representatives should have at least 50 per cent of the seats at all levels of policy-making.
2 These representatives should be shop-floor workers elected by their fellows, and directly accountable to them.
3 Workers' Councils should be elected to run the plants locally, to which plant managers would be accountable.
4 The trade-union function should be retained in the new structure, as a separate organization from the Workers' Councils, and the right to strike should be retained.

These demands received not a nod of acknowledgment from official Labour, whilst Mr Wedgwood Benn and his colleagues held office. Mr Benn has since repudiated many of the sins of omission and commission of those days, but at the time he and his colleagues were too busy promoting the further 'rationalization' of the industry, and encouraging the Rolls-Royce aero-engines division to embark upon the ambitious fixed-price contract to supply the Lockheed Aircraft Company in America with the RB-211 engine. When Rolls-Royce was forced into bankruptcy by its inability to meet that contract without incurring insupportable commercial losses, a Tory government, acting against its own official ideology, carried out an act of partial nationalization. Although this may have caused the Government some political embarrassment, its action implied no conversion to the views of the shop stewards. On the contrary, it was merely fulfilling 'the historic function of the neo-capitalist state; nationalization, an act which evoked public thanks from France, and from NATO, and a bid for co-operation from Germany. The outcome is likely to be in the case of Rolls-Royce, as it will be in the case of Lucas and the ailing Leylands (on the verge of bankruptcy in late November), centralization of capital on a European scale'.[12]

The Government has made it clear that it does not propose to nationalize the profitable sectors of the company—that is to say, the motor-car and oil-engine divisions, which between them ac-

12 Robin Murray, 'Rolls-Royce', *The Spokesman* 'London Bulletin' section (March 1971).

counted for 20 per cent of the turnover of the whole combine. Instead it is to take over the loss-making aero-engine and small engine divisions. Moreover, the assets to be acquired will be vested in a company with limited liability, all the shares of which will be held by the Government. This form of nationalization will make it easier, as Mr Barber, the Chancellor of the Exchequer, explained to the House of Commons, 'for private capital to participate in due course'. The purpose of this 'lame duck' operation is, according to the Government, to ensure the continued service of the Rolls-Royce engine division to the Royal Air Force, to many foreign air forces and to 200 of the world's civil airlines. Moreover, the Government has been anxious to save a number of collaborative projects into which the company had entered with Western European aircraft companies, including the Italian multi-role combat aircraft (the MRCA) the Anglo-French Jaguar strike fighter, the Anglo-French 'package' of three helicopters, and the Anglo-German VFW 614 airliner.

The Government has made it clear that it does not propose to retain even the aero-engine part of the company indefinitely in government ownership; it is interested in the idea of a European consortium comprising Snecma (the French State-owned company), Motoren-und-Turbinen Union (MTU) of Munich, and the public section of Rolls-Royce. Nor has the Government ruled out collaborative agreements with American aero-engine companies. For the rest, it has already been reported, in February 1971, that Lord Stokes of British Leyland is interested in acquiring the profitable and prestigious car division. He put it rather delicately a few days after the bankrupcty was announced : 'If there is anything we can do to help we shall be only too happy to do so.' The tens of thousands of workers threatened with redundancy, both in Rolls-Royce itself, and more widely in the hundreds of companies which provide components for the company's products, weigh nothing on the Government's scales. The Government even precipitated the bankruptcy (by withholding further financial aid in respect of the RB-211 project) and ensured that a receiver was appointed before making its partial nationalization bid, thus avoiding any kind of legal obligation for covering the outstanding debts and contracts to the component firms! Its other significant demonstration of loyalty to its traditional supporters was to appoint Lord Cole (earlier Chairman of Unilever), the former Chairman of Rolls-

Royce, and Mr Ian Morrow, the former Deputy Chairman, to assume these same roles in the nationalized company.

To sum up, this latest instance makes it perfectly plain that centralization of control, whether partially or wholly in 'public ownership', which is the standard medicine prescribed, by both Labour and Conservative governments, in one form or another, for industries with long-term structural and commercial weaknesses, is not even the most modest move towards the creation of islands of socialism and industrial democracy in the general sea of capitalism. The case of Rolls-Royce should finally disperse any illusions which linger in the Labour and trade-union movement on this score. Moreover, the trend towards European levels of centralization merely heightens the contradictions, and further clarifies the nature of public participation in capitalist forms of organization. As Robin Murray puts the matter :

> As long as capitals compete in the market, the contradiction, which we may call the contradiction of gestation,[13] will always be there. The fall of Rolls-Royce, Harlands, Leylands, will not be caused by workers refusing to accept cuts in their living standards. It will be caused by the structure of the economic system of which they form a part.
>
> By refusing to press claims, the workers in such firms will not avoid the culmination of this contradiction. They can only momentarily delay it. What the Labour Movement should do is to demand a socialist structure which alone can develop rationally the forces of technology and production.[14]

This is not to say that the aircraft workers were wrong to draft a blueprint for nationalization with workers' control. By doing so, they are now able, like the steelworkers and the dockers, to define their own goals and purposes against those of the neocapitalist State, an exercise which assists greatly in the understanding of things as they are. Now that some of these aircraft workers are in the public sector, they can begin to appreciate the

[13] Murray coins this phrase to describe the 'ever widening gap in time between the beginning of development *for* production and the coming into play *of* production. This is a gestation lag which is devoted to the production of the means of production. Firms like Rolls-Royce have been, and are working on projects which it is expected will take over fifteen years to realise any surplus'. And this of course was precisely the situation at Rolls-Royce with the RB-211 engine.
[14] Murray, op. cit.

need for a wider alliance, which should embrace the whole of that sector, since all workers within it face a common problem, a common boss. Since they are face to face with the State itself, and since their acquiescence in corporate planning and wage control is an essential factor upon which governments increasingly rely, the working out of a co-ordinated strategy of trade-union demands can become a key factor in the advance of workers' control.

Shipbuilding

In mid-June 1971 there broke the latest and most severe of all the crises of retrenchment which have resulted from the Heath government's 'lame ducks' policy: close on the heels of the Rolls-Royce collapse, the Upper Clyde Shipbuilders' consortium became insolvent, and was placed in the hands of the liquidator. 7,500 Clydeside workers, employed in the yards of Charles Connell, Alexander Stephen, Fairfield (Govan), and John Brown, faced redundancy. Behind them stood an estimated 25,000 other workers employed by firms supplying the yards, and in ancillary concerns.

UCS was created in February 1968 as a result of the merger of the four Upper Clyde yards with a fifth, Yarrow, a naval construction yard, which left the consortium in February 1971. The Govan yard, formerly known as Fairfield, had been established upon governmental initiative with the State holding 50 per cent, the unions 15 per cent, and private enterprise 35 per cent. This much-publicized experiment had been launched in January 1966. By July 1967 a working party of the Shipbuilding Industry Board, chaired by Mr Anthony Hepper, who was later to become Chairman of UCS, recommended the fusion of the five yards. Sir Iain Stewart, Chairman of Fairfields, became a vice-chairman of this new consortium, but he subsequently resigned because of policy disagreements. The merged concerns carried over from their parent yards a volume of substantially unprofitable orders, which became even more unprofitable as the effects of accelerating inflation made themselves felt. By the beginning of 1971 the managing director of the consortium was to tell the subcommittee on Trade and Industry of the House of Commons, that 'UCS was a group of five yards which would certainly, if they had been left on their own, have gone bankrupt'. British shipbuilding in general was in difficult straits, but the Clyde in particular was suffering from aggravated structural problems which made its very survival problematic.

During its tenure of office, the Wilson government had been careful not to complicate its relations with the rest of industry, let alone its money-lenders, by nationalizing shipbuilding. Accordingly, great amounts of public money were made available on loan to the shipbuilders. Up to 1969 £24.8 million had been put into the yards concerned in this argument. The latest date of substantial government assistance to the yards was December 1969, when the Ministry of Technology provided loans of £7 million, together with certain other guarantees of liquidity. After the accession of the Heath administration to office, Mr Davies proved an altogether tougher bargainer, however, and in February 1971 he told the Commons that 'no new public funds are to be provided to UCS'. At this time, Mr Davies was already aware of the meaning of his statement, for, in October 1970, the Government's own accountant in the consortium had reported to the Department of Trade and Industry that, 'on the figures he had seen, UCS must inevitably go broke within a few months'. This report produced a temporary suspension of the 1969 government guarantee to both bankers and shipowners that credits would be available to ensure the continued operation of the yards. By the time the guarantee was restored, its suspension had blocked £6 million worth of credit. In the context of stringent inflation, together with the removal of investment grants, and the restriction of suppliers' credit (accompanied, in some cases, by the limitation and cutting off of supplies), the yards faced an acute shortage of working capital.

On 14th June, 1971, the Cabinet met to consider an inevitable request from the directors of UCS for further financial assistance. The crisis was in the open, and the result was, first, the decision not to grant the request, and, subsequently, the announcement of the appointment of a provisional liquidator.

There is no doubt that shipbuilding is in a state of great difficulty in many countries of the world, and is often only kept alive by subsidies from the governments concerned. Inflation has made the prevalent fixed-price contracting system extremely difficult to sustain, and the recent boom in construction appears to have run its course. Yet the order-book of UCS was in an unusually brisk state, even though inflation made important sectors of it commercially marginal. Thirty ships, valued at over £90 million, were in commission. The order-book for the whole of the shipping industry in the UK stands at 312 ships, worth £690 million: so that UCS accounts for slightly below 10 per cent of the ordered tonnage, and as much as 13 per cent of the value, of the whole shipbuilding industry today.

THE FULL ORDER BOOK AT UPPER CLYDE

Tonnage	Ship Type	Owner	Delivery
CLYDEBANK DVN (formerly JOHN BROWN)			
5,000	drilling rig	Rimrock (UK)	
2,000	train ferry	NZ Government	end 1971
18,000 (2)	Clyde Cargo ships	John Samonas & Sons	1971
18,000 (3)	„ „ „	Haverton Shipping Co.	1971–2
26,000	bulk-carrier	J. and C. Harrison	1972
26,000	„ „	Reardon Smith	1972
27,000	„ „	Lyle Shipping	1972–3
GOVAN DVN (formerly FAIRFIELD)			
15,400	suction dredger	Costain/Blankenvoort	1971
6,860	„ „	Brazil Government	1971
25,000 (2)	bulk-carrier	Cardigan Shipping	1971
25,000 (2)	„ „	Reardon Smith	1971
26,000	„ „	Cardigan Shipping	1972
26,000	„ „	Irish Shipping	1972
26,000 (2)	„ „	„ „	1972
27,000 (2)	„ „	Hogarth & Sons	1972–3
SCOTSTOUN DVN (formerly CHARLES CONNELL)			
18,000	Clyde Cargo Ship	Haverton Shipping	end 1971
18,000	„ „ „	Seafern Shipping	1972
26,000	bulk-carrier	Gowland Steamship	1972
26,000	„ „	J. and J. Denholm	1971

SOURCE: *The Times* (15th June, 1971).

Sir Iain Stewart, a representative of the 'dynamic and abrasive' school of management so close to the hearts of the Labour front bench, who, having presided over the Fairfield yard, was subsequently to resign from the vice-chairmanship of UCS, claims that this order-book was itself a liability. Writing in *The Times* (on 24th June, 1971), he said:

The real responsibility for the collapse of Upper Clyde Ship-builders goes back to the board decision and policies in the first three months of 1968. The decisions at that time were made by the old shipbuilders on the Upper Clyde which had been criti-

E

cized, thoroughly criticized and more criticized than by anyone else in the Geddes Report.

When the merger came together the board's first idea—and Mr Anthony Hepper was the man who promoted it—was to get a full order-book. So off he went round the world and picked up millions of pounds worth of work which in fact was profitless. The labour force simply sat back and said 'what's the point of carrying on with this productivity situation and working harder when work is all there?'

The new management approach was to go back to the old days. They could get no discipline from the unions. The unions simply felt that they were back in the hands of the old guard and behaved accordingly. At Fairfields, we had a productivity figure of something like 61 man hours per ton and we were aiming to get them down to possibly the forties by the end of 1968. But under the control of the new management, productivity moved towards the 100 mark. Therefore what was a profitable contract under our control became unprofitable under theirs.

Of course, the state of the order-book alone does not determine the employment policies of any industrialist; but Sir Iain felt that these contracts were part of a general policy which could only aggravate the difficulties of surviving in a hostile environment :

Orders were one thing. The other was that we considered the key to our relationship with the unions lay with the central joint council which embraced all the unions—including the boiler-makers.

Around September 1967, we had got to the point of negotiating a double day shift with the agreement of the Boilermakers Society, led by Mr Dan McGarvey. When the new lot came in they thought that Danny McGarvey should be handled separately because the Boilermakers preferred traditionally not to sit around the table with the other unions. So a relationship was built up between some members of the Upper Clyde Board and some of the boilermakers' leaders, which enabled Danny McGarvey to break away. And so they put Danny McGarvey back in the driving seat—and that is where he still is.

If all the policies spelt out by the working party of the Ship-building Industry Board had been carried out the present situation would not have arisen.

One of the main conclusions of the working party was that the labour force should be reduced from 13,000 to 8,000. At Fairfields we thought this made sense from the point of view of the Upper Clyde's future as a whole, and on that basis we reluctantly gave up our independence, and joined the merger in the belief that their philosophies, and what we considered modern practices, would be adopted. Within a month it was clear to me that the UCS management had no intention of adopting the working party report. So I cleared out.

Quite clearly, the intensification of labour is a first principle of this innovating school of management. At Fairfields, notable advances in productivity had been gained, and Sir Iain wished to extend these to the whole consortium. His confessions in *The Times* are, from the trade-union point of view, engagingly frank :

Rather than face up to the redundancy of 5,000 men, Mr Hepper guaranteed them two years full employment—5,000 people at £1,200 a year is £6m, in two years it is £12m. If you are going to pay out £12m and get nothing back from it, you go bankrupt. I said that UCS would go bankrupt in 18 months. I was wrong. They were bankrupt in 15 months—and bankrupt three times since.

The management techniques required at UCS were those we had applied at Fairfields. When we went into the yard the men were not really doing two hours work a day, not because they did not want to, but because there was not enough work for them to do. The materials were not arriving at the right time, the painters did not have any paint, the plumbers did not have any pipes and the steelmen did not have any steel.

There was no control system, there was no flow of materials and there was no attempt to have the labour force in the right place at the right time. Through simple planning and network analysis we were getting, by the time we finished, about five hours out of eight we were paying for.

Payments were based on proven performance. And on that basis our fellows got better pay. The other yards were mad about it because they were getting demands from the unions for similar rates and they have no system of measuring them. So the industry as a whole, and especially the Clyde, set out to cut our throats. And they did. The Shipbuilding Industry Board was receptive to the shipbuilding lobby and they were anti-Fairfields from the start.

In my view Fairfields was a practical demonstration that shipbuilding could be made viable, given the unions' freedom of operation and management's freedom to inject the modern controls and flexibility which other industries enjoy and which shipbuilding has never done.

I think that without the merger John Brown's would have gone bankrupt, and Connell's and Stephen's were probably heading for bankrupty, too. That was why they were in such a hurry to get into the merger. If you look at how quickly John Brown's produced £1.7m to underwrite the rights issue for the investment in the merger, you can see how damned keen they were to get out with the QE2 sitting there. They had no orders ahead that carried any profit at all. It might have been saved if the working party report had been carried out. The whole merger was killed by management's guarantee to labour—which as I mentioned was £12m down the drain. Labour does not respect that sort of attitude. They would much prefer to have a tough management.

But what is frequently ignored by socialist critics of capitalist rationalization policies is the fact that the pursuit of high labour productivity naturally involves the imposition of even tighter degrees of managerial control. Sir Iain Stewart's critique of UCS is particularly revealing on this score :

I don't think that UCS applied what we would call professional management. At Fairfields we had financial control in every aspect of the business. Whatever happened to these control systems in UCS I do not know.

Shipyards, and a lot of other industry in Britain too, have been running on this sort of 'back of an envelope' system of accounting. They depend on their auditor's report, the balance-sheet, and the profit and loss account. Everything is geared to that. So they do not know from one year to another whether they are making a profit or loss. According to Mr John Davies's statement, the Upper Clyde Board could not even tell what was going to happen in 1973. They simply cannot have applied the systems that we left there.

The combined intensification of work and managerial control is scarcely possible in modern conditions without important changes in labour relations practice. From this point of view, Sir Iain's commitment to 'participation' as a management technique for rationalization, is of great significance.

When UCS came in there was no room for trade unions on the board. There was no attempt to carry on the co-operation and collaboration we had set up. Trade unions did not know what

was going on in management and they still don't know. At Fairfields we had a two-tier board system. We had a policy board of
which I was part-time chairman, and on which two executives
also sat.

The rest were outsiders, a merchant banker, other industrialists
and two leading trade unionists. This board established policy
and left management to implement it. Now the executive
management board had three trade unionists sitting in. In other
words, management reached decisions after knowing what the
trade unions thought about it.

So you had trade unions involved in management decisions
without being responsible for them at policy and executive levels.
But if there were any management troubles it was the management board that carried the can. Trade unionists were not
party to those decisions.

Another big factor of labour was killing the redundancy
bogey. Once we got them accepting discipline and had started
loading them up with work we guaranteed them employment for
three years and that took the heat off. We were guaranteeing
to establish with training and retraining flexibility and mobility
provided we could make that work and turn an unprofitable
company into a profitable one.

The fangs of rationalization policy may not be readily visible in
the smiling discussions of participatory reform : but the fangs are
there, and Sir Iain was engagingly frank about the implications
of his doctrines for the future of UCS :

Anyone who is given *carte blanche* to reconstruct UCS now
would have to cut the labour force in half. But the attitude of
the unions must be questionable as things have deteriorated a
lot since 1968. I doubt whether one would get the same
freedom with the unions as we had and whether he could get
ahead with a double day shift. We now have the Industrial
Relations Bill, and with the rising unemployment figures unions
are quite understandably anti-productivity.

All of this adds up to an extraordinarily telling critique of the
given social order. Today, the rights of capital demand that whole
industries be closed. The rights of labour, of the human beings
involved in those industries, can only be asserted in direct opposition
to the pursuit of solvency, commercial rationality, managerial
authority. Not only are needed ships not built, while many thou-

sands of skilled men are faced with unemployment; not only do artificially engendered crises of liquidity in this, and many other older industrial sectors, prevent the application of that very productive effort which alone can solve the underlying difficulties of the British economy; not only does the authoritarian management of this key industry stand indicted of inability to manage : yet the only cures which the establishment can offer for these maladies involve their intensification. What is wrong with the 'rationalizing' solution of Sir Iain Stewart? Clearly, in seeking to intensify the efforts made by a sharply reduced labour force, in the context in which he is compelled to operate, he can only aggravate the acute social distress of all those who are displaced, who on his own calculation must number as least as many of those who 'benefit' from the process. Neither the old guard of conventional capitalist management nor the 'innovators' can offer any hope at all for this vast force of condemned men. And yet, given the limited encroachment of welfare rights which has been made up to this time, even the balance-sheets argue against closing the yards. Poor as public relief standards are, unemployment costs money. The fact that one government department refuses to bale out the shipbuilding industry simply means that another government department will have to pay for its collapse.

Taking the assumptions that the Government has made, the grotesque folly involved in orthodox economic calculations has been lucidly exposed by Frank Field, of the Child Poverty Action Group, writing in *Tribune*.[15] The costs of dole and social security payments alone will almost certainly mean greater losses to the Government than those involved in continuing to support an unprofitable industry :

There has been no official estimate of the number of jobs which will be lost. Unofficial estimates vary greatly. The *Economist* puts 5,000 jobs at risk although it adds 'there will be real hardship for some men', adding 'Scotland is not a good place to be unemployed in'. At the other end of the scale—and no doubt more accurately—the Scottish TUC puts the number of lost jobs at 27,000. . . .

So if we take the lower prospect of 5,000 unemployed, 3,500 will be in jobs after six months. On the assumption that half the

15 14th July, 1971.

wives work (and so disqualify the family from receiving supplementary benefit) 50 per cent will just receive unemployment
pay and the wage related supplement and the other 50 per cent
will have their income supplemented up to current SB rate. Flat
rate unemployment pay is £5 but workers earning £9 a week
gain a 5p a week wage related supplement and those earning £30
or more a week gain a £7 benefit. If the mid-point between these
two extremes is taken, the unemployed will gain £5 flat rate
plus a £3.50 wage related unemployment benefit. In other words,
£8.50 per week.

Those without working wives will be eligible for SB. The
assumption is that these families have two children, so 90p
family allowance has to be deducted from their entitlement of
£4.50. This gives a total payment of £13.60 a week.

Of those unemployed for more than six months 45 per cent,
on current trends, will be in jobs by the end of the year, but
those remaining 55 per cent will still be on the dole. We will
assume that, on average, these men will be idle for three years.

The same assumptions hold for the largest estimate of unemployed, the 27,000.

We get the following totals if these assumptions are used in
calculating the cost of unemployment pay and supplementary
benefits. If it is assumed that only 5,000 men will be made idle
the cost will be nearly £1.9 million. If the assumption is 27,000
unemployed, the cost is just over £10 million. Even if the mid-
point is taken, the cost in unemployment and related pay is
greater than the Government has saved by closing the UCS. If
the cost of redundancy payment is included then the Government will certainly be paying more than the £6 million required
by UCS.

But this of course ignores the human cost of making men idle
and the loss in national income resulting from each unemployed
man.

The application of such criteria of social cost demands that the
shipbuilding industry be kept open. The established commercial
structures cannot meet such a demand. As the workers in the yards
have already clearly understood, it is therefore necessary that
their plants be nationalized.

Does this mean that a nationalized shipbuilding industry could
continue to operate, oblivious of costs? Of course it does not.
But what it does mean is that even public ownership of shipbuilding will not in itself be enough to meet the implications
of this particular crisis: since, even if production is organized

with the most active involvement of the workpeople concerned (and indeed, to the very extent that this involvement succeeds in raising productivity) it will be necessary to guarantee extensive new areas of redeployment in productive work, at levels of earnings and expectations similar to those prevalent in the parent industry. Nationalization will need, if this problem is to be met, not only co-ordination with the Steel Industry already in public ownership, but also the State take-over of other key sectors of the engineering industry.

In their reactions to these problems, the UCS workers have shown a clear ability to profit from the lessons of the past few years. They have responded with militant determination, coupled with a keen awareness of the need to carry with them the widest popular support. In their first lobby of the Prime Minister, on 16th June, 1971, their spokesmen were admirably clear. As *The Times* reported :

After an hour-long meeting with the Prime Minister at 10 Downing Street during the morning, a delegation of seven shop stewards and councillors were left in no doubt that the Government had no intention of changing plans for reorganizing Upper Clyde Shipbuilders.

'We were offered sympathy, and only sympathy,' Mr James Airlie, Chairman of the joint shop stewards committee, said bitterly afterwards. 'It wasn't sympathy we came to London for, but something more concrete.'

The men, he said, would fight the Government all the way. *'We will not leave the yards,' he said with what can only be described as barely controlled fury. 'If he wants to get us out he will have to come and try to get us out himself.'* This government will be moved far more quickly than the men of the Clyde.

'They will need to get the soldiers from the Bogside to get us out of the Clydeside,' added Mr William McKinnes, a stewards' convener from Linthouse.

The decision to occupy the yards, approved by a mass-meeting, and supported also by Anthony Wedgwood Benn during one of his many visits to Clydeside, was a very wise one. No other possible action could clarify so graphically the issues in the public mind, and mobilize so effectively support for the workers' cause. Lobbies and petitions, important though they are, are by themselves quite inadequate to the task of defending the employment possibilities in the industry. The Government has shown itself contemptuous of orthodox political pressures. Only the most decisive action can break the doctrinaire front which is currently shaping up against the Clydeside workers.

Chapter 10

Trade-Union Strategy in the Public Sector

Discontent in the nationalized industries must be running at a higher level than ever before in their history. During 1970-1 we saw spontaneous unofficial strikes, on a national scale, in the mines (in protest against a wage offer) and in the Post Office (in reaction to the dismissal of the Chairman for political reasons). These have been joined by a whole round of official actions, usually less than strikes, but involving, for instance, working to rule in electricity generating and on the railways; and at their most severe, producing the longest and largest dispute for a very long time in the postmen's struggle for their wage claim.

Friction in the public sector about wage levels is not by any means a new phenomenon. The reason for this is simple. Every major move towards overall, national wage control that has been initiated by successive governments since the commencement of the structural crisis of the British economy, has begun with an offensive against workers in the public sector, and has hit these workers harder and more effectively than almost any other group. The scandal of the Selwyn Lloyd pay-pause, which brought the first direct governmental intervention in traditional arbitration procedures, turned first of all on the decision to set aside findings which favoured employees in Admiralty dockyards. From that time on, the conditions of public service workers, and employees of nationalized industries, have always been in jeopardy, but never more than recently, under the Heath administration.

Although the Conservative Election Manifesto in 1970 specifically denied that the inflationary upsurge of the past year had resulted from trade-union pressure, and claimed with some justice that it resulted from governmental taxation and restraint policy,[1]

[1] See Michael Barratt Brown's evidence to the Wilberforce Committee, on the wage claim of the power-workers, presented on behalf of the Institute for Workers' Control and published as *Trade Unions and Rising Prices* (IWC, 1971); and John Hughes's evidence to the same inquiry.

there has in fact been a consistent onslaught on public sector wage claims from the very moment that the Heath administration took over. That Mr Carr has come to admit this in public is not surprising.[2] It has been apparent to each successive public service union negotiating team in turn, as its claim has moved towards the front of the queue for settlement, and into the centre of press and television limelight, that every form of pressure, direct and indirect, was being mobilized in order to reduce the level of each successive settlement below that of its predecessor.

After the strike of local council workers in autumn 1970, the Scamp Inquiry, which was established to recommend the terms of settlement, awarded a £2.50 increase, with a 10 per cent conditional increase for those workers not covered by productivity bonus schemes. In justifying this finding, the inquiry reported : 'Given the pace of inflation in the country as a whole, there is no chance that it can be arrested by a somewhat smaller pay increase for local authority employees. All that would achieve for certain would be a deterioration in their position without a significant benefit to the country as a whole.' In response to this moderate and obvious judgment, Mr Heath went on television to denounce it as 'blatantly nonsensical'. He did not stop at publicly excoriating the results of the inquiry, but went on later to take physical reprisals against at least one of the members responsible, Professor Hugh Clegg.

A settlement having been imposed upon the miners, conceding much less than their stated demands, the next major upsurge came in the power stations. The Wilberforce Inquiry which was established in order to consider that case was given quite extraordinary terms of reference, which charged it to take into account the 'public interest'. All this had only one obvious intention, to intimidate the court into constructing an award within the framework acceptable to government policy. Although there are different interpretations of the actual percentage value of the award which was finally made by Wilberforce, the Government still to this day adamantly claims that it was consistent with the general phased reduction of public sector settlements. This pattern continued with the postmen's offer, and, up to the time of writing,

[2] See, for instance, the report in *The Times* of Mr Carr's meeting with leaders of the CBI (7th April, 1971).

has culminated in the lowest offer of the whole series, which has been made to the railwaymen.

All of these settlements compare very unfavourably with the best private sector settlements on two grounds : the net percentage increases are worse, and the bases from which the increases were calculated were almost invariably lower. The only exception to this trend has been that of the policemen's claim : and in the context in which the Government is settling itself, it is hardly surprising that it wishes to buy the loyalty of the constabulary.

So far, this story is one which is common knowledge. It is also common knowledge :

(a) that a main argument for nationalization, in the days in which it was an active preoccupation of the Labour Movement, was that the Government 'should set an example' as an employer, and (b) that the largest concentrations of low-paid workers are to be found in direct government and local government service, and in nationalized industries. It is quite true that the lowest paid workers of all are to be found in the old sweatshops of the worst Wages Council industries : but the nationalized industries still employ greater numbers of low-paid workers than all the others, and still tend to pay rates which are closer to the established minima than are those of other industries. Low pay is still, to a disgraceful degree, a problem of the public service above all others.

Yet again, it is also common knowledge that the co-ordination of claims in the public sector has not, from the unions' viewpoint, been advantageous, to put the matter as mildly as possible. The power dispute of manual workers was almost followed, four months later, by one of engineers in the same industry. But during December the engineers shelved plans for action in order to keep services running as well as possible.

The postmen's extraordinary sacrifice having been ended, there began a railway dispute which, had it coincided with the earlier stoppage, could have blocked the major alternative channel for parcel distribution which remained open for the whole period in question. It was revealed after the return to work of the postmen that the Post Office made 'a profit' out of the strike, since no wages had been paid out, while the service normally runs at a loss which, in this event, was not incurred. But the telephone service, which is very profitable, enhanced its income, and, it is almost impossible to believe, but it remains true : the Post Office engineers' own claim remained to be processed later in the year.

These are but a few examples of a chronic lack of trade-union co-ordination.[3] One might add that, had the miners maintained their threatened strike at the end of 1970, power stations in parts of the country would have been left with only a week's supply of coal. But the miners' claim was settled before the power dispute began. To put the matter in this way is to pose the beginning of the obvious answer. The Government is able to deal with each and every separate claim which arises in the public sector, since it never comes under co-ordinated pressure. By sectorizing the argument, it is enabled to manoeuvre freely between the territories which it has, itself, chosen. Why, for instance, is there a Coal Board, and a plurality of separate bureaucracies to organize the Gas and Electricity Supply industries? No one can claim that planning considerations argue for such an arrangement. An Energy Board would be able to arrange its production effectively, and cut through a host of problems which today appear absurdly intractable from the consumers' point of view. The simple and obvious joke about the digging of separate holes in the same street in order to lay electricity and gas mains is only one by-product of segmental organization. Certainly we shall never have a sane transport policy while railways are separate from road haulage, and both compete to do inefficiently what a planned division of labour might accomplish with high efficiency. If it is said that 'supra-boards' are unwieldy, then why not decentralize their administration into integrated regional units? The anarchy of the present arrangements does have a powerful effect on trade-union bargaining power, to say nothing of its role in diminishing the effective voice of the workpeople in the positive government of their industries. From such chaos, however, the Government can profit even if the community at large loses. The main 'profit' for Authority comes in the greater ease with which separate labour forces can be manipulated. Even when a nationalized industry is highly profitable, it has in the past proved perfectly possible so to arrange its accounts as to reveal a very slender

---

[3] Since this section was written, important changes have taken place, beginning a move towards the policies recommended here. It is still too soon to judge whether the public sector unions will be able to operate effectively in harness, and there are good grounds for scepticism. But it would be churlish not to note that some very positive developments have taken place as a result of the lessons learned during the postal strike.

surplus.[4] But in the nature of things public enterprise is liable to incur losses, especially when the prices of its products are held artificially low as a matter of social policy. No one can argue that it is not a good thing to have, for instance, cheap fares. But if travel were made free, which would be a good idea, we could hardly expect busmen and train-drivers to work for nothing. If the Government wants steel to be artificially cheap, it must meet the deficit, not beat it out of the steelworkers' ribs.

This loss-making propensity of nationalized industries will be greatly aggravated when the present Government's policies of selling off the most profitable parts of public enterprise to private concerns takes effect, assuming the unions do not find the necessary means to put a stop to all such plans. The table below provides a list of the ancillary activities of State firms. It shows that many are very profitable, and indicates that the balance-sheets of many State boards could be made to appear very sorry after all the greater plums had been distributed among enterprising businessmen.

FINANCIAL INFORMATION ABOUT ANCILLARY ACTIVITIES

	Turnover	Operating profit	Average net assets	Operating profit as % of net assets
	£m	£m	£m	
1 NATIONAL COAL BOARD 1969/70				
Coke ovens	60.6	7.5	22.7	33.0
Sales depots		1.3		
Estates and farms		0.6		
Royalties from licensed mines	49.8	0.6	20.7	13.2
Road transport, wagon repair shops, etc.		0.3		
Processed fuel plants	15.1	2.0	19.2	10.3
Chemical by-product plants	3.7	−0.1	2.4	−3.7
Brickworks	3.1	−0.3	3.0	−11.3

[4] Documentation on this point can be found in *A Plan for the Miners*. This publication showed how large net surpluses could be, and were, translated by the NCB's accountants into the smallest of widows' mites when profits were announced. It caused great controversy between the union and the NCB, and was vigorously denounced by Lord Robens at a NUM conference!

	Turnover	Operating profit	Average net assets	Operating profit as % of net assets
2 GAS BOARDS 1969/70				
Sale of appliances	95.9	(−4.7)	—	—
Contracting	14.6	—	—	—
Hire purchase finance	3.3	—	—	—
Rental of appliances	1.3	—	—	—
3 ELECTRICITY BOARDS (excluding NORTH OF SCOTLAND) 1969/70				
Sale of appliances	87.0 ⎫			
Contracting	39.0 ⎬	5.3	24.0	22.0
Hire purchase finance	4.9	—	46.7	—
4 BRITISH STEEL CORPORATION 1960/70 (26 weeks)				
Structural engineering	31.1	−1.2	30.7	−3.8
Iron foundries	24.4	1.4	23.0	6.0
Wiremaking	11.8	0.8	8.0	10.3
Forges	11.2	−0.5	10.4	−4.9
Overseas subsidiaries	10.4	0.6	21.4	2.8
Coke ovens and chemicals	7.7	0.6	10.0	5.6
Pipework engineering	4.3	0.1	6.5	−2.0
Steel foundries	3.0	−0.3	2.9	−10.5
Stockholding	2.8	0.2	1.7	10.5
Brickmaking	2.0	−0.3	1.9	−17.0
Concrete pipes	1.8	—	2.6	1.0
Plant and machine tool manufacture	1.1	−0.3	2.0	−14.3
5 BRITISH RAIL* 1969				
Workshops	94.8	0.5	29.3	1.8
Ships	26.9	4.5	29.6	15.3
Hotels	13.3	0.9	11.2	7.7
Non-operational property	4.3	2.7	(31.1)	(8.6)
Harbours	3.4	0.3	9.7	2.9
Hovercraft	0.6	−0.3	2.6	−11.0
6 NATIONAL FREIGHT CORPORATION 1969				
Tayforth, etc.	13.5	0.5	—	—
Pickford's	12.8	0.7	11.9†	7.2†
Atlantic Steam Navigation ⎫	7.2 ⎰	0.2 ⎱	8.1	−1.8
Associated Humber Lines ⎬	⎱	−0.3 ⎰		
Harold Wood and other special traffic	5.5	0.2	—	—

* Net fixed assets excluding land
† Includes Harold Wood and other special traffic. Net assets at end of year

	Turnover	Operating profit	Average net assets	Operating profit as % of net assets
7 POST OFFICE 1969/70				
Giro	5.3	–6.0‡	—	—
National Data Processing	2.8	—	8.2	–0.5
8 ISOLATED UNDERTAKINGS				
Thomas Cook (1968/69)	164.0§	1.1	6.6	16.1
Lunn-Poly (1969; 10 months)	12.0§	–0.1	—	—
State pubs (1969/70)	4.6	0.3	2.2	11.7

‡ After interest
§ Travel business handled and sales of travellers cheques

SOURCE: Richard Pryke and Michael Barratt Brown, *Stop Messing Them About* (Public Enterprise Group, June 1971).

The auctioning of Thomas Cook, or Pickford's, or the Special Steels division of the BSC, would add to the process of erosion, since these are not normally classified as 'ancillary undertakings' but are, of course, easily detachable and attractive commercially. The point is often made that the sale of all such undertakings would not change the basic facts of nationalization in the major part of the public sector : and in terms of investment, or employment, this may be a more or less valid statement. But to cut the profitable fringes of nationalized concerns, at the same time as their major activities are suffering a general squeeze, is to harm them very considerably.

For the purposes of this argument, it is quite clearly the fact that sectoral resistance to the process by individual unions will not get far. Joint organization, joint policies, joint counter-plans and joint action are the absolute precondition for effective trade-union resistance to such a devastating onslaught.

The immediate round of wage settlements in the public sector is coming to an end, and for this reason the obvious goad to trade-union co-ordination is not at its most pressing. At the time of writing, claims are outstanding in local government (for white-collar workers), electricity generating (engineers), steel (process workers and craftsmen), the Post Office (POEU), British Rail and London Passenger railway employees. The 37,000 railway shop-men also have an outstanding claim under consideration.

But the overall pay position in the public sector is still serious

enough to compel trade unionists to think seriously about intensified co-operation and co-ordination : and the structural changes
which are to be expected as a result of government policy can only
intensify this necessity. The appalling concentrations of low-paid
workers in several key areas of the nationalized industries (Post
Office, mines, gas) and in local government and elsewhere in
public service employment, which places many tens of thousands of
them below the poverty line, will not see any marked improvement
unless they can develop a far more aggressive and far more integrated bargaining strategy than they have elaborated up to now.

The stark facts concerning the lack of a joint trade-union
response to these conditions were graphically explained by Tom
Jackson, in a strong article he contributed to *Tribune* on the 9th
April, 1971. He wrote :

All that the struggle of local government workers, the miners,
the electricians, the railwaymen and Post Office workers proves
is that the trade union movement is disorganised.

Perhaps this last example is the best we can find at the
moment. For here the trade unions were not involved in some
massive political battle. They were just doing their jobs :
trying to prevent the standard of life of their members from
being depressed. And yet each union, or group of unions, met
its moment of truth in its own particular way and in isolation.

It is true that the UPW had lots of sympathy—bucketfuls!
We even had £200,000 in direct donations and we could have
raised more interest-free loans than we could afford to accept.
But we were alone.

Despite the fact that the TUC's Nationalised Industries
Committee discussed the problem of public service workers'
pay in September 1970, despite the fact that the General
Council was resolved not to see individual groupings in public
service workers 'picked off' in isolation, despite the fact the
problem was identified in September, no solution was found.
Brave words aplenty, action no !

I suggested to the General Council on September 23 that
pay claims in the public service area should be cleared through
the TUC and that once such claims were approved, mutual
aid and assistance should be available between unions. The
inability of the General Council to face up to such a proposal
set the scene for the current wages de-escalation policies which
are reducing the public service workers' standard of living.

What was at stake was autonomy, the sacred right of each

individual union to make its own decision. There can be no co-ordination of policies, no teeth and no 'general staff' without the giving up of autonomy. And yet when discussion on this subject takes place, trade unionists, both Right and Left, reach for their individual rule books and brandish them like scimitars. The rules of individual unions are meant to protect and promote the interests of their members not to destroy real co-ordination and reduce trade union effectiveness.

Of course we all know what we want; some of us even know what we don't want. What we don't know is how to get the one and reject the other. And in a way, that statement is not true. For, deep down, most trade unionists would admit that our present lack of central directions and disunity is to the disadvantage of workers generally. Most would agree that co-ordination is necessary and then go on to find a million 'rule book' type reasons that doing nothing seems right. In this the Left in the trade union movement is no better than the Right. . . . It is this attitude that has prevented, and will go on preventing, a centrally directed logical trade union structure. It is this that has been the Tory Party's greatest asset in our campaign against the Industrial Relations Bill. It is this which is helping to grind down public service workers. It is this which will render us impotent as a movement. We have learned nothing and forgotten nothing.

The TUC's Nationalized Industries Committee was established after Arthur Horner moved a resolution at the 1949 Congress, calling for increased co-operation between both unions and boards in the nationalized industries. He urged a joint council of boards, and a special committee of TUC affiliated unions to promote co-operation in the public sector. Certainly the committee which resulted has never, even remotely, seemed likely to provide an effective strategic response for workers in the public services. This body meets, and presumably discusses something : but it very seldom finds anything to talk about which merits the briefest mention in the Annual Report of the General Council. Each year a perfunctory report of five or six lines is added to all the other hundreds of pages, normally saying very little more than that the committee exists, and recording its membership.

Something much more serious than this will be required if the crisis in the public sector is to produce anything other than a carve-up by Authority, in the unlikely, but very real, persons of Mr Heath and his acolytes. Perhaps the time was not really ripe for Arthur Horner's initiative in 1949. It is certainly overripe today. Can we not ask, at least, that an official delegate conference of all relevant unions be convened, if necessary, by the TUC Committee, to discuss all those matters affecting public service and nationalized industry unions, and to hammer out joint policies? If such a gathering were summoned, could it not, at least, agree that poverty wages must be abolished in the public sector? Might it not agree to submit a joint and combined claim for a public service minimum wage at least two pounds a week above the public relief-rates for a family of four? If a joint claim were submitted, could not joint action be elaborated to back it? And if the abolition of poverty wages could provide the issue for a joint campaign, could not present working conditions, the lack of workers' rights in production, and the failures of overall public responsibility in and to the nationalized sector, be put under common trade-union scrutiny and, with a minimum of goodwill, confronted by a co-ordinated trade-union policy?

Can the public service unions continue, any longer, to ignore these questions? One hopes not, if trade unionism is ever to be taken for a serious social force.

Chapter 11

Trade Unions and Free Communications

It would be remiss to pass on from the consideration of workers' control struggles without giving some brief attention to an extremely important theatre of operations : the mass-media.

Of course, the crisis which afflicts other sectors of the British economy has not bypassed the press and the television companies : as competition escalates, the need for concentration and rationalization has struck the national newspapers with considerable force. We have witnessed the closure of the old *Daily Mail* and *Daily Sketch,* and the launching of a new tabloid out of their joint resources, which is attempting to compete with the other popular newspapers, now effectively controlled by three other giant concerns, publishing respectively the *Daily Express, Daily Mirror* and *Sun.* Newspapermen are experiencing the same insecurities that have become familiar in the wake of other mergers, and print-workers have begun to react with the same kinds of demand.

Yet the press is not just any industry. Whilst it is quite clearly true that people nowadays tend to be somewhat sceptical of what they read, it remains undeniable that newspapers can exercise a considerable influence upon public opinion, and, at crucial times, actually manipulate the whole climate in which overall decisions are taken. What newspapers print, and sometimes what they do not print, can make all the difference to a particular situation. And nowhere have newspapers been more active than in the development of public concern about the allegedly unbridled power of trade unions. For many years now, the press has carried on what amounts to a systematic campaign of distortion about the nature of trade unionism. One has only to recollect some of the recent scandals—the famous 'noose-trial' story from Cowley, which broke out during the 1966 General Election; or the story of intimidation of Midlands road hauliers, which followed; or the ludicrous accounts of 'force and violence' in the 1970 miners' strike—to realize that any stick has been good enough for some newspapers to beat the unions with. True, if one reads carefully, and follows a story from page 1 (on the early, sensation-making days) to the bottom corner of page 6 (when the unions reply, much later), one can sometimes piece together a different picture. The fact remains that most workers do have quite extraordinary ideas of their brother trade unionists, which can only originate from the miscalled communications media. Shop stewards are commonly assumed to be predominantly selected from the Communist Party or further left, even when the academic surveys that have been conducted in industry make it plain that for many years the growth of factory representation has been encouraged by management, and that the opinions of stewards very directly reflect those of their constituents. It is always a surprise, even to groups of militant trade unionists, to discover exactly how unusual demarcations disputes are : because the attention accorded them in the press totally distorts the reality, and presents them as a major industrial problem. Strikes are reported with general disapprobation and, if they persist, may well lead to witch-hunting of the kind in which individual militants are hounded. A full dossier on misrepresentations of this kind during the past two or three years alone would fill a fat volume, and that would not cover the gravest sins, which are invariably sins of omission. For instance, during the work-to-rule of power-workers in December 1970, the popular press suddenly discovered hypothermia.[1] Old people might die of cold if the electricity supply failed, we were told—told, moreover, loudly and insistently. In point of fact, old people die every winter, in horrendously large numbers, because they are too poor to find money for the meters, or cannot afford a bag of coal. Since we have been agitating, for years, for free fuel for old-age pensioners, we think we have a right to point out that the silence of the media on this question has, normally, been deafening. Or again, when incomes policy was the music of the day, and the unions had to be persuaded to sign on the dotted line, the newspapers discovered low pay. 'Fair shares' became the

[1] This was only one of the more extreme publicity stunts which were current during that dispute. The newspapers in general blanketed out all news of the unions' plans for emergency services, and seemed to be hellbent upon actually creating emergencies. The story was graphically documented by Mr Frank Chapple in his evidence to the Wilberforce Inquiry, which followed the dispute.

watchword, and every demagogic egalitarian utterance by ministers was given splash coverage. But when the charter of the Prices and Incomes Board was approved in Parliament it said nothing whatever about 'social justice', and indeed the Board did not begin work on the issue of low pay until years later, when it was on the brink of dissolution. Year by year under the incomes policy, the poor got poorer. When did the popular newspapers reveal this fact? Not until the beginning of the 1970 election campaign, in the majority of cases.

The distortion of trade-union news is not primarily a result of conscious bad faith. It flows from a whole series of implicit attitudes, which can easily be brought to the surface if one analyses the famous case, a few years' old now, of the girl in the lavatory. The story ran like this. In a Midlands factory a young girl spent a long time in the lavatory. When she returned to her job she was sacked. Her workmates struck work and demanded her reinstatement. Every headline screeched about the wickedness of this response. Here was the hidden cause of the balance-of-payments crisis! How could someone be defended for spending an hour in the toilet? When would the workers see how disgraceful this behaviour really was? And all this ran for several days as a lead story, apparently seriously intended. What did not run was any discussion of the underlying significance of the incident. To begin with how many journalists, let alone editors and newspaper proprietors, are ever timed on their visits to the lavatory? If someone followed a press lord to the door marked 'Peers' in the Upper House, and stood attendant with a stop-watch, wouldn't this, quite rightly, be generally regarded as a gross breach of privacy? But more than this: even supposing that all the implications of slothful conduct by the girl were justified (and there was no evidence on this matter), what did her action tell us about the nature of her work? If her job was so boring, or so exacting, or so restricting in its demands, that she found the lavatory a freer place to be than her work-bench, what do we have to assume? That she was 'lazy'? Would it not be at least reasonable to assume that there was something wrong with the job? Any one of the pressmen who helped to hound this young lady would be expected, in polite society, to treat her with far greater deference if she were to be, let us say, his guest. Yet because she was 'at work' she was expected to conform, not to the standards of polite society, but to industrial discipline, which can only allow that workpeople have bowels, and natural functions, if these are submitted to the control of a clock, and cannot allow that they have feelings at all.

The ultimate debasement of objective standards of news presentation came, however, with the debate around the Industrial Relations Bill and the struggle that this produced. Every major non-socialist newspaper welcomed the news that the Bill was forthcoming, and when it was finally published it received an almost ecstatic reception. Polls were published to show that it had the support of a great majority of trade unionists and these were given headline display. (Very much later the *Daily Express* was to reveal, in a modest report, poll results which showed that a majority of the population had *not even heard of* the Bill.) A one-sided 'debate' raged, in which all the standard prejudices against trade unionism had a field day. When strikes broke out in protest against the measure, they were reported, albeit with great disapproval, as insignificant events. When they recurred, every attempt was made to break the front of the unions concerned, by grossly exaggerated accounts of the unwillingness of some few workers to participate.[2] On television one report covered the impending national protest strike of AUEW members by interviewing some women outside a Midlands factory. They did not want to strike at all, they said. Oh yes, they'd certainly be going to work. They weren't going to take orders from the unions at any price! Only at the end of the piece of film concerned did it become clear that the women interviewed were members of the NUGMW, which had not only not called out its members, but which was actively opposed to strike action of any kind.

When 150,000 trade unionists rallied in Hyde Park to support the TUC's campaign against the Bill, this event, the build-up to which had been virtually ignored, was covered as a 'picnic', a 'good-natured stroll in the sunshine'. Subsequently, the mass strike which accompanied the TUC's special conference in Croydon was reported not as the largest political strike ever to take place in this country, but as a very low-key affair indeed. One wiseacre

[2] See analysis by the Free Communications Group in *The Spokesman*, No. 9, p. 22. See also the report of the ACTT 'Television Commission', which monitored television news and current affairs programmes from 8th to 14th January, 1971 (reported in *The Spokesman*, No. 11, p. 22).

from the union side commented that if there was a general strike about the Bill, it would appear in the news on television in a brief flash after the story that Brian Close had been re-established as captain of the Yorkshire cricket team.

This humiliating mixture of hullabaloo about slanted and distorted accounts of what are sometimes insignificant matters, and calculated silence about major issues, has turned many trade unionists very sour about the media. Increasingly, justified suspicion about the press prevents trade unionists from attempting to put their views across. The television pillorying, by David Frost, of a group of rank-and-file workers from the power stations, has had the effect of discouraging workpeople from collaborating even with some of the most highly qualified and transparently honest reporters from other media. TV personnel who have wanted to prepare objective documentaries on the problems of industrial stress and safety at work have, to their surprise and distress, been denied vital co-operation by shop-floor workers who have come to regard all intrusion into their affairs by journalists or commentators as, by definition, hostile.

This response can be a very damaging one. From the point of view of the new unionism, a very much more positive development has been the growing awareness, by workers in the media themselves, of the need to exercise vigilant supervision over the use of newspapers and television to prevent their manipulating public prejudice against the unions. A Free Communications Group has been formed, bringing together journalists, producers and technical personnel from the press, radio and television to work for democratic accountability in the various media and control of their content by representative staff bodies subject to overall public responsibility. This group has begun to publish a lively journal, *The Open Secret*,[3] which documents the concentration of power in the media, the hidden histories of take-overs and mergers, and the successful attempts of journalists and workpeople in newspapers and television, at home and abroad, to exercise a degree of responsible control over what their media report or do not report. *The Open Secret* has made available accounts of the struggles of the staffs of *Stern* and *Figaro* on just these issues,[4]

[3] Obtainable from 30 Craven Street, London WC2.
[4] See *The Open Secret*, No. 1 (1969); also the FCG pamphlet *In Place of Management*, Appendices A and B.

and encouraged debate among widening circles of trade unionists and professional newsmen. Stimulated by this growth of concern, the ACTT, the television crews' union, set up a monitoring service to cover the transmissions of the television companies during the outbreak of struggles against the Industrial Relations Bill. Its report aroused widespread comments and began a useful union counter-attack against the traducers of trade unionism. Similar documentation has been encouraged and published by the Free Communications Group itself.

At the same time, the deepening anger among print-workers, as the mischievous effects of misrepresentation of trade-union activities have become increasingly plain, has given rise to a series of direct actions. Notable among these was the demonstration in December 1970 by workers on the *Evening Standard* against a particularly offensive drawing lampooning the unions, by the paper's resident cartoonist, Jak. By insisting upon the right to a rejoinder, these workers established an important point. The media may be owned by a tightly knit oligarchy, or controlled by authoritarian cliques, but they cannot perform their work of manipulating popular opinion if they meet serious united resistance from the workpeople they employ. The Editor of the *Evening Standard* was so discountenanced by this action that he published a long article in *The Listener* condemning his employees for attempted censorship, and claiming that the workers' control movement must inevitably lead to such censorship.[5] The truth is the exact reverse. The workers on the *Evening Standard* demonstrated their clear understanding of the issues, and their commitment to freedom of expression, when they demanded, not the suppression of Jak's cartoon, but the right to reply.

This initiative caught on. In January 1971 the *Bristol Evening Post* tried to publish an account of a union meeting, and its afternoon editions were stopped when the Editor refused either to correct it or remove it. In March, during the Ford dispute, the *Southend Evening Echo* tried to conduct a 'ballot' of Ford workers on their strike, by printing a 'ballot-form' and urging strikers to return it in boxes specially provided at the newspapers' offices. The NATSOPA chapel at the *Echo* objected, and after

[5] 24th December, 1970. On 11th February *The Listener* published part of a reply by Ken Coates, the full text of which appeared subsequently in *Socialist Leader*.

the management's failure to agree that the conducting of 'ballots' was no part of a newspaper's proper business, work was stopped and the paper did not come out.

Up to now, journalists have lagged behind print-workers in insisting on their rights, as workers, to serve the cause of providing objective information, and to prevent the misuse of their talents for purposes of misrepresentation. But it is absolutely clear that journalists, too, can only gain from the exercise of democratic responsibility over their products. To condemn trade unionists of seeking to 'suppress' opinions in such cases as these is quite absurd : the opinions in question are all too widely ventilated, since they are the opinions of those who own the means of production of opinions. What is at stake is the right of all of us to hear *other* people's ideas, the opinions of ordinary people : and the right of those ideas to be heard.

This struggle, for true freedom of expression, cannot be left to newspapermen, printers, television journalists and crews. Their own initiatives deserve the widest support from the trade-union movement as a whole, but this movement needs also to enter the field of communications on its own account, and to deploy its vast human resources to ensure that the growing demand for real democracy in industry and society is not frustrated by the artificial constraints of our unfree press.

Chapter 12

Trade-Union Structure: Impediment or Stimulus?

We have already made the point that trade-union organization is hard pressed to keep pace with the changes in industrial organization, and that this is particularly noticeable in two main respects. First, the frontiers between 'industries' are constantly changing, so that trade-union arrangements which were rational twenty years ago are often seriously inadequate today. Second, the concentration of scale and ownership shifts the focuses of power in industry even on to the intercontinental plane, while unions remain organized in narrow national segments.

Urgent reform of trade-union structure is thus vital for elementary self-protection, let alone advance. A concrete example will spell out what this means in the 1970s. If we look at the coal-mining industry, we find within it three trade unions affiliated to the TUC: the Colliery Overmen and Deputies (NACODS), the National Union of Mineworkers (NUM) and the NCB Labour Staff Association.[1] In all, 322,000 members are organized in these bodies. Outside the TUC we find a professional body, the British Association of Colliery Managers, engaging itself in repeated debates about affiliation. This arrangement is almost the nearest thing in Britain to a model of industrial unionism. True, not one but four bodies exist, stratified by status and responsibility. But only in very few industries does a single union, like the NUM, cover the territory so exclusively, taking in clerical workers and craftsmen alike, as well as all grades of manual workers. Once, in their heyday, this structure served to make the miners a spearhead of trade unionism, placing them in the forefront of the whole movement. Today they are in a very different position. This is not primarily a result of organizational defects. As we have already shown, the powers of the mineworkers have been tapered away by a catastrophic series of events set in the general context

[1] TUC *Report* (1970).

of severe decline in the industry. Why? Was the whole process inevitable? If one sees mining as a self-contained constituent of the economy and society, the answer is, inevitably, yes.[2] But if one sees coal as a part of the total energy supply of the nation, then the process is nothing like so clearly preordained. A National Union of Energy-workers which included power-station operatives, refinery workers, gas-workers and oil drillers as well as miners would, at all times, have exercised prodigious powers, more than adequate to defend those of its members, in coal-mines, who were exposed to the ill-effects of new technologies.

Yet not only did the NUM find it quite impossible, from within its given structure, to formulate a strategy for assembling such an alliance : worse, it has been quite unable to adapt adequately to the structural changes which have taken place within the National Coal Board itself. At no point has the union been organized in units matching those developed by its employers. When the old five-tier organization of the NCB was replaced by a three-tier structure, the already inappropriate county organizations of mineworkers were, by and large, left almost exactly as they had been previously. What this means is that the Coal Board's men have never been adequately matched and paced by appropriate members of a union oppositional team. Research and other services were never very extended in the NUM, but even the modest resources which did exist were unable to shape up to the possibilities, in such a dysfunctional set-up.

If we write about the problems of the miners, it is not because they are more than averagely unfortunate in the organizations which represent them. The tests which technological changes pose for most other sections of workers leave similar reproaches at the doors of their respective unions. An obvious example is the printing industry. Here we find, in 1970, six unions affiliated to the

[2] This is the tragedy involved in the careers of such dedicated men as Will Paynter, former General Secretary of the NUM. In his book *British Trade Unions and the Problem of Change* (Allen & Unwin, 1970) Paynter reveals the extent to which the structure of industrial unionism has blinkered his vision. Authoritative over the problems of the coal-fields, he seems almost completely unaware of the rhythms of every industry but his own, and is certainly quite unable to draw lessons for the mineworkers from the experience of, say, the engineers. Although he makes a strong statement of his belief in industrial unionism, his arguments notwithstanding, the evidence offered by his book points in an entirely different direction from the one he wishes the unions to seek.

TUC, representing 391,756 workers. A few years ago printing unions were far more numerous and the problems of new techniques have certainly assisted in precipitating agreement upon the need for union mergers. Yet, in 1970, we had the National Graphical Association and the Scottish Typographical Association representing compositors; SOGAT, representing all the many semi-skilled trades, the machine operators and numerous specialist skills such as binding; SLADE for the lithographic designers and process workers; and the specialized union of wallpaper workers. To have narrowed the field to three main bodies is progress indeed, even though one has subsequently redivided. Nevertheless, the explosion in lithographic printing, the enormous technical advances in cold type-setting, in which today six or seven typists can be fully occupied in keeping one small computer fed with hard copy, which it in turn will automatically translate into justified galley proofs, and the enormous advances in photographic processes, taken together, speak very sternly of the need for one *single* print union, if any of the old print-workers' controls which have been troublesomely established through the entire long history of printing are, tomorrow, to be defended. While key sectors of the printing unions, such as those employed by the major newspapers, can be relatively well protected because of their very concentration, which itself troubles all trade unionists, it remains true that it will be impossible to achieve the requisite degree of fluidity of response to new technologies throughout the whole industry unless the old divisions between yesterday's crafts and skills can be replaced by a union integrating all the trades.

If this is true within industries which remain recognizably tied to the same general line of business, what of those industries whose old frontiers have been totally recast by innovation? The disadvantage of old-fashioned industrial unionism is at its plainest in such cases. The struggle to establish an inclusive organization for one single industry is itself a tough one, without taking account of the need to do it all over again once a decade. New materials, new processes, new machines, new combinations of products, all act together to recast the social division of labour. Unions are bound to reflect that division of labour : but they are also bound to reflect it through a time-lag. They must always, alas, to some extent, respond after the event of industrial change. This means that they must always seek to develop organizations which are adaptable, and as sensitive to new forms of production and industrial organization as is compatible with organizational solidarity.

There could be no clearer example of the vast melting-pot into which technological change is casting the old industrial frontiers than the case raised by the third London airport. The apparently conclusive decision of the Government to site this at Foulness, at the mouth of the Thames estuary, is not perhaps at first sight relevant to questions of trade-union structure and strategy. But, in fact, this decision has far-reaching implications for the future of the location of industry, its ownership and control, and the degree of cohesion or sectionalism with which the trade-union movement responds to these issues.

The technological revolution in cargo-handling methods, which includes the widespread adoption of the container system for traditional general cargoes, the development of the giant special-ized bulk-carrier for the shipment of many raw materials—oil, ores, grain, etc.—and the attempted rationalization of internal movement of freight through British Rail's freight-liner service, combined with the need to discover sites for new industrial and urban development away from existing centres of congested in-dustry, have led the planners to define and discuss a concept which has been given the inspiring initials MIDAS—Maritime Industrial Development Area Scheme. During the 'sixties there was continual speculation about possible locations for such a grand design, and the spectacular growth of Europoort, around Rotter-dam, lent credibility to the concept. The Humber, the Wash, the Thames estuary, sites on the south and west coasts, and the Clyde estuary, were amongst the locations discussed in the literature of transport economics and in the publications of the National Ports Council. In turn, each of these locations was pictured as the scene of intensive development, which would include a modernized port, with deep draught to accommodate mammoth tankers and bulk carriers, integrated through-transport systems linking the port to other centres of industry via freight-liner trains and trunk roads, and an on-site complex of industrial plant for the treat-ment of bulk cargoes—food-processing, oil refining, chemicals, and ore-processing (steel, etc.).

The ever-increasing scale of the super-tankers, however, elimin-ated one after another site from consideration, since very few coastal areas of Britain provide sufficient depth of water to allow these dinosaurs of the sea to berth or to manoeuvre. On these grounds, the Clyde emerged towards the end of the decade as the most likely candidate for MIDAS's application. Yet in the absence of any adequate planning authority in charge of port development, let alone any overall institution through which to harmonize the concurrent schemes of oil, chemical and steel concerns with those of the transport industry, no clear decision emerged. And meanwhile the existing ports, inland transport systems and shipping companies stumbled through a series of investment decisions which dealt in a haphazard way with the container revolution : decisions which still leave the final shape of the port system undefined and uncertain.

Thus, the freight-liner routes of British Rail were aimed towards the south-east coast and the Thames; the shipping companies' consortia, Overseas Containers Ltd and Associated Container Transport, concentrated their attention on the development of Tilbury and Southampton as terminals for trans-continental trade; whilst the port authorities of the major and medium-sized ports constructed container berths and specialized handling equipment in order to capture at least some of the new traffic. The established conventional dock systems competed for the dwindling amount of old-fashioned break-bulk cargoes. Every port and shipping company wanted to be in on the act, whilst no authority was charged to account either for the commercial losses involved in the creation of over-capacity in cargo-handling facilities or for the social cost incurred as a result of the non-decisions which led to the decline in activities in the older dockland areas. The antipathy to 'lame ducks' expressed by the Conservative Government, and its persistent discrimination against the British Steel Corporation, have both added further irrationalities to the continued drift of port-and-industry locational decisions.

The Mersey Docks and Harbour Board was one of the first 'lame ducks' to suffer the consequence of competitive over-development of port facilities. Its own modernization scheme, involving new container berths at Seaforth, and large oil and ore terminals, was started later than others and is still not complete. Consequently, the port of Liverpool has been losing trade to Southampton, Bristol and east coast ports such as Felixstowe, whilst the relatively small port of Preston has containerized much of the Irish traffic. Ironically, the very inefficiency with which the

OCL/ACT freight-liner development has taken place, has meant that the full effect of Liverpool's backwardness has not been felt by the port, and there is still some expectation that Merseyside will retain a major role in the general cargo field. But there is general agreement that the new capacity, which will come into service when the Seaforth development is complete, is already *surplus* capacity which will simply add to the competitive scramble for traffic between the ports. The ore terminal at Seaforth was commenced in the expectation that Hawarden Bridge, the British Steel Corporation's works in nearby Flintshire, might prove to be the site of a large new green-field expansion of steel-making capacity.

The Clyde Port Authority received government approval in October 1970 for the construction of a new £12 million ore terminal and general user port at Hunterston to handle ships of up to 200,000 tons. At the time it was said that this greatly increased the chances that BSC would construct its new green-field site on the Clyde in the late 1970s. Thomas Craig, the BSC chief in Scotland, enthused : 'The decision to permit construction of a major deep-water ore terminal at Hunterston is important to planning the future development of the British steel industry.'

Included in the Clyde development was a site for a new oil terminal, and adjacent land was allocated for the Chevron Oil Company to build a refinery, although the company was undecided at that time about whether to build. Nevertheless, something like a MIDAS looked to be 'on' for the Clyde in the latter part of 1970. Despite all this, the BSC was reported in 1970 to be searching for its green-field site on the south or south-eastern coast of England. (The Corporation has also incurred criticism from some quarters for missing out on the opportunity to locate new capacity at Immingham, on the south Humber bank, where there is an existing ore and coal terminal, an oil terminal with associated refinery developments, and where land is generally available for MIDAS-type industrial expansion. The Corporation preferred to build new plant at its existing inland site of Scunthorpe, though it is certain that short-term commercial, rather than social cost consideration for the welfare of the Scunthorpe community, was instrumental in arriving at that decision.)

To this increasingly speculative picture was added a final confusion when the Government cut the BSC's projected price increase early in 1971. The Government has not only denied the

Corporation in this matter, but is also preparing to sell off its profit-able divisions to private industry. Under such dispensation, the Corporation is foredoomed to continue in deficit. Government policies are responsible for the lameness of this particular duck, yet this does not deter the Government from the conclusion that it would be wrong to approve large-scale capital develop-ment by such a persistently loss-making section of public industry. Of course, at present prices, the BSC itself does not believe it can make new investment 'pay', but argues rather that it can well afford to raise prices to profitable levels without losing out in competition with world steels. The Government, however, will not allow price freedom to the Corporation. In other words, the Government is creating a situation in which Britain may not have an independent steel industry in the future.

BSC originally planned to spend £4,000 million on long-term capital renewal and modernization. £1,000 million of this total was earmarked for the great new green-field project. But this project will be the biggest casualty of the Government's restrictions on British Steel. The project will not go to the Mersey, or to Hunters-ton (Scotland could be without a steel industry altogether in the not too distant future), and the ore terminals in both those places now appear likely to join the growing list of white elephant investments which are beginning to litter the British coastline.

It began to look as though the great new works would fail to materialize anywhere, even on the south/south-east coastal site which the BSC apparently favoured. Foulness *had* been a pros-pective site, but only as part of a MIDAS which would grow up around the third airport. Cublington was going to get that airport. Then suddenly Cublington was *not* going to get it, but Foulness again. Even that decision could not itself save the green-field project, however. The Government was still not going to 'pour tax-payers' money' into the lame-duck steel industry. But then, towards the end of April 1971 and close on the heels of the Foul-ness airport decision, the press began to report . . . an offer of foreign cash! The German steel industry wants coastal sites for production and has apparently discussed joint products with BSC. There had been a proposal for a joint Hoogoven-Hoesch steel-works at Rotterdam, but this had been rejected. There is now a possibility that the Germans and Dutch will take a share of a major British expansion, sited at Foulness for easy access to the

F

Rhine. Finally, and again discreetly separated by a few diplomatic days, the news emerged from a meeting between Mr Davies, Secretary of State for Trade and Industry, and the Labour MPs of the power and steel group, that 'the Government is prepared to consider proposals, *from whatever quarter*, for the establishment of a site for the production of steel at Foulness'.[3]

We now perceive, therefore, that—perhaps by accident, perhaps by design (what *has* gone on between the Government, the Common Market steel giants, the BSC, the airlines, the oil companies and the shipping companies?)—the by-product of apparently disconnected government decisions and non-decisions, involving the siting of airports and the financial squeeze on public sector steel, is the nearest approximation so far to a MIDAS, which is to be sited not on the basis of public discussion or social-cost considerations, but in order to meet the interest of private German and Dutch steel masters.

If the MIDAS really does develop at Foulness, its evolution will be directed not only by European private capital from the steel industry, but also by the major shipping companies and the refinery owners. Perhaps the new 'third-force' private airline will even find an appropriate voice in the affair.

In the light of all this, it is instructive to look back to the proceedings of a two-day conference held in October 1970 and convened under the auspices of the British Productivity Council. It concerned the potential development of Foulness. Amongst those present were a Mr H. H. Pusey, General Services Manager of Field Aircraft Services, Mr Anthony Howard, a director of the Thames Estuary Development Company, Mr David Thornton, Managing Director of the Thames Aeroport Group, Mr G. Collard, Managing Director of Silvertown Lighterage Services, Mr John Black, the Assistant Director of the Port of London Authority, Mr J. J. Johnson, an 'oil industry consultant', Mr D. Grenville, of Rio Tinto Zinc Corporation (which is a shareholder in the Thames Estuary Development Company), Mr Kenneth Warren, MP, an 'air consultant', and Mr P. A. Satchwell, Local Services Planning Manager of British Rail.[4]

During their deliberations Mr Collard looked forward to a big boost for London's lighterage industry from the Foulness develop-

[3] *The Times* (12th May, 1971)—our italics.
[4] Details taken from a report in *The Port* (8th October, 1970).

ment, whilst Mr Howard envisaged a seaport providing facilities for vessels up to 500,000 tons and 85 feet draught. (The congestion of sea-lanes leading through the Channel to the Thames, and the associated collision and pollution dangers do not seem to have been considered at the conference!) An extremely interesting observation from the same speaker about the cost of the project should have led—at the very least—to the tabling of some pertinent questions to the Government from Labour MPs. 'This is the only airport site,' said Mr Howard, 'which has attracted the attention of those who gamble—if this is a gamble—in London, Paris and Zurich. There would be no cost to the tax-payer.' He also reported that four major oil companies were prepared to share an oil terminal, that some oil facilities could be ready by 1976, two airport runways and access facilities could be built between 1976 and 1982, that some port and industrial facilities could be available by 1978, and runways 3 and 4 could be ready by 1985 (just one year after the fatal date on which Britain is due to become 'Airstrip One . . . the third most populous of the provinces of Oceania', according to George Orwell). Mr Howard put the total cost of the entire project, including dredging for up to twenty-five years, at £169 million.

A patriotic note was struck by Mr John Black. 'It is this appreciation of the advantages of planned location that has led to the post-war development of Europoort, Antwerp, and more recently, the Golfe de Fos near Marseilles. It lies behind ambitious proposals for Dunkirk, Le Havre and elsewhere.' Without similar development at Foulness, Mr Black feared that traffic would be increasingly directed to the continental ports and that industry which would otherwise come to the UK would be sited on the other side of the Channel. He envisaged that oil and ores would be a major feature of Foulness seaport. The proportion of ships of over 200,000 tons in the world tanker fleet would rise from the present 10 per cent to 75 per cent by 1985, and 'with the relentless growth in oil traffic and the competitive prospects offered by the Thames estuary we have no doubt that the provision of a deep-water terminal to service these large ships will be needed in a very few years'. He foresaw iron ore, petrochemicals, cereals, forest products and timber as other major industries at Foulness.

Mr Grenville predicted an increasing import of ores from Australia, South Africa and South America into Europe, coming in vessels of increasing size. 'Why must they use continental ports and have their cargo transhipped to Britain? It could be cheaper for Britain's iron and steel industry for them to come direct to Britain, and Foulness would appear to be a logical site for such a development.'

Mr Warren spoke enthusiastically about the growth of air freight, which he predicted would rise from 10,000 million ton-miles in 1970 to 60,000 million in 1985. Mr Thornton spoke of creating 'out of the crumbling ruins of the economy of the Port of London . . . a brand spanking new port'. (Mr Peyton, Minister of Transport, delivered a stern 'lame-ducks' speech to the port employers of London in April 1971, in which he warned them that the financial deficits of the Port of London Authority would not be relieved by government subsidy. As with Merseyside, so with the old port of London; it must make way for bigger and brighter things, financed by the gamblers of Zurich.) It remains to add that Mr Satchwell dutifully promised the assembled moguls that British Rail would lay on a direct high-speed rail link between London and Foulness.

This then, in the eyes of some of the interested parties, is the technological, multi-national, corporate-financed splendour which will grace Maplin Sands and the south-east coast of Essex. But one very significant anxiety clouded the brows of the Foulness enthusiasts, namely the 'labour problem'. The project 'could lead to a new generation of who-does-what labour problems. *And the conference spent a great deal of time dealing with this possibility,*' said *The Port*.

The report of the conference goes on :

> . . . pleas were made for early negotiations with the trade unions and, assuming Foulness comes about, *for separate labour forces* [italics added] for the air, sea and industrial sections of the complex to reduce the effect of labour disputes.
>
> No official consultations have yet taken place with the unions, delegates were told. . . .
>
> Delegates expressed the opinion that labour problems would be as big a hurdle as technological and social problems in getting Foulness off the drawing board.
>
> 'There must be separate labour forces,' said Mr H. H. Pusey. 'We must be very careful in arranging the manning for facilities handling traffic from many different modes of transport.'
>
> With a single labour force, he said, a dispute could paralyse the centre complex.

'Even with separate labour forces a dispute could easily spread from one section—say the seaport—to the airport. . . .'

. . . And Mr David Thornton . . . warned : 'Labour problems would be among the most difficult to solve. BOAC made it part of their argument against siting an airport with a seaport at Foulness. They said that bad industrial relations in the docks could spill over into the airport. An urgent and essential part of the preplanning exercise is to test the reaction of the unions to the project.'

So—co-ordination, mutual assistance and international co-operation stretching from Rio Tinto Zinc's mines in South Africa to the Anglo-German steelworks in Britain is the planned pattern for the employers and financial backers of the project, whilst 'separate labour forces' is the planned stratagem for the workers and their unions.

The registered dockers, in pressing (against all the resistance of Government and employers) their claim to handle all dock work within a defined area surrounding the river and the estuary, are at least thinking ahead to ensure some control over the labour force of any future port at Foulness. But, as the employers dimly recognize, much wider issues are at stake. If the existing patterns of British trade-union structure are simply transplanted on to a vast new multi-industry project such as Foulness may become, the employers will not have to scheme very hard to guarantee 'separate labour forces'. The unions with potential interests at Foulness include a fair-sized chunk of the 160-odd affiliates of the TUC. The steel unions (BISAKTA and NUB), the rail unions (ASLEF, NUR and TSSA), the transport unions (TGWU, NASDU, URTU), involving in the case of the TGWU *separate* trade groups for dockers, road-haulage workers, and airport workers, are among the most immediately concerned. It is difficult, *but necessary*, to conceive of a concerted strategy being evolved by say the BISAKTA and the dockers, with the same ease and fraternity with which the representatives of big business sat down for a week-end to carve up a corner of England.

Nor is it simply a question of co-ordination of strike actions between different sections of the cargo-handling labour, though the employers intelligently apprehend that possibility. Certainly the unions should appreciate and use the great potential bargaining power presented to them by the funnelling of so much wealth and hardware through such a narrow and vulnerable entry and exit. The key question is : for what ends should the bargaining power be deployed? Will the unions adopt the commercial enthusiasms of the project designers, and forget the social consequences of this concentrated development for their brethren in Scotland, the Mersey, the East End of London and elsewhere? Will they concur in the rationalizing zeal of Hoesch-BSC, and neglect the wider social purposes which could emerge from dialogue with the German steelworkers? Will they identify with the false nationalism of the Foulness employers, and fail to establish common cause with the dockers and transport workers of Dunkirk, Le Havre, Rotterdam and Antwerp, all of whom will be subject to the same siren appeal to compete with their counterparts across the Channel? The corporate giants which will employ labour at Foulness will switch production and cargoes to the continental ports as indifferently and easily as they now do between Scunthorpe, Scotland, the Mersey and the east coast, provided always that they can maintain 'separate labour forces' in England, France, Holland and Belgium (Airstrips 1, 2, 3 and 4!).

Perhaps the internal and international divisions between trade unions are such that co-ordination and positive, aggressive, alternative social planning is beyond them. Perhaps. The structural crisis which modern neo-capitalism creates for the trade unions is indeed a deep and critical one. The adaptation of trade unions to new structures of industrial ownership and control is so often slow, and so often inadequate. Undoubtedly the workers themselves will build a liaison for themselves if and when Foulness becomes a reality. There will probably be unofficial, *ad hoc*, rank-and-file liaison committees. They in turn will have at least the possibility to compel more formal structural changes in the unions, and the potential to effect shifts to higher levels of social and class consciousness, breaking down sectional barriers between workers. One of the unions which will be intimately concerned, the TGWU, may well contain within its own structures (through the eventual mergers which can be anticipated with the merchant seamen, the lightermen, the stevedores' union and others) the possibility of strategic thought and behaviour embracing the whole transport industry. But ultimately what we are seeking may not be achievable *in trade-union terms* at all, though trade unionism will be the essential institution through which workers reach forward to the necessary international *socialist* strategy. Trade unionism may meet and contain the neo-capitalist 'planners' of Foulness; eventually only a workers' *political* strategy can *overcome* the manipulations and the dominance by private interests to which all the Foulnesses of the advanced capitalist world are subject. Foulness could become a gigantic demonstration of the basic contradiction between the social nature of production and the private ownership of the means of production. Yet, if trade unions need to respond on a higher level of integrated understanding and action than ever before, they are virtually hamstrung by the present fragmented nature of their present organizations. How can policy be made by a complex of bits and pieces? How can action be co-ordinated by bodies which are jealously autonomous?

All these needs point inexorably to the only organizational pattern which is conceivable for modern unions: the only model which can permit the degree of flexibility required by industrial change is that of general unionism. This is already very apparent from the figures. In 1971 the Transport and General Workers' Union counted over 1,600,000 members, and the AUEW substantially over a million (1,200,000). Together with the General & Municipal Workers, who in 1970 claimed 803,000, the Electricians and Plumbers (EETPTU), which numbered 392,000 and the Shopworkers' 316,000, we find that now, not far short of half the affiliated members of the TUC belong to unions which, whatever their antecedents, and however they have evolved from such diverse origins, have all acquired the main attributes of General Unions. In short, the workers are voting for this form of organization of unions by the simple process of joining up.

Yet, once posed, this question implies another. What conceivable reason can there be for organizing a plurality of general unions? Consider what it means. In a huge proportion of the larger British factories which are unionized, there are working alongside one another members of at least the TGWU, the AUEW and the NUGMW. Each of these unions will have to assign at least one professional officer to concern himself for some of his time with the affairs of the membership in that factory. But few factories can split their employees between several unions and still allow a sufficient concentration of membership to permit the engagement of a full-time officer exclusively dedicated to their affairs. Each such officer will thus find himself spread over membership in a whole number of enterprises. Such servicing as may be required will thus, very likely, be done with unnecessary amateurism, by unnecessarily overstretched personnel, unnecessarily duplicating the efforts of others. This accounts, to some degree, for the serious loss of control which unions may have from time to time over their middle-ranking officers. During the Ford dispute of 1969, for instance, the leaders of both the AUEW and the TGWU were severely embarrassed when, quite rightly, they rejected the imposition of an agreement to accept managerial practices which were clearly incompatible with their unions' basic policies, only to be informed in the press that local officers of their own organizations in other parts of the country had previously concluded absolutely identical agreements with other employers. In such cases, neither the leaders nor the membership of unions are able to exercise effective supervision over actions done in their name.

The logic of this situation points to a simple solution, and indeed, early in 1970, two major unions began to discuss the only sensible answer : merger. But when the NUGMW and the EETPTU opened abortive negotiations for fusion, their predominant motive was not trade-union efficiency, but political convenience, in that they wished to conclude an effective conservative alliance in order to defend, more vigorously, the overwhelmingly corporatist atti- tudes upheld by their leaders. Much though Lord Cooper and Sir Leslie Cannon disliked what they were prone to regard as the rabid leftism of the growing new unionism, and much though they wished to join forces to oppose it, they were to prove constitution- ally incapable of consummating the marriage so devoutly to be desired. The former represents an old-established doctrinally founded conservative current in the Labour Movement, while the latter was the voice of a quite instrumental conformity of a markedly different species. This mixture would not gel, and for a reason which brings us to the crucial point in this discussion.

The answer to industrial flux, the displacement of skills and the recasting of the overall division of labour, is truly simple and time- honoured : we need one big union. But one union will not meet the needs of its members for adaptability, strength and quick- ness of response, just by being big. However large their organiza- tion, trade-union leaders alone can never rise to meet these modern demands simply by employing professional staffs, although they certainly should expand and improve their organizational, advisory, research and educational services. Whatever administrative improvement they make, however, the key to successful response to rapid change will remain, firstly and always, active involvement by those confronting it. One big union is not enough. It must be one big *democratic* union, or it won't work. Indeed, we can see the inadequacies of sheer size very plainly when we observe the progress of the NUGMW, which over two decades has run as well as it could to stay exactly where it began in terms of membership. Since it is general enough to cushion its losses in areas of decline, like the gasworks, by gains in what have been parts of the growth sector of the economy, such as engineering, there is no 'objective' economic explanation for this stagnation analagous to that which explains the decline of the industrially based unions of mineworkers or railwaymen. But the 'subjective' reasons for it can be clearly understood if one looks at the oligarchic bureaucratic structure of the organization, so graphically exposed during the dispute of Pilkington's glass-workers at St Helens in 1970.

In April 1970 a miscalculation of wages provoked a spontaneous strike in one of the departments at Pilkington's. There had been no major strike there for a century: and the NUGMW, which organized the company, had both a closed shop and a long-standing policy of collaboration with the employers, come what may. The fruits of this policy were long hours and low wages for the workers (£25 average for a 52-hour week). The April outbreak, however, came at a time when Ford workers at Halewood, close by, had recently won a £4 a week wage rise : which contrasted starkly with the 7½d an hour, phased over several months, negotiated in the Pilkington plants during the same period. Within two days of the stoppage in the Flat Drawn department of the Sheet Works, all of Pilkington's branches in St Helens were struck. The union branch supported the strike and most of the men imagined that the strength of their case would bring immediate recognition of their dispute by their national officers. This was not to be the case. From the beginning, the national officers denounced the strike as unofficial, and demanded that it end. In all, the strike dragged on for seven weeks. When it concluded, hundreds of workers were dismissed. 350 were subsequently re-employed with loss of entitlements : 250 were, according to the strike leaders, 'shut out and blacklisted'.[5]

[5] *The Pilkington Struggle* by John Potter—Secretary, Pilkington's Rank and File Committee (published by the Committee, 1970).

True, a £5 increase in weekly wages was agreed by the union's
representatives with the management: but at the price of a solid
front between union and management against the strike leaders,
who found themselves in open war with the officers of their own
union. During this battle, Lord Cooper not only resorted to remarkable stratagems to get his members back to work, but went so
far as to invite the Home Office to investigate the 'intimidation'
of the strikers, while his executive formally charged that 'hooli-
ganism, violence and intimidation' were rife. There was no substance in these charges, as is made perfectly clear in the exhaustive
account of the strike, by Tony Lane and Kenneth Roberts, published in the following year.[6] Neither was there any truth in the
allegations which the union's leaders freely made, that 'subversives'
from outside were playing a major role in prolonging the dispute.
What *was* true, from the beginning, was that the union leaders
were determined to crush the slightest sign of autonomous initiative,
leave alone 'unofficial' action, by their members.

The Pilkington affair was a dramatic, but none the less typical,
example of the meaning of the corporatist policies of the NUGMW.
When the leaders of the TGWU and AUEW established, at Ford's,
the principle that union officers would not sign agreements until
the relevant membership had ratified them, this was regarded by
Lord Cooper as an 'abdication of responsibility'. 'Responsibility'
in his union goes to extreme lengths, of course : the most celebrated
occasion upon which it was demonstrated was during the unilateralist debate in the Labour Party. When the NUGMW conference voted the wrong way in this debate, it was solemnly re-
convened, in order that it could reverse the decision and thus
guarantee the dominance of Hugh Gaitskell's leadership in the
Labour Movement as a whole. It should be added that the
NUGMW has always played a keen role in the management of the
Labour Party itself, and that its representatives have, for many
years, made their presence felt in the Conference Arrangements
Committee of the Party, which has considerable power to prevent
the agenda from unduly embarrassing the given platform.

The structure of the NUGMW, which upholds this orthodoxy,
consists of over 2,000 branches, based either on areas or work-
places, and organized in ten regions. Each of these is organized by a

[6] *Strike at Pilkington's* (Fontana Books, 1971.)

full-time officer, and some 140 other professionals who are deployed throughout the regions. Each region has a council whose members are elected from the branches. Nationally, an annual conference elects a chairman (for two years) and agrees the main lines of policy to be applied by a general council consisting of the Chairman, the General Secretary (elected for life in a membership ballot) and fourteen lay delegates appointed from the regions. A smaller National Executive Committee is the effective government of the union, however, since the General Council only meets quarterly. This NEC has one representative from each region, and half of those chosen must be lay members. At no level are elections for professionals open, since the NEC has the absolute power to disqualify candidates it believes to be 'unqualified'. In sum, this adds up to one of the most powerfully entrenched bureaucracies in the trade-union movement, individual members of which tend to rise by preferment rather than open election, and, once ratified in office by a single ballot, remain thenceforward irremovable. It is possible to administer a union democratically when it has appointed officers, although difficult. But the solid precondition for democracy in such a context is that executive bodies must be overwhelmingly composed of lay members, under the constant control of their constituents. An indication of the distance between the NUGMW and such norms is to be found in the degree of nepotism that rages within it : the evidence has been partially recorded by Hugh Clegg.[7] A list of full-time officers of the union shows that David Basnett, a district officer at the age of twenty-four and now a national officer, is the son of Andrew Basnett, a former district secretary; that Lord Cooper, the present General Secretary, who became a clerk in the Manchester district office of the union at the age of twenty, was the nephew of Charles Dukes (later Lord Dukeston), a former general secretary; that Jack Eccles, who became a district officer at the age of twenty-six and later a national officer, was the son of Tom Eccles, a former Lancashire district secretary, who first held full-time office in the union at the age of twenty-seven, and was himself the son of Fleming Eccles, an earlier Lancashire district secretary; that Fred Hayday, who became a union clerk at the age of fourteen and is now a national officer (and Secretary of the International Committee of the TUC

[7] H. A. Clegg, *General Union in a Changing Society* (Blackwell, 1964), pp. 211-17.

General Council), was the son of Arthur Hayday, a former Midland district secretary; and that Lord Williamson, who was Lord Cooper's predecessor as general secretary, was the nephew of T. Williamson, a former Liverpool district secretary.

The existence of this elaborate network of kinship and mutual obligation has to be added to a highly centralized constitution, and a rigidly collaborationist ideology. In form, if not in content, the nearest parallels to this type of structure are to be found in the more conservative communist parties, those so far unaffected by the winds of revisionism and pluralism. The same instrumental freemasonry of 'cadres', and the same rabid fear of heresy and independent initiative, are to be found in both institutions.

It would be difficult to find a more apt summary of the meaning of these facts for trade unionism than is contained in a study of one officer of the NUGMW, Alderman Cunningham. Under the headline 'Tynesides' Moderate Union Boss', the *Financial Times* published the following graphic profile of this functionary:

While the boilermakers and their colleagues in the craft unions of the Tyneside shipbuilding industry periodically reinforce the reputation of North-East labour for toughness and militancy, with banner headlines about disputes with employers, the Northern Region's biggest union, the General and Municipal Workers, with its 99,263 members, is doing a great deal to replace this unfortunate image with one of reasonableness.

Regional secretary of the GMWU is 59-year-old Alderman Andrew Cunningham, generally known as 'Andy' and also as one of the region's more colourful political figures. Since he took office four years ago [1965] it is doubtful whether the union has been directly responsible for a single strike. Its anti-strike policies have in fact been the cause of some disharmony with other unions.

In 1968 the GMWU in the North disowned an 11-day stoppage in the shipyards caused by 54 militant gangers on Tyneside which was holding up construction of two oil tankers. Cunningham was outspoken at the time. 'Shipbuilding on Tyneside,' he said, 'is on the dole. Both employers and men are living on taxpayers' money and unless they realize this they are finished.'

The GMWU has differed dramatically with other unions in the region. The Government's White Paper 'In Place of Strife' is an example. While others demonstrated against Barbara Castle and took part in May Day token strikes, the GMWU supported the proposals more or less to the hilt.

For a union leader who was born into the large family of a Tyneside coal trimmer and who spent his early youth labouring in the militant environment of the Tyneside water front, these may seem bizarre policies. Yet there is little doubt that Andy Cunningham's appointment as region secretary has paid dividends.

In 1965 GMWU membership in the Northern Region stood at 80,000. At the last count during August it was within an ace of 100,000, and Cunningham remains one of the few union officials with a reputation in the North for commanding instant obedience from his membership.

An efficient administrative machine occupying modern offices in Newcastle, and a staff of 50, helps the GMWU negotiators to anticipate and intercept discontent before it crystallizes into action. By all accounts the union is possessed of a good system of feed-back from factory benches to full-time officials. This, together with its policy of avoiding a militant stance during negotiations, has contributed something important to the relaxed relationships the union enjoys with local management.

In his own view Andy Cunningham's success is very simply explained by the fact that he speaks to the men on the shop floor as often as possible and in their own language.

There is, however, rather more to his success than mere gift of the gab. To understand it one needs to look more closely at the labour scene in the Northern Region. Like a good many other beliefs held about the area, labour's reputation for toughness has not got a great deal of substance. The miners were militant, but that was a long time ago; their battles have been largely won—or lost. In shipbuilding work is hard and conditions unpleasant. There are too many different unions involved to eliminate squabbling, and it would also be possible to name more progressive employers.

Trade unionism in the North is taken seriously. An estimated 70 per cent of the labour force is in membership of one or more unions compared with 40 per cent for the country as a whole. Compared with other parts of the UK apathy to union affairs is less of a problem.

A large number of people half expected a return to the old conditions and tend to regard the union in the same light. Disruptive elements find little to work on in this situation. The local Communist Party is small, claiming a membership of only 800. Shop stewards carry less influence than even minor full-time officials.

It is also necessary to look more closely at Cunningham himself. His success with management may be because he seems less concerned with the idea that all men are born equal and more with the reality that life tends to make all men's motivations similar—especially where matters like money and power are concerned.

His union career has been and still is closely linked with numerous other roles he plays in the region. He is a member of the National Executive of the Labour Party; chairman of Newcastle Airport Committee and chairman of the newly-formed Tyneside Passenger Transport Authority. Until recently he sat on the Northern Economic Planning Council and in the Chair at Durham County Council, Durham Police Authority and the Northumbrian River Authority. For a time he was a director of Fairfields shipyard on the Clyde.

His detractors, and some of his friends, say he has left the working class and is in danger of losing touch with the ordinary worker. His house with its lawns and ancient street lamp in the drive—a slightly modish gift from the Northern Gas Board—is very comfortable. His two sons are members of the professions. He has two cars and personally drives an electric-blue Jaguar. In appearance he could be a business man.

All this is less important than his popularity with the membership. The job he does for them may be because of his life style, not in spite of it. Certainly it makes management more at ease in his company. By way of a demonstrative answer to the contradictions, he cultivates a patch of leeks in the middle of his rose garden which, he says, proves he is still a proletarian.

Will the GMWU's amiable relations with the bosses in the North continue? Andy Cunningham thinks they will. He takes an arrestingly sanguine view of the future.[8]

It is perfectly apparent that this type of 'general' unionism is a model of what is *not* needed by a Labour Movement which is in increasingly open conflict with both the growing oligopolies and the governments which emerge to uphold their basic interests. The benefits of being organized across the board apply to aggressive organizations which are actively seeking to advance their members' interests. Generality becomes almost a defect when it is applied to retrogressive policies like those of the NUGMW, which require a high and permanent level of membership apathy in order to survive. In such a context the absent legions, conveniently proxied in massive card votes, can be deployed with final decisiveness against any local outbreaks of lively dissent.

[8] 'The Moderate Trade Union Boss', *Financial Times* (23rd September, 1969).

For this reason, the rationalization of the General Unions will be a difficult and conflict-ridden process.

Outside Lord Cooper's domain, matters have been evolving very differently. During the first years of Jack Jones's succession to the general secretaryship, a number of internal reforms and new initiatives have been undertaken with the Transport and General Workers' Union.

The first point to notice is that the union continues to grow at an impressive rate. Each recent year has seen expansion, and now, whether there are new mergers or not, the TGWU makes enough new recruits each year to add up to the equivalent of a fair-sized new union. The union has undertaken a special drive in the white-collar field, and its 'subsidiary', the Association of Clerical, Technical and Supervisory Staffs, is constantly expanding. Agreement on 'spheres of influence' has been reached between ACTS and the Clerical and Administrative Workers' Union, which specifically refers to the unions' determination to exclude the employers from any involvement. (An old trick of employers is to offer sole recruiting rights to one union to keep out a more militant union. The ACTS/CAWU agreement prevents this from happening. The lesson of the Steel Corporation's promotion of the anti-militant Iron and Steel Trades Confederation amongst their white-collar staff, to the exclusion of CAWU and Clive Jenkins's union, has been well learnt.)

A further field of recruitment opens up with the growing discontent in the ranks of the General and Municipal Workers' Union. After the Ford's strike in February 1969, which the T&G supported but which was vigorously opposed by Lord Cooper's NUGMW, the Ford's Halewood branch of the latter union wound itself up, and transferred its membership *en bloc* to the T&G. If similar mass transfers were to take place in other sectors of engineering, and in the public service sector, the brakes on transfer operated by the Bridlington Agreement against 'poaching' might prove less than fully effective in protecting areas of inefficient trade unionism.[9]

In the engineering industry, the T&G has been operating fully

---

[9] 'Poaching' is traditionally regarded as a sin against good trade unionism. Whilst the Bridlington Rules, as interpreted by the TUC, have in the past sometimes operated to protect bad trade unionism, and to deny genuine trade unionists the right to join the organization of their choice, their enforcement pending the repeal of the Industrial Relations Act seems vital to the TUC's campaign of non-co-operation with that legislation.

with the AUEW in the campaign to revise the York Agreement of 1922 which, as we have already pointed out, imposes on the unions formal recognition of the 'management's right to manage' and which allows employers to operate changed conditions unilaterally, whilst the union must pursue a grievance procedure which involves months of delay. The unions have threatened to withdraw altogether from the agreement unless a provision for the operation of a *status quo* in any proposed change in conditions is included. This would write into the agreement what amounts to a workers' veto over unilateral management action.

Within the union, rule changes were made in 1970 that bring to an end the old system of regional trade group committees and introduce in their place district committees, either on a trade group or industry basis (where the district is large enough for several specialist committees), or on a composite base in smaller centres. The effect of this change is to increase the number of active rank-and-file members who are engaged on policy-making committees, and to bring together the shop stewards of each industry in the localities. The old regional trade group committees were more remote from the shop floor, and tended to be dominated by the full-time regional trade group officers and their close associates in the branches. The breaking up of these older centres of power, which often harboured the survivors of the Deakin era, is to be welcomed. (Yet, such is the autonomy possessed by the regional secretaries and their committees, that this revision of the committee structure is being effectively resisted and delayed in some regions.)

A further consequence of the introduction of district committees on an industrial or trade basis is to bring the structure of the TGWU closer to the pattern of the AEF district machinery, in which shop-floor representation has normally been more effective. Since discussion of a full-scale merger between the AEF and T&G is an overdue necessity, any steps along these lines are to be welcomed.

Other moves have been announced to bring the union's national headquarters and its national negotiating activities into closer touch with the shop stewards, and the regions. A Telex system has been installed, giving instant communication between regional offices and Transport House. A mailing-list of senior shop stewards has been compiled in Transport House, so that a speedy report back on national negotiations in key industries and companies can be dispatched direct to the stewards. The new-style union newspaper, *The Record*, had made a good start, using techniques from the popular press, without deteriorating into a gimmicky tabloid. Of course, this process of democratization must develop or stagnate : and the lay committees which formally control the union will feel that they should sustain and carry further the 'reforms from the top' which have been initiated. The T&G is not a monolith, despite the prominence which is inevitably and rightly given to the statements of its leading officers. Very real and considerable effort is still required to carry through the democratization of the union, and to kill for ever the tradition of officer-dominated committees and officer collusion with employers. And the union's excursions into the field of *political* control, including the intention to revise its parliamentary panel of sponsored MPs and candidates, needs to be taken further. Only a politically conscious and militant lay leadership can ensure that the reforms do not get stuck half-way.

There is little doubt that Jack Jones, Harry Urwin (the Assistant General Secretary) and many of the more recently appointed officers as well as the new generation of younger shop stewards who are emerging in the process of internal reform, are fully committed to the concept of democratic trade unionism, under rank-and-file control. But the union is so large, and its presence so widespread across industry, that it is of course fully exposed to all the pressures for incorporation of stewards and officers which stem from new techniques of management, including productivity bargaining. An open, but inevitably complex process, has been set in train by the union.

This process has been accompanied by closer working unity, on every level at which they come in contact, between members of the AUEW and TGWU. The AUEW, which has always been formally organized on a hyperdemocratic model, has seen a formidable development of energetic self-government by its rank-and-file enterprise and workshop bodies, since it elected Hugh Scanlon as President in place of Lord Carron. Of course, shop stewards' committees have been developing their own forms of organization ever since the Second World War : but accession to the leadership of a key spokesman of workers' control and rank-and-file supervision of all activities of the union have markedly concentrated and reinforced the tendencies which were already very apparent.

Even when Hugh Scanlon casts his vote against the most militant voices, he invariably does so in the name of the democratic majority decisions of their less advanced brothers. The degree of change is remarkable. Lord Carron was constantly usurping the decision-making powers of his committees and their memberships, and maintained a running commentary of adverse criticism on his union's militants, who, on one famous occasion, he characterized as 'werewolves'. Up to now, if the activists have been able to carry the majority of their members with them, they have found, since the downfall of the Carron regime, that they have been pushing at an open door.[10]

None of this implies for a moment that the new leaders have been beyond criticism. All that is being said here is that the democratization of decision-making in the major unions constitutes a major step forward. An even bigger step forward would be made if the members of these unions were to take up the demand that the two great giants should begin to move towards unity, and to build upon their merged strengths, the foundations of the unified, aggressive and socially aware trade unionism which is desperately needed in the next decade. Once this task is begun, the atavistic and moribund old unions, the prototype of which is the NUGMW, will either be galvanized into joining in, or disintegrate under the pressures which the new movement will exert upon them.

At the same time that union members call upon their major organizations to close their ranks, they should also insist that, as they do, they open their structures to the fullest democratic controls. Unless trade-union members can freely determine the direction in which their army is marching, there is no good reason why others should wish to enlist. But if they do enlist, if they are free to fight their own wars, and not skirmishes of other people's making for other people's profit, then they need the same assets that any other army requires for success : strategic integration, tactical flexibility, decentralized initiative and overall co-ordination. There is no recipe for such a mix outside the widest and most thoroughgoing democracy. At a time when the State itself will be doing its utmost to curtail such processes, the fight to develop them will certainly be difficult, and may be long.

[10] Cf. 'The State of the AEU' in Ken Coates, *The Crisis of British Socialism* (Spokesman Books, 1971); also J. D. Edelstein, 'Democracy in a National Union: The British AEU', *Industrial Relations*, Vol. 4, No. 3, (May 1965).

Chapter 13

A Political Arm for the Unions

The work of transforming the social structure is of necessity a complex one, and even if trade unions were restructured in the manner we suggest, it would still be necessary for them to seek ways of developing an effective political instrument capable of defending and advancing the overall interests of their members : not only as producers, but also as consumers and citizens. Certainly the abolition of private ownership of industry is inconceivable as a *simple* trade-union act, however much control over industry the unions may be able to exert. It is also inconceivable that a social revolution of this kind could ever produce a more desirable, more civilized society if it were not based upon the widest freedom of thought and the most developed democracy imaginable within the ranks of the political movement which brought it about. In Britain this has been understood : the main political party of Labour was established by the trade unions, following upon a serious offensive by employers' organizations to curtail union rights, which culminated in the Taff Vale judgment against the South Wales railwaymen, who were compelled to meet, from their union funds, the damages inflicted upon the Taff Vale Company by their strike. This ruling obviously put all union funds at risk in the event of any industrial dispute. The Labour Representation Committee, which had been established for the purpose of representing and voicing the trade-union interest in Parliament, grew rapidly with the campaign for legislation to protect unions from the adverse results of the Taff Vale decision.

From the beginning, the Committee consisted of an inclusive alliance of trade unions and socialist societies, and after it transformed its name to *The Labour Party*, subsequent to its electoral victories in 1906, it still preserved its federal structure intact from the days of its foundation. In the early days the unions were affiliated alongside the Fabian Society, the Independent Labour Party and the Social Democratic Federation—the latter dropped

out and later reaffiliated. No socialist party or group was excluded
by fiat, and the only left-wing societies which remained outside
were those which chose to do so.[1]

It was after the First World War that the Labour Party adopted
a new constitution, including the socialist commitment in its statement of aims (Clause IV, which was to become the occasion of a
notable dispute in the days of Hugh Gaitskell's leadership). This
constitution allowed individual membership for the first time.
Gradually individual membership grew, while the socialist societies
played a diminishing role. The Social Democratic Federation
became the British Socialist Party, a substantial part of whose
members helped to found the Communist Party after the Russian
Revolution. On Lenin's insistent advice, the communists applied
for affiliation with the Labour Party, only to be firmly rejected.
After the MacDonald débâcle in 1931, the Independent Labour
Party broke away,[2] to maintain a diminishing handful of Members
of Parliament until the 1945 elections. The socialist societies within
the Party were thus reduced to two small professional bodies, of
doctors and teachers; the Fabians; and the Royal Arsenal Co-
operative Society, which was placed with the other societies because
there seemed nowhere else to put it.

For many years the main body of socialist opinion outside the
Labour Party was organized by the communists. A number of
attempts were made to enable them to affiliate; but after the
Second World War, when it looked as if their campaign for
affiliation might begin to succeed, the rules of the Labour Party
were changed to prevent any such contingency. Other outside
socialist groups, like the short-lived Commonwealth Party formed
during the war, and the majority of the old Independent Labour
Party, were largely absorbed back into the individual members'
section. In 1949, the Trotskyist Revolutionary Communist Party
dissolved itself, and its supporters joined the Labour Party as individual members. Meantime, the Labour Executive had developed a
tactic of 'proscribing' socialist bodies which it felt ran too close to
communism, and with the outbreak of the Russian peace offensive
in the early 'fifties, the list of proscribed organizations became

[1] Compare the regime in the Fabian Society during the heyday of Guild
Socialism, as it is described in Margaret Cole, *The Story of Fabian
Socialism* (Heinemann, 1961), pp. 148 *et seq.*, with the present attitudes of
leading Parliamentarians to new developments in socialist thinking.
[2] Cf. R. E. Dowse, *Left in the Centre* (Longmans, 1966), pp. 152–84.

a filled page. Soon the institution of proscription, applied originally to the communists and then later to outside bodies like the British Peace Committee and Artists for Peace, was developed into a full-scale internal police weapon, and in the early 'fifties the oppositional newspaper *Socialist Outlook*, which had a strong Trotskyist orientation, was added to the banned list. When nuclear disarmament became a key issue of the day, attempts were made to proscribe its organizations and expel its major spokesmen, notably Bertrand Russell. In short, throughout the Cold War and beyond it, the tendency in the Labour Party leadership was to identify and forbid a succession of heresies, each of which was in fact further and further away in spirit from the original heresy of communism. Today at least as many non-communists and independents find themselves *persona non grata* as do orthodox upholders of the banned creeds.

For many years trade unions not merely went along with this process, but actively applied it themselves. A whole number of unions applied restrictions which made it impossible either (in some cases) for communists or (in others) for members of any proscribed organization to hold office within them, or on their behalf. For many years the Transport & General Workers' Union itself applied such rules, which even had the effect, upon their imposition, of removing one of their union's representatives from the General Council of the TUC.[3]

Two things began to undermine this rigorous orthodoxy in the 1960s. First, the nature of communism began to change, as the monolithic pattern of communist rule broke up. The existence of Russian, Chinese, Cuban and Yugoslav models of communist government, and of Italian and French styles of communist opposition, tended to introduce a strong pluralist element to the hitherto solidly and dogmatically integrated British Communist Party. Secondly, the trade unions themselves began to move into opposition to the successive governments of their days, and to find bans and proscriptions anachronistic interferences with their most efficient functioning. The question which remains, however, is whether trade unions which have rejected policies of thought-control over their own officers and members, will continue to allow such principles to apply within the dominant Labour Movement.

[3] For an account of these restrictions, cf. Jim Gardner, *Key Questions for Trade Unionists* (Lawrence & Wishart, 1960), pp. 42–7.

At the same time that orthodoxy has been more and more rigorously defined by the Labour Party, so the options of radical change and democratic reform have been further and further relegated to the indefinite future. 'Gradualism', which began as a strategy for reform, has become an alibi for accepting the given order of things.[4]

In his presidential oration to the Labour Party Conference in 1923, Sidney Webb fiercely rebutted the charge that the Labour Party was unfit to govern. Such an accusation could no longer be made by 'any instructed person of candour', he said. When Labour took office, of course, it would not expect to usher in an instant millennium: 'once we face the necessity of putting our principles first into Bills, to be fought through Committee clause by clause; and then into appropriate administrative machinery for carrying them into execution . . . the inevitability of gradualness cannot fail to be appreciated'. By 1924 we had the first instalment of gradualness, which was brief. All the indications are that Ramsay MacDonald soon wished to be relieved of his high responsibility, and it is very clear that he ultimately chose to resign upon an absurd issue rather than continue to defend the scant achievements of his administration. The month before the 1924 election he confided to Beatrice Webb that he was 'sick of it', and that he hoped not to win, because 'the Party was not fit to govern'.

Whatever may be said of the Party, MacDonald himself was not greatly improved when he regained office in 1929. It is hardly necessary to say anything about the resultant mess, except that gradualness was nowhere to be seen in the plummeting employment figures or the drastically reactionary governmental measures which these provoked.

In 1945, however, a reforming administration was elected. But the lack of inevitability associated with such gradualness became fairly obvious by 1951, and Mr Crossman subsequently explained the defeat of the Attlee administration by confessing that it 'had run out of ideas'.

Now we have come to the end of the Wilson era, and it is difficult to imagine that there is any instructed person, whether of candour or otherwise, who will have the temerity to defend the proposition that gradualism works for anyone but the Devil. Under

[4] Cf. Ralph Miliband, *Parliamentary Socialism* (Merlin Press, 1964) and Coates, *The Crisis of British Socialism.*

Mr Wilson the poor in general got gradually poorer in relative terms, while some became abruptly poorer in absolute terms. The unemployed figures became larger, without much gradualness. The powerful oligarchs of the great combines gradually concentrated even greater power with the enthusiastic support of Mr Wedgwood Benn's ministry. The unions became gradually more disillusioned, while Labour voters became quite suddenly and dramatically more difficult to mobilize. Such stalwarts as Mr Greenwood, whose audacity in the verbal resolution of the housing problem was in inverse proportion to the number of actual dwellings completed, perfectly exemplify this policy. Far from offering the electors a blinding light on the road to Damascus, the Wilson team hoped to offer a benumbing darkness, as if a fog of official rhetoric and bombastic apologetics might anaesthetize the voters into forgetting that all their grievances of 1964 remained to be redressed, and that they had in addition accumulated an augmentation (gradual, to be sure) of their burdens.

Instructed persons of candour, if such there be, will at once draw one conclusion : that if Mr Wilson is not a total villain, there is, today, some structural impediment to gradual reform. Judged upon its record, there is no particular reason why anyone who defected at the polls in 1970 should seek the restoration of the Wilson administration in 1975. For the unions, the need for repeal of the Industrial Relations Act will make a Labour victory in a General Election a crucial necessity : but only because the alternative is even worse.

Discussion which limits itself to the question of how Labour is to win the next election will be self-defeating. The unions must face this fact. What bait should be offered the electors? A guaranteed minimum income? An incomes policy to secure social justice, instead of a wage-freeze? Universal reform of the education system? The elimination of poverty? Or, perhaps, a humane technological revolution? Full employment? The nationalization of growth points in the economy, and the creation of public enterprises among science-based industries? An independent foreign policy? People forget easily, but it would be remarkable if they forgot that easily.

The question which the Labour Movement now has to answer is, what steps does it propose to take to implement such measures, given that balance-of-payments crises will not go away; that the bankers will never be more tractable than heretofore; that 'our allies' will continue to be robbers, brutes and bullies until they, too, are overturned by a radical alternative with the resolution and integrity so sadly lacking in the Wilson team? No conceivable alternative exists, other than one basing itself on the rapid overturn of established power, the dismantling of industrial authoritarianism and control of the economy by propertied elites, and the mobilization of what Mr Wilson once referred to as the 'extraordinary initiative of the working people' for political purposes.

In a word, the crisis of the Labour Movement is a crisis of strategy. Is Britain to become a socialist country? If so, how? If not, does it matter a jot whether we are governed by Labour conservatives or Conservative conservatives? Let us assume that we still cannot inaugurate the millennium in a fortnight. Even so, can we not expect a Labour Government to make measurable progress towards the establishment of socialist priorities within a normal term of office? And if we can nourish such an expectation, then what are those priorities and how will they be asserted? A discussion on these questions would help to decide what the Labour Movement is about. Any argument which forswears such an inquiry and limits itself to the problem of how to restore Mr Wilson to the premiership is irrelevant.

If the Labour Movement is to begin a serious elaboration of socialist policies, it ought to be very clearly understood that this is a difficult choice, and that a great deal of largely negative experience has to be critically dissected if we are to accomplish what is necessary: the training of a whole school of socialist trade unionists and activists, upon which the real work of transformation will fall. And this leads back to our original problem. A large proportion of active socialists are not permitted to be members of the Labour Party, and so can play no part in such discussions. Back in the 'twenties, the communists were excluded from membership of the Labour Party because they had adhered to the Comintern and worked for a soviet revolution. Today the Comintern is dead, and the British communists no longer appeal to a strategy involving soviets. What rational reason can even the most parliamentary of socialists retain for excluding them? Perhaps the British Parliament is even less sovereign today than it was in 1920, having yielded up authority not only to civil servants, corporate businessmen and bankers, but also to such uncontrollable international organizations as NATO : while the power of transnational companies grows every day. The impotence of Labour Party policy in the late 'sixties owes a very great deal to these processes of erosion, through which the popular conception of Parliament as a governing body has, in reality, been very largely nullified. If this is so, then no sensible socialist programme can ignore the fact, and it becomes absurd to maintain a whole series of bans and proscriptions upon a growing variety of socialist societies which have expressed their disbelief in the inevitability of gradualism. If such groups as the International Socialists, or the Socialist Labour League, or the International Marxists, or any similar bodies, were to renounce all parliamentary forms of politics, they would be mistaken : but such a renunciation could not be seen as simply absurd, in the light of the fiasco of the past six years. What is now necessary is the evolution of a practical set of policies which can 'walk on two legs', in the words of Mao Tse-tung. That is to say, we need socialist activists in Parliament to work in concert with other socialist activists in factories, trade unions and neighbourhoods, in order to be able to reach into the very heart of the working population and prepare for change among the people who alone can either make or benefit from it. Bans and proscriptions are a ludicrous anachronism in such a context. They aggravate the intolerance which is in itself a serious disorder of the Left.

As we have shown, the Labour Party began as an inclusive alliance of trade unions and socialist societies. Regardless of who leads it, such an inclusive alliance is precisely what is needed today. How can new ideas emerge and old ones be digested if such discrimination is continued? Already it is fair to say that the bulk of creative socialist thinking and writing goes on either outside the Labour Party, or in its underground. Writers like E. P. Thompson, Raymond Williams, Perry Anderson and Ralph Miliband are scarcely less outsiders in the present climate than such maverick Fabians as John Hughes or Peter Townsend. No one in the higher councils of the Party takes any notice of what the latter say. One wonders, indeed, if there is anyone left in those councils who reads anything at all beyond the digests of editorial opinion in the financial press. Whatever may be said about the Webbs, or Cole, or Laski, their work did unwind itself in the centre of the Labour Movement as part of a living discussion. Today, the intellectual lethargy which is cramping the leadership of the Labour Movement will negate any

positive attempt to make or mend its policies, unless Labour men
and women insist that they are old enough, and clever enough, to
think for themselves in the heat of a free discussion.

Certainly no one can suggest that all the answers which have
escaped the established Party machine are to be found among the
nostrums of the myriad socialist societies operating on the political
fringes. The point is not that the old Labour leadership proscribed
all the right ideas and was therefore left with the wrong ones :
it is rather that the effect of proscription was to close down all
energetic debate about how to transform British society into a true
social and industrial democracy, and thus to alienate not only
the young people who are clustering into the new socialist groupings, but, far more important, to drive away many thousands of
others, including key trade-union activists, who see no prospect
for radical change within the given political structure. Of course,
there has always been a core of people in the Labour leadership
who have been determined to do just that. Today, however, some
of the main trade unions have reached the collective view that
there can be no middle-term security for their conditions without
deep-going structural reforms of society. It is crucial, if this view
is to be translated into action, to attempt to clarify the issues
involved in it. This can only be done by rational discussion and
co-ordinated action involving all those who seek change.

Of course, any political party needs safeguards of its integrity
and cohesion. A democratic party should seek democratic safeguards.
An inclusive socialist alliance would need rules which upheld
freedom of speech and organization, and which penalized any
attempt, from whatever direction it came, to hamper such freedom.
Such rules would of necessity be upheld by an appropriately judicial
body of elected lay members, and would be jealously enforced. If
any affiliated society were unwilling to abide by such rules, it
would place itself beyond the pale, whether it were a small socialist
society or a trade union organizing hundreds of thousands of
members. But such rules should be procedural and neutral, not
motivated by dogma or received opinion. People might be expelled
from a democratic organization for behaving undemocratically,
but not for believing peculiar beliefs. Leaders would certainly
be held accountable for their actions, and agreed policies would
be binding upon the representatives entrusted to implement them :
but opinion would remain free at all times.

Even with an inclusive socialist movement, trade unions in Britain have a difficult path to blaze. Many old responses will no longer serve, and many new approaches must be attempted experimentally. The poor are waiting to be organized, and there are millions of them. The frustrated young people are organizing themselves, but outside the ranks of the Labour Movement. The technicians and professional workers have already begun a vast process of self-mobilization into trade unions, but these lack plausible political expression and cohesion of movement relevant to the needs of today.

Labour could win elections, taking them in its stride, if it directed its energies towards meeting these problems, unleashing the changes which are long overdue in the British social and economic structure. But if it is content to remain a faint echo of a dying establishment, of course it will not want the company of socialists, or noise about workers' control, and it will tread its own gradual path to oblivion.

Part Three

Participation

Chapter 14

The Responses of Authority, and Some Answers

We have already described briefly the evolution of 'workers' participation' at plant level, which has hitherto been primarily construed within the framework of joint consultation, but which may well be about to assume quite novel disguises. In discussing this development, it is necessary to make one fundamental point as clearly as possible : to wit, 'participation' never falls from the sky. Employers are not born with a hunger to devolve, let alone to share, responsibility, for the very apparent reason that true responsibility is inseparable from power. Offers of participation invariably follow demands for control, and will not normally be actively canvassed in the absence of such insubordinate cries, simply because they may well result in the stimulation of a greater appetite than they were designed to assuage. There is no latent democracy in industrial authority, burning to escape. What there is, is a concealed totalitarianism, seeking to dissemble. The result of this situation is that trade unions which begin to assert their own prerogatives may well, if they are strong enough, call up a 'concessionary' response, which will be deliberately designed to neutralize their direct pressures.

The matter has never been expressed more forthrightly than it was by G. S. Walpole, in a tract published during the Second World War, canvassing support from employers for joint consultation :

What joint consultation does for industry is threefold in character. It provides higher management with an additional source of information, warning and advice—particularly valuable because it covers a field in which conventional channels of information and advice are too often biased and ineffective. It also provides the means for transmitting to employees information and explanation without which their attitude towards the work or their management is liable to be prejudiced. Thirdly, on the psychological side, *it canalizes the legitimate aspiration of labour to have* a voice in the industry to which it contributes so much.[1]

The price of this 'canalization' may not be very high, and the employer may well find it worth while to pay it, but there is a price. P. F. Garner, a worker at Ley's Malleable Castings in Lincoln, sums it up rather well : at his enterprise 'the pattern of procedure is as per the national agreement, seven workers and seven from the management side . . . the chair is always taken by the owner's son, who is extremely fair. . . . The effect that this has on our departmental managers is quite something, as they hate to have anything concerning their department mentioned before the owner's son. Hence greater co-operation'.[2]

Whether the degree of blackmail this offers the workpeople at Ley's is sufficient to restrain intermediate management from depredations it might otherwise engage in, is an open question. Far from representing an extension of grass-roots influence in a widening democracy, it is an improvement in the capacity of managerial bureaucracies to centralize their effective powers. Authority all too easily collapses in its middle levels. And it is often difficult for the top man's left hand to keep track of his right. (Chinese Emperors faced the continual problem of controlling the excesses of their tax-collectors, who were constantly tempted to go beyond their briefs and raise a little extra from the peasants with which to endow their own estates. The Emperors found a simple answer : castrate the tax-collectors, and recoup their ill-gotten gains by having their estates revert to the sovereign upon their death. The problems of intermediary managerial bureaucracy in modern

---

[1] *Management and Men* (Jonathan Cape, 1943), p. 43. We would recommend Walpole's blunt account to Carole Pateman, who takes us to task in her *Participation and Democratic Theory* (Cambridge University Press, 1970) for 'lack of clarity', since we do not understand that 'there can be no control without participation', or that 'where industrial democracy exists there are no longer "sides" in the existing sense'. Walpole understood that the other 'side' needed to have its 'legitimate aspirations' 'canalized', as does virtually every businessman who experiments with participatory forums. When there really are no 'sides', we should like to be able to discuss with Mrs Pateman what the world looks like; but we fear that day will be after our time. Even in the most democratic of socialized economies 'sides' are still very much in evidence : and for us, the key to progress is to win for the subordinate 'side' the maximum chance to assert itself.

[2] A report on joint consultation in the Lincoln area, by members of the day release class organized by the WEA and Nottingham University Adult Education Department, 1968.

industry are a little too complex to solve with gelding-irons, but the principle involved here is not too dissimilar. Instead of aborting their hopes of family life, you could threaten, in a controlled way, to throw one or two of them, from time to time, to the peasants.) In general, however, this kind of side-effect is the most cogent reason given by workers today for placing any value whatever on consultative devices. In the early 'fifties, the Acton Society Trust did a careful survey of the results of the extensive panoply of consultative mechanisms developed by the National Coal Board. The Board published a monthly journal, organized the verbal transmission of information through its staff, held regular consultative meetings from pit level upwards, called special conferences, and, on one occasion, delivered a personal letter from its chairman to miners' homes. All this effort produced no positive response from the men. The Trust found that it was either not assimilated, or 'taken the wrong way'.

All of this goes a long way to nullify the optimistic predictions of G. D. H. Cole :

> It is impossible to stop at joint consultations : it is bound to turn either into joint decision of policy by collective agreement, or into actual joint management. These two, however, are by no means the same, although they both involve an acceptance of responsibility. The essential difference is that decision by collective agreement leaves the execution of the agreed policies entirely to a managerial authority of which the trade unions form no part, whereas joint management would mean that the trade unions would become participants in executive action as well as in the shaping of policy.[3]

The fact is that there was a third option : that the whole pantomime would be seen to be very largely an irrelevance, and ignored by the workpeople. Yet, at the same time as they speak of consultative committees with open contempt, active trade unionists will frequently appeal to some ideal of 'proper consultation', in which they will be consulted *before* innovations are made, and, possibly, decide to veto them. Once again, workers' control demands often make their first appearance in the language of the given order of things.

In general, the participative content of consultation is now

[3] Cole, *An Introduction to Trade Unionism* (Allen & Unwin, 1953), p 281.

G

virtually nil, which is to say that the device no longer has the capacity to persuade workpeople to allow their 'legitimate aspirations' to be 'canalized' by it. A survey by the Industrial Welfare Society in the early 'sixties summarized the position in this way : 'The general impression gained is that the majority of firms do not fully believe in and practise formal consultation and all that it implies, but use it rather as a forum for company pronouncements and the airing of employee irritants.'[4]

This kind of appreciation, we have already pointed out, persuaded Professor Clegg to revise his opinions about the central significance of consultation as a constituent of industrial democracy. But his alternative theory, which we have discussed, has a great disadvantage from the point of view of capital. It is too honest. If what we have is already industrial democracy, then it is profoundly unsatisfying to vast numbers of working people. New devices will be necessary if their aspirations are to be guided into channels, which will leave the realities of industrial autocracy at peace. And the more insistently and effectively the trade unions take up the demand for workers' control, the more urgent it will be to discover these devices. The most likely form which they will take was briefly examined by the Donovan Royal Commission on Trade Unions and Employers' Associations.

The Donovan Commission limited its consideration of possible overall reforms of the patterns of industrial authority to one basic type of proposal, for what it terms 'workers participation in management'. Even this type of proposal was treated very cursorily, occupying only three and a half pages of a report of more than 350 pages. And within those three and a half pages, members of the Commission found themselves in disagreement, so that two possible views are sketched out in the Report.

The TUC had given evidence to the Commission, recommending three different, but linked, levels of workers' participation in management.

 1 At plant level they thought a workers' representative (e.g. a shop steward) should sit on 'whatever body . . . takes decisions on the running of that plant'.

 2 Trade unions should, they submitted, also be represented at

[4] D. Llewelyn Davies, *Formal Consultation in Practice* (Industrial Welfare Society, 1960).

'intermediate' levels, either at regional level or wherever authority over a particular produce was centralized within a particular concern.

3   Legislation should, they felt, be enacted, to enable companies to allow for union representation on boards of directors.

These proposals should be promoted by voluntary negotiations. The TUC hoped that the Confederation of British Industry would 'take a strong lead in encouraging its members to follow the spirit of their proposals'.

The Commission argued that the reform of collective bargaining would do more to assist workers to influence the administration of their enterprises than either of the TUC's first two proposals, for workers' representation below board level. At the same time, they felt that such reforms might stop management from operating freely. Management 'must . . . be free to discuss policy without being preoccupied with the risk that what they say may be misunderstood and lead to confusion on the shop floor', says the Report. It also suggests that any intervention by unions at this level would be countered by the fact that management representatives would caucus beforehand, so that all decisions would be cut and dried before the unions were ever involved.

As for workers on the boards, the Commission was neutral. The majority, although they noted that German industries operate neither 'more nor less efficiently' *with* worker-directors than do British industries without them, thought the TUC's third proposal should be rejected for the following reasons :

1   Workers' directors would be under obligation to represent the 'interests of the company as a whole' and as such would have to support unpopular decisions. This would result in loss of confidence by their constituents.

2   It would be difficult to define the personal responsibility of workers' directors for the conduct of the company's affairs.

3   Appointment of worker directors might be a pretext for *not* reforming collective bargaining.

4   'The appointment of a small number of worker directors,' thought the majority, 'would not change the real share in control of the majority of workpeople.'

Five members of the Commission disagreed with these ideas. They did not think the board need be, or in practice normally is, free of the pressures of special interest groups. Indeed workers had, at present, no protection against such groups. For instance, share-holders might vote to sell out to a rival who wished to close down their company. Workers could not meet such threats simply within the collective bargaining machinery.

Lord Collison, Professor Kahn-Freund and Mr George Wood-cock thought that the snag about legal responsibility could be met by appropriate legislation, and that then progress could be made by voluntary agreement between unions and individual companies. Messrs Shonfield and Wigham wanted compulsory participation, which would involve new legislation on company law. They pro-posed that

1   Worker directors should act as guardians of the workers' interests in the stage of policy formation.
2   They should participate in Board meetings on the same footing as other directors, with the status of non-executive directors.
3   They should be appointed by the relevant unions, after con-sultation with the TUC.
4   They should not engage in collective bargaining with the company while serving on the Board.
5   Although larger Boards might have more, no less than two workers' directors should serve on *every* Board employing more than, say, 5,000 workers.
6   They should share all the general duties of directors to ensure the overall prosperity of the concern.
7   They would report to their constituency in the same way that their colleagues reported to shareholders.
8   Workers would have access to their directors, but could not *control* them. They would act in their own responsibility, not upon any mandate. They could not be recalled by their work-mates.
9   They would serve for a fixed term, with legal responsibilities as close as possible to those of other directors.[5]

Although the majority of the Commission reported against worker-directors, the subsequent White Paper, *In Place of Strife*, announced that it favoured experiments with them, and that the Government would consult further on how this was to be done before presenting

[5] *Royal Commission on Trade Unions and Employers' Associations: Report* (HMSO, 1968). Cmnd 3623, pp. 257–60.

the Industrial Relations Bill.[6] This ill-fated measure never survived
the deadlock between the Wilson Cabinet and the TUC, however,
so that the consultations never materialized into solid proposals.

After the defeat of *In Place of Strife* the Confederation of
British Industry appeared to be ready to revise its policies. 'The
emphasis now,' reported *Industry Week*,[7] 'is that workers should be
given a direct say in management.' The journal went on :

> Employers who have been expecting the Tory party to take a
> firm line with the unions if they come to power have been under-
> standably bewildered by some of Mr Heath's recent remarks.
> Mr Heath has said that owning a business does not give a man
> the right to run his affairs as he likes.
> Members of the CBI were puzzled—and some angered—by
> similar remarks by Mr Campbell Adamson. In his April letter
> to members, the CBI director-general told them that 'managers
> do not—if they ever had—have a divine right to manage. There is
> no automatic prerogative to make decisions and expect them to
> be carried out. The process of decision-making will have to be
> more and more justified and demonstrated to be right in order
> to command the respect not only of the people working in the
> company, but the community as a whole'.

However, in spite of himself, Mr Heath won the 1970 General
Election and, temporarily at any rate, found himself so completely
preoccupied with curbing the rights of trade unions that he had
little time to contemplate necessary limitations to the divine right
of ownership. Mr Campbell Adamson has also been more reticent
upon the question since that election. For the time being the notion
of participation is out of favour.

Even so, many trade unionists remain reluctant to let employers
forget about it. Their attitudes, in the main, spring from a desire
to explain the ambiguities of the employers' position, although it
must be admitted that there is a certain degree of risk for the
unions themselves in such an approach, since workpeople are
themselves not by any means immune to the danger of taking an
ambiguous view of the realities which confront them. While it is
true that, with growing strength, unions are less and less likely to
allow the 'legitimate aspirations' of their members to be 'canalized'
into safe channels, it is also true that clear ideas are themselves a

[6] *In Place of Strife* (HMSO, January 1969), Cmnd 3888.
[7] 24th April, 1970.

major source of effective union power. For this reason it is worth while for unions to think very carefully about 'participatory' proposals. Some of the notions canvassed in certain quarters in the Labour Movement can be dismissed out of hand. The concessionary rhetoric of some of the main industrial relations spokesmen of the Wilson administration, which became more and more pronounced as the harmful proposals of *In Place of Strife* were crystallizing, represented, as the draughtsmen's leaders claimed, the 'sugar coating on a poison pill'. The same cannot be said when such convinced advocates of trade-union democracy as Jack Jones enter the argument. His pamphlet *The Right to Participate: Key to Industrial Progress,* based on an address given by him to an Industrial Society conference on 'Involvement at Work', and originally delivered in November 1970, represents his vision of a democratic trade unionism, 'trade unionism with a human face', as he has expressed it elsewhere. It is invested with a compassionate concern for his membership, with a deep humanitarianism, which leads him to reject not only autocratic forms of management but also paternalism and 'phoney' consultation devices, as being entirely inadequate answers to the industrial condition. His prescription for the *amelioration* of that condition has reflected the growing sense of outrage which exists in the minds of a new generation of shop stewards and active trade unionists, the generation which has known capitalism working at its best : that is to say, a capitalism with full employment, providing substantial material gains for fully employed workers in their capacity as consumers, which nevertheless subjects them to continued and intensified subordination and exploitation, and which has increasingly dehumanized its 'industrial relations'. Yet, for all that, the prescriptions in this pamphlet offer somewhat limited remedies even to the problems of post-war boom capitalism, and are quite inadequate to meet and hold off the growing harshness of capitalism in crisis. Trade unionism in the 'sixties did, at its best, build on the aspirations towards greater workers' control which have been the foundation of shop-steward activity, and which produced leaders like Jack Jones. In a world of goodwill based on economic prosperity, we might have expected that those aspirations would have been welcomed by an enlightened and disinterested management, and *fostered.* There is plenty of evidence to suggest that the management-style of the late 'fifties and early 'sixties *did* in fact foster the growth of those earlier, less demanding, less self-confident shop stewards of Macmillan's cosy era. If Britain had been objectively capable of achieving sustained and crisis-less economic growth, matching the performance of the so-called West German economic miracle, then it is possible that many employers would have been led, some haltingly, others with liberalizing zeal, to yield genuine concessions to the reform programmes which have been the most interesting product of the changed leadership of Britain's largest and most 'general' trade unions. In those circumstances, trade unionism in the 'seventies might have achieved a smooth development of the kind hoped for by Jack Jones himself : 'The developments at the grass-roots of our movement have been of great significance. What remains is to translate these into changes throughout the whole of the trade union and industrial structure.'[8]

Certainly this ambition is still an honourable one. But in his formulation of the perspective for trade unionism, and in particular in his emphasis on the prospects for 'constructive' participation, Jack Jones fails adequately to meet the counter-revolution which has been developing, both among individual employers and the government that represents them, which seeks to thwart and resist every advance which democratic trade unionism has made in recent years. This establishment feels that it has less room for manoeuvre and concession than at any time since the inter-war slump. For this reason, the formulations in Jack Jones's text seem at times to be designed for a social context that is different from the newly apparent one in which trade-union rights and functions have been, and continue to be, challenged and restricted in a most systematic way. Just as Alexander Dubček's attempt to realize the vision of a 'socialism with a human face' was ploughed under by an extremely repressive, hard-centred conservatism, which met all his very sound arguments with the occupation of his country by Russian tanks, so Jack Jones's humanism is opposed to an increasingly unfeeling and reactionary set of powers.

For this reason, we would hope to see a clearer definition of the purpose for which a humanizing trade unionism seeks greater 'involvement' and participation in industrial decision-making. In *The Right to Participate* Jack Jones writes :

. . . keeping up with the speed and racket of the assembly lines

[8] *Trade Unionism in the Seventies* (TGWU, 1970).

or the machine shop, or working in some of the hells of foundries
and forging plants, *means our people wait and hope for retirement.*

Not enough attention has been paid to make life worth living
in the factory—to develop interest. It's doubtful whether changes
will ever come if management-worker relations remain as they
are.[9]

He cites an American trade-union slogan that inspired a recent
strike against General Motors—'30 years and out!'—which expressed a demand for an earlier retirement age to get workers out
of the 'sweat-shop' after thirty years' work. Whilst he would no
doubt support such demands, Jack Jones seems to be implying here
that the purpose of participation and reform is mainly to humanize
factory conditions, and to make them tolerable in the meantime by
developing the workers' 'interest'. But this is a very limited formula.
For many workpeople the object of workers' control has already
become much wider : to speed the process of transition to socialist
social relations under which assembly-line and machine-shop
labour is progressively *abolished*, not simply made more 'interesting'. Every rational trade unionist will agree that we should try the
limits of reform within the given order of industry, but it is also
important that we should resist the temptation to formulate our
ultimate ambitions so that they conform to those limits. We have
written elsewhere : 'A democratically run sand foundry is a far
better place than one run by order : but in a world where some
men ride round the moon or sing in *Fidelio*, a foundry-man is not
a *free* man.'[10] Of course, the workers who obtain early retirement
have solved the problem of the physical and psychological oppression in the workshops only for themselves and only partially; they
remain part of an alienated society in their retirement. And certainly it is true as Jack Jones argues in his pamphlet that

As we live longer, having been educated better, do you think
that the assumption will continue to be made that a man loses
his employment faculties at 60 or even 65? No, we shall have to
respond to that demand, welcome the contributions made by
people in these age brackets, instead of writing them off.

But at the same time, the demand for the right to early volun-

9 TGWU pamphlet (1970), p. 3.
10 *Workers' Control*, ed. Coates and Topham, p. 441.

tary retirement (and also, we would add, for a drastically reduced working week) is still as positive an assertion of the values of socialist humanism against the political economy of capital as it has ever been since Marx first identified it as such. A man's dignity can never depend, for a socialist, simply upon his ability to sell his 'employment faculties'; a fundamental contradiction in Jack Jones's humane trade-union programme is that it seems to interpret the demand for leisure as a *wholly* negative phenomenon, as basically an 'escape' from work.

All this apart, his programme for participation in industry contains a number of familiar recommendations.

He sees progress 'very much in terms of managers and shop stewards acting in combination'; he seeks 'the direct contribution from workers' representatives and individual workers to improvement in work routines, lay-outs, processes and products' and 'comprehensive provision of information . . . extensive consultation and agreements . . . when management is handling change (whether in processes, work-load, capacity use, wage system, or labour requirements)'. He recognizes the threat of concentration of industrial ownership, and proposes to contain the growth of elite management powers through 'representative participation'. He acknowledges that this method 'will not resolve all conflict' and therefore rightly insists that the unions should avoid 'collaboration' and retain the method of 'confrontation', which recognizes that there are 'differences of interests' whilst reflecting 'certain objectives which can be mutually advantageous'. The result should be that it will be 'possible to hammer out agreements which injure neither but benefit both'.

All these objectives arise out of Jack Jones's unrivalled experience of the living trade-union movement. The scene at present is one of militancy, brinkmanship, collaboration, hesitancy, a forward-backward movement in a hundred different industries and countless plant, local and national disputes and agreements which certainly do not add up to a coherent strategy. It is a bit of a mess, and it remains essential for the trade unionist caught in this situation to persist in the effort to clarify and define a strategy, such that the confusion is progressively eliminated and the range of conflict rationalized outwards rather than confined and moderated as the employers certainly desire. A mess like the present one is certainly preferable to a mindless bureaucratic rigidity in the unions, but the reason it is preferable is that it challenges trade unionists to elaborate and specify their own goals.

Jack Jones advances these goals in one breath: 'Units of industry,' he believes, 'should eventually be seen as a series of self-governing communities, within which working people increasingly assume the role of policy-making and controlling . . .'; but in another breath he is anxious that in casting the unions 'in the role of champions of individual freedom in industry' he should not be accused of making 'a statement about wages versus profits'. Perhaps here his tongue is in his cheek. He wants to break down the barriers between negotiation and consultation, and is utterly scathing about the inadequate promises of 'more information' which the Tory Government has offered as part of its Industrial Relations legislation, while remaining prepared to demand 'statutory provision' for safety inspection by workers, yet it seems reasonable to suppose that the effect of such measures might not be very good for profits. Jack Jones sees the reforms which have been agreed between the unions and company in the case of the ICI Works Councils, under which the shop stewards have taken over the role of workers' representatives on those bodies (which were previously regarded by the unions as anti-union devices) as an entirely positive step. He may be right, if the workpeople concerned *do* effectively augment their powers and understanding of the forces they are up against. But they will find this process easier when they speak the language of 'control' than when they go along with that of 'participation'.

This they are increasingly keen to do. The democratization of their unions, which, although it has been an uneven, up-and-down process, has reached a very great deal further into the heartland of the trade-union movement as a result of the initiatives of Jack Jones and Hugh Scanlon, can only accelerate matters. The ghost of participation has by no means been laid, even though the whole subject is, for the time being, more or less taboo for authority. How long the idea of participation will remain in cold storage depends very much on how far the trade unions are pushed into adopting defensive postures by the Industrial Relations Act. We can be perfectly certain that no one in the CBI, or the Department of Employment and Productivity, will strain himself to raise the question from the point of view of abstract justice. It will emerge again when the political and economic powers of workpeople bid to enlarge themselves to a degree uncomfortable to the present directors of affairs. At that point, the neglected ideas of the Donovan Commission's minority will become again the object of strenuous discussion.

When next the kite of participation is flown by men of power, there can be little doubt that their ideas will greatly depend upon the models established in West Germany. For one thing, the German system of *Mitbestimmung* has run for a long time, and is, to a great extent falsely, held responsible by many authorities for the relative peaceability of German industrial relations. (Better explanations exist, based on an understanding of the post-war 'German miracle', which depended in its early years on a virtually unlimited flow of cheap labour from East Germany. This followed a long period of artificially low wage-levels; it was followed, after the erection of the Berlin Wall, by new supplies of cheap labour from as far afield as Turkey and Persia. In such conditions, the passivity of labour may well stem more from blocked opportunities than from that discipline inherent in the German national character.) Furthermore, the European Community which, in some countries, experiences a very different level of intransigent trade-union militancy, seems very likely to move over *en bloc* to a two-tier system of boards, imitating the German arrangements. For this reason it is necessary to discuss *Mitbestimmung*.

'*Mitbestimmung*' is normally translated as 'co-determination'. It is a woolly term, far less precise than most of those we have dealt with. Hammer and anvil could be said to 'co-determine' the objects forged between them : but that is hardly a lucid description of their function in the hands of a blacksmith. In the words of the rude limerick, the key question is 'Who does what, and with which, and to whom?' One can detect in the idea the German genius for abstraction, here no doubt stimulated by the post-war efforts of socialists schooled in a very doctrinaire and rarefied form of sterile Marxism, to get along with Catholic social philosophy. The Western allies, who occupied what subsequently became the Federal German Republic, had in the early days after the war a lively distrust of a good section of the German business community, for the good and sufficient reason that it had been thoroughly integrated with Nazism. The anti-Nazi unions had no such taint. In the Ruhr, in particular, enterprises began post-war production under the aegis of workers' councils, working alongside the unions. Up to the end

of the war the powerful steel industry had dominated mining:
but after the Allied victory this control was broken up. Under
the pressures of de-Nazification, key steel enterprises rushed
to offer 'co-determination' rights to workpeople and unions. Later,
in 1951, the principle was extended to the mines. After this, the
Cold War eroded the independent influence of the unions (while
the British Labour Government fell) and subsequent co-determination laws (in 1952 and 1956) put the seal of subordination on the
workers' powers within industry.

These laws cover mining and steel production wherever units
employ more than one thousand workers. Under them, boards of
directors, normally numbering eleven, are selected, five from the
workers' and five from the shareholders. The 'odd man out' is
agreed between the two blocks as a 'neutral'. Workers' directors
will include at least two representatives of the revelant workers'
council in the firm itself, approved by the unions, and three union
nominees. These boards appoint an executive committee, which
must include a labour director, who may not continue to hold
office if he loses the support of the workers' side of the board.

All this is co-determination at its strongest—in its two bastions,
coal and steel. If a firm develops into other produce fields, so that
activity in those industries is reduced below 50 per cent of its total
turnover, these laws no longer apply and it must be governed by
the Works Constitution Law.[11] This edict covers the majority of
firms in West Germany. Under it, firms are overseen by a supervisory board, which is charged to uphold the shareholders' interest,
but which is also composed of one-third of elected worker-repre-
sentatives. It meets at quarterly or four-monthly intervals and has
ultimate control of investment decisions, the appointment of top
management, and the preparation and presentation of accounts to
the annual general meeting. It also appoints executive directors,
who are not allowed to sit on both the executive and the supervisory
boards. The executive boards do the real work of management,
and, if they do it well, can normally exercise a big influence over
the two-thirds of the Supervisory Board which is appointed by
shareholders. Furthermore, although executive directors cannot

[11] For an official account of this law, see Dr Alfons Klein, *Co-determination
and the Law Governing Works Councils and Staff Representation in the
Public Services,* Social Policy in Germany, Monograph 23 (German Federal
Ministry of Labour).

be supervisory directors in their own firm, they *can* be appointed to supervisory boards in other firms, provided they are not already serving on more than fourteen other boards at the time of appointment (fifteen boards in all is the maximum). At supervisory board level, the banks play a crucial role.

According to a report in the *Financial Times*

There have even been cases where banks have publicly gone against the management, and refused to accept the accounts, for instance. Very often the chairman or vice-chairman is a banker; these appointments carry special responsibilities and those holding them must be consulted on matters concerning investment, finance and its timing.

The big three Germans banks—the Deutsche, the Dresdner and the Commerz—are most involved. The Deutsche Bank officials between them are estimated to hold 400 board appointments; one in three of the non-employee places on the supervisory boards are held by bank representatives.

The reasons why the banks play such an influential role are not hard to find. The bulk of share dealings in Germany is handled by the investment departments of big banks, and with the proxy system which they have, they control something like 70 per cent of the quoted shares in public companies in Germany. This proxy system gives general voting rights on a continuing basis and sometimes the banks exchange these rights between each other, in particular when they feel that one bank can deal better with a situation than another.

Further, no dealings in shares can take place until one year after the registration of a new company, and therefore in Germany new companies depend upon the banks for finance and the banks keep a very careful watch during the early stages of a new public company. In fact one can say that in general German companies depend to a great extent on the banks for making a market in their shares. The banks are automatically in very close touch with industry, they are equipped with technical departments, and obviously pride themselves on their ability to take industrial decisions.[12]

Under the Works Constitution Law there are other stipulations which affect the process of 'participation'. Shop committees analagous to joint shop stewards' committees in England, have a major influence upon the works council, which is defined in the law as having special powers of liaison, consultation and certain joint

[12] David Nicholson, 'The Executive's World' (17th February, 1971).

powers with the executive board. The shop committees also participate in works assemblies.

But what does all this add up to? Meino Bühning has summarized extensive researches into the effects of co-determination as follows :

1   The employees consider co-determination more than a mere regulation of the Co-determination Law and the Works Constitution Law. They generally consider co-determination as having a direct influence on all economic and social questions in the firm.

2   A majority of the employees desires and welcomes such a far-reaching co-determination.

3   Nevertheless, most of the employees have very little knowledge, or none at all of the factually existent institutions of co-determination. Most well known are the Shop Councils and the Labour Directors.

4   The employees expect a noticeable improvement of their situation from co-determination. They tend to be disappointed if this does not occur. Most important for them are their wages and their immediate working conditions. Changes in the heads of work management and their effects generally remain unknown to them.

5   The employees find a large difference in prestige, power and income between themselves and 'those up above'. The latter often include the workers' representatives in the Board of Directors.

6   They are suspicious of their representatives, consider them easily corruptible, incapable, and powerless against the entrepreneurs.

All observers agree that the qualified co-determination has not markedly altered the social order; not many important social changes have been brought about within the framework of this order. The participation of the Labour Directors in entrepreneur associations offers a good example for the social significance of co-determination. The Labour Directors are strongly represented (to an extent of 33%) in the Employers' Association of the iron and steel industry, which conducts wage rates discussion with the trade unions. On the other hand, the Labour Directors are hardly represented in the economic affairs extraneous to the firm itself.[13]

[13] 'Mitbestimmung: A Midpassage', *International Socialist Journal*, No. 19 (February 1967), pp. 94–111.

An altogether stronger assessment of the moral limits of participation was given by Professor Kenneth F. Walker, in his
Times Management Lecture for 1970 :

> . . . the impact of co-determination upon the work situation
> of the rank and file worker has been minimal. One study found
> that although about three-quarters of the workers knew that
> co-determination had been introduced into their enterprise,
> 'only half of the interviewed workers had any concrete ideas
> about the actual meaning of co-determination and most of
> these knew the name of their labour director'. In one big com-
> pany in the Ruhr only 14 out of 733 workers who were inter-
> viewed knew how co-determination worked. Half of the workers
> interviewed in another study stated that co-determination had
> led to improved conditions but only a fifth thought that they
> had gained personally from it. Perceptions of the labour director
> varied; in one survey 64 per cent of the workers interviewed saw
> the labour director as their representative, 21 per cent regarded
> him as representing both management and workers and 6 per
> cent regarded him as part of management. Nearly half of those
> interviewed perceived his main task to be a kind of arbitration
> between various conflicting interests.
>   A review of the experience of workers' participation in
> management in the Federal Republic of Germany concludes
> that : 'The individual employee usually feels hardly at all directly
> affected by its procedures. Though he is able to put forward
> complaints and suggestions, and some information of vital concern
> is given to him regularly, he has little chance to play an active
> part in shaping relations at his own workplace.' Thus the Ger-
> man experience suggests that 'integrated' workers' participation
> at the board level does not necessarily democratise management
> at lower levels in the enterprise.[14]

These reactions are not altogether surprising when one looks at
the overall effects of this system of working. Erhard Schumacher
has pointed out[15] that no adequate statistics of wealth distribution
exist in West Germany, and that a succession of governments have
sedulously avoided commissioning any. But Professor Krelle, of
Bonn, has calculated that in the mid-'sixties over 70 per cent of

[14] *Industrial Democracy: Fantasy, Fiction or Fact?*, published as a brochure
by *The Times* (1970), p. 27.
[15] Cf. Elmer Altvater, 'West Germany: The Soul Massage', *International
Socialist Journal*, Nos 16/17 (November 1966).

the productive capital of the private sector of the German economy was owned by 1.7 per cent of the population. This is hardly a massive discouragement to the Confederation of British Industry to follow the trails blazed by its German counterparts, should trade-union pressure in Britain for real control become effective.

Yet the very ambivalence that employers rejoice in, when they settle for participation schemes, leaves a whole number of questions wide open. A militant trade-union leader, Herr Gefeller of I.G. Chemie, speaking at the 1966 Congress of his organization, expressed the question very well by actually calling for an extension of *Mitbestimmung* downwards to the workshops, and upwards and outwards through every level of the economy, embracing regional and national economic plans :

> The employers know as well as we do what is at stake : a penetration of their sphere and of that field of power that they think is destined to remain forever their own private domain. To our demand their reaction is hard, preconceived and without possibility of compromise. We must recognize this situation and be prepared to face it. They see the enterprise as their own exclusive domain which must be ruled today as yesterday by unchangeable laws . . . their attempt to throw off the risks of the crisis on the weak must meet with our firm resistance. We do not want to be simply an object in the economy any longer.[16]

The same demands, especially that co-determination be extended to shop-level, have been widely canvassed in the metal-workers' union, I.G. Metall.[17] Of course, at the level of the job itself, 'co-determination' would come to mean something very close to what English workers call 'mutuality', which, where the shop stewards are on the ball and the unions are strong, amounts to a workers' veto over unpalatable management decisions. In this way, 'participation' can be transformed from a device to incorporate workers in the structures designed by capital, into a lever for extending the struggle for direct control by the workers. The banks will not find life so easy on the supervisory boards if the workers are fully able to determine how things shall be run at the point of production itself.

[16] In *Free Labour World* (ICFTU, February 1971).
[17] See especially Fritz Vilmar, *Demokratisierung der Wirtschaft*, Arbeitshefte 110 der I. G. Metall; also the same author's *Betriebsdemokratische Strategien in Europa* (Köln, 1971).

Summing up, we could do far worse than to reproduce the view of Elmer Altvater, a German socialist who has been warning about the dangers of co-determination for many years.

> *Mitbestimmung* can mean two very different things. It can result in the institutionalization of class conflict, as has been sustained, for example, by the sociologist Dahrendorf. In this case, it produces more or less the same effects as the policy of savings formation, in that it contributes to the integration of the working class. But it can also evolve into a politically and socially advanced demand for the abolition of capitalist rule in the factory and in society. If we want to be realistic, we must unfortunately admit that at present *Mitbestimmung* does not have this second meaning, and for several reasons. In the first place, as long as *Mitbestimmung* is limited in its application to the large and very large firms, it will remain an abstract idea. Under these conditions, the workers actually have no part in the direction of the firm, because the representatives of the 'workers' in the board of managers cannot really be considered as 'workers' themselves. *Mitbestimmung* at the top is not paralleled by a similar system in the factory and in the various departments of the factory, and this is the only way in which this highly abstract project can be made concrete. . . .
>
> Two things must be done. First, clarify *Mitbestimmung* to the workers and trade union cadres as a concrete working class claim in opposition to a capitalist rule and as a positive step in the direction of self-management. Secondly, clarify the consequences of this claim. *Mitbestimmung* at the level of the individual firm will always be a farce unless it also exists at the inter-firm level, and this means in planning. But for planning to really be in the interest of the working class, power must be wrenched out of the hands of capital, and this means socialization.[18]

All this argues that the ambiguous element in 'participation' as an employers' strategy can, perhaps, backfire, and help to arouse the very demands it was designed to forestall. Even so, trade unionists should not allow this hope to encourage them to accept such schemes. It is always best to try to see the world the right way up, and to fight shy of mystifying projects which are designed to alter the appearance of things without changing their reality. How much easier it is for trade unionists to fight from a base of firm ground can be seen in the example set by the Belgian Trade

[18] 'West Germany: The Soul Massage', op. cit., pp. 400–1.

Union Movement. The positive response to all this comes from Belgium. At the end of January 1971 the Belgian socialist TUC (General Federation of Belgian Workers, or FGTB) met in an Extraordinary Congress to agree on a strategic programme for the middle-run future. Among the documents discussed and ratified was a major text of 62 large pages on workers' control (from which the extract below is taken). This was designed to advance the powers of workpeople within the Belgian framework on industrial relations, and at the same time to meet the challenge of the European Limited Company, proposed by a commission of the EEC and based on German principles of co-determination. Under the guise of the European Limited Company, *Mitbestimmung* would be exported all over the Continent.

> For the FGTB the concept of workers' control covers an orient-ation of trade union action which requires the transformation of a number of habits and routines even more than it necessitates the creation of new institutions . . . workers' control can only be exercised by the workers, organised in unions. Solidarity and cohesiveness within the workers' organisation is the guarantee for the defence of their interests. . . . The essential conditions of workers' control are to be informed, in time, which is to say before decisions have been finalised, and not to be confronted by accomplished facts . . . to have the opportunity, but not the obligation, to exercise the right to contest decisions which implies the right to put up alternative proposals. . . . Workers' control must establish itself at every level (enterprise, combine, region, sector, nation) in close association with all the workpeople con-cerned.[19]

Reporting on the acceptance of this programme, the General Secretary of the FGTB, Georges Debunne, wrote in the journal *Free Labour World* :

> The FGTB has never limited its aims to fighting for direct or indirect wage increases and it has always refused to become part of the capitalist system; hence it has never agreed to restrain its action according to limits fixed by management. Our organis-ation has, in fact, adopted an attitude of being in constant opposition, with the aim of transforming the entire system. It

[19] *Congrès Controle Ouvrier* (Brussels: FGTB, October 1970), pp. 7–8. For an English translation, cf. *A Trade Union Strategy in the Common Market*, ed. Ken Coates (Spokesman Books, 1971).

constantly rejects the different methods, adopted in some countries, of participating in economic power . . . workers' control as we understand it implies the complete independence of the trade unions vis-à-vis the employers. Workers' control enables the trade union movement to accept responsibility for certain limited items during a specific time at a moment and under conditions which it can freely choose itself. Frankly speaking we accept a certain amount of responsibility, deciding ourselves how far it should reach, but we refuse to shoulder the responsibility for all the decisions of the employers who intend to keep all economic power for themselves, but are willing, when things go badly to share the responsibility for their actions with the workers' representatives.

The very fact that the trade union organisation is represented in a whole series of organs could give rise to the fear that it might be integrated into the existing economic system. However, all depends on the way the trade union representatives interpret their part in these bodies. According to the personality of the delegate, his presence in these organs may either serve to strengthen the union's contesting power or make him in the end part and parcel of the economic and social structures concerned, without, however, giving him any real grip on the social and economic realities. In fact, there is a world of difference between integration and taking on certain responsibilities which the trade union movement has in full autonomy decided to accept. Membership in certain institutions must be considered not as an end in itself, but as a means of speeding up the transformation of society.

Since its beginnings, the trade union movement has endeavoured to limit the employers' arbitrary powers and to reduce the area in which employers can take economic and social decisions without considering anyone else; for this reason, the FGTB has always set itself the goal of securing for the workers a participation in economic and social decisions so that eventually these decisions may be transferred to the community.[20]

The Belgian trade unions advance two strong reasons for developing a struggle for workers' control : the need, in the context of rapidly changing technologies, to advance trade-union policies to maintain effective control over unemployment; and, in face of the increasing intensity of work, with the consequent loss of job satisfaction and fulfilment, to assert the worker's right to develop his talents and effective social powers. Clearly the goal of the unions

[20] *Free Labour World* (March 1971), pp. 20-3.

has to be self-management in industry and society. But as an immediate programme the FGTB sets out a charter of demands for the co-ordination of trade-union strategy on public planning and regulative social bodies for the strengthening of safety and health committees, and for the provision of far more information than is currently made available to works councils at enterprise level. This last demand is a complex one, and it is worth quoting :

> One important step towards workers' control consists in ensuring the complete information of the workers' representatives in these councils about the whole of the economic and human problems connected with the life of the enterprise.
>
> This information must precede decisions and influence the intentions of management which will put at the disposition of committee members the documents or facts necessary for giving in due time an opinion on the choices open to the enterprise and enable members to get a clear view of the prospects, position and results of the enterprise as well as staff policy. In the case of undertakings which are decentralised or established in a number of different places, information must be given at the same time for each technical unit and, at least once a year, on the global position of all the technical units or establishments together. The workers will be entitled to demand precise and detailed information on the financial position, trading policy and productivity of the enterprise. The legal provisions concerning the composition of the Works Councils will have to be revised so as to give the trade union appointeees seats among the workers' representatives.
>
> But in no case must the activity of the Works Council be restricted and bound up within the limits of the horizon of the individual enterprise; hence it will be necessary to co-ordinate the action of the Works Councils to ensure liaison between them in the economic field.
>
> The staff policy, the possible activities of the personnel department and the social services, the organisational or technological changes, and the organisation of the work must also be the object of monthly reports and of consultation with the workers' representatives in the Works Council.
>
> The information about the personnel policy must concentrate on the means for making the best possible use of human resources (recruiting, selection, reception, vocational and social adaptation, retraining, human relations, discipline, etc.). With regard to these matters, details will have to be given about objectives, means, material, the people in charge, the workers concerned and the results obtained.

The information concerning the organisation of the work should *inter alia* specify the planning and the division of the work, the manning and placing of machinery and equipment, the organisation and practice of time and motion studies, changes in working hours and working methods, changes in the material and human environment which may affect the way human resources are utilised (reduced demands on skill, loss of independence, mobility of labour, higher cost in human terms).[21]

In order to underpin this programme, the FGTB is expanding its education and research services, and extending its training programmes. There can be little doubt that a thorough attempt to develop such policies and extend their effectiveness to the limit will be far more productive, from the trade-union viewpoint, than will the blandishments of the European Limited Company.

[21] *Congrès Controle Ouvrier.*

Part Four

Self-Management

Chapter 15

Towards Self-Management

'No man is good enough to be another man's master,' wrote William Morris. It is a profound thought, if a simple one. In a world in which masters dominate, the social arrangements over which they preside are so arranged as to obscure its truth. Myths are created, with the prime object of justifying the right of rulers to rule, owners to own, managers to manage. These myths cannot succeed in their prime object, however, if they do not, at the same time, achieve a secondary effect: the undermining of the self-confidence, critical judgment and independent initiative of all those over whom rule is exercised.

This is a common story. In the United States black people have been dominated, ever since the overthrow of direct slavery, as much by their own carefully implanted sense of inadequacy as by the force at the disposal of authority. When Malcolm X and his friends began to preach 'Black is beautiful', and the movement for Black Power started rolling, the first and key element in the up-surge of the black population was a new self-recognition. Black people had to recognize themselves, but they also had to learn to like what they recognized. In the same way, the movement for Women's Liberation has to begin with an attack on all the complex of attitudes *held by women* which contribute to their subordination. And with working people, things are not fundamentally different. It is a mental police force, first and foremost, which holds the trade unions in a subject role. Whilst workers take for granted their right to political suffrage, they are prevented, by attitudes which pervade their whole upbringing, from conceiving industrial suffrage as natural or just.

What are these mental policemen? In the old days they were savagely distorted religious ideas, which not only placed God over Heaven just as the King ruled the State, but went further, to uphold the notion that the King derived his own authority directly from God, to whom alone he was accountable. If there are modern

workers who believe in God, there are few among them who would
be prepared to accept that He appointed the Chairman of the
Board of Directors, and fewer still who see the lineaments of
divinity in the inconsiderate and impolite fellow who, all too often,
is entrusted with the immediate supervision of their work. More
subtle myths, rationally founded, are required to justify the present
industrial order.

We must necessarily examine two of these. The first is the myth
of intelligence'. Some men, we can all see, are cleverer than others.
You have to be clever to run a factory. If you are clever, provided
you are not *too* clever, you'll get on. All these common-sense per-
ceptions have now been systematized into an extensive theory of
intelligence, which, however often it is questioned or discredited,
still persuades many people that they are too stupid to know how
to conduct their own collective affairs. The theory, in its crudest
form, states a number of propositions. One is that intelligence is a
quality which is secreted in individual heads. Another is that the
capacity to secrete it is determined genetically, so that it can be
inherited. A third used to be that this capacity was fixed, and
unchanging, so that it could be objectively measured by an
intelligence quotient. An extension of it, commonly made, is the
fourth proposition that people in subordinate roles occupy them
because they are inadequate in intelligence, and could not do other
than what they are doing. All four propositions are questionable.
We prefer to regard intelligence as a social product, resulting from
the social interaction of people. Whilst all kinds of characteristics
can be inherited, most people who are not mentally handicapped—
in a strictly medical sense—are capable of learning up to the highest
standards, provided that the learning starts early enough, that the
teaching is effective and that the process is not subject to counter-
influences from the labour market, which discourage the learner
and distort the role of the teacher. Because it is a social development, the capacity of people to show 'individual intelligence' is
very variable indeed, and can be drastically affected by changes in
the social environment. And people in subordinate roles occupy
them because people who aren't in them like to keep things that
way.

And yet it remains true that workers need to learn much before
they can manage their own factories. If teaching facilities were
made available to them by the factories, they could acquire the

right knowledge relatively simply. But the factories are organized in ways which prevent them from being taught, so that the whole process of management appears to be out of reach.

The second myth is that property is the whole basis for a free society. This myth used to be a great deal truer than it is today. In the Middle Ages, when 'town air was free air' and the guilds were at their height, a workman would own his tools, his shop and his product. Apprentices would learn their skills and subsequently become masters. Property in scissors, needles and cloth was indeed the very foundation of the freedom of the tailor, or the glover, in such a society.

But property in the vast concert of machines which are currently working towards the manufacture of the RB-211 aero-engine is a very different story. Those who own this equipment can only do so at the expense of the freedom of all those who have to work it. Unless this ownership becomes truly social, that is to say communal, it is bound to restrict the general freedom, not advance it.

None of these arguments prevents many workers from seeing things differently. If you ask ten engineers at random whether they believe in, say, the nationalization of the engineering industry, at least three or four of them will say 'No' : and when pressed for a reason, answer : 'How would you like it if you worked all your life to build up a sweetshop, and the Government came along and took it?' Of course, sweetshops aren't aircraft industries and might well be left for ages to the control of individual shopkeepers, who might, indeed, feel the freer for the fact. But when workers make this equation, which is wrong, they do so because it corresponds to the 'normal' assumptions of the culture they inhabit. It is 'normal' for factories to be privately owned and autocratically managed. It is 'natural' for workers to be allocated to jobs which do little or nothing to develop their capacities, and subjected to disciplines which are calculated to restrict their initiative to minimal levels. If these things are usual, then they all too easily become accepted as unavoidable and, even when resented, may well be seen as, in some sense, 'fair'.

Yet the idea that no man is good enough to be another's master constantly recurs. It can be traced throughout the history of industrial capitalism, from its very dawn. The goal of social self-management has never really been purged from the body of the

trade unions, or the political parties of Labour. With every crisis
of the established order, it is wont to reappear. It is repeatedly
announced to be dead, outdated or primitive. Men who have re-
nounced it repeatedly secure preferment after the fact. Its partisans
are frequently reviled and sometimes persecuted. None the less,
it keeps coming back, and has done so ever since the beginning of
socialism.

The lineaments of self-management are to be found clearly
exposed as far back in British Labour history as the struggles of the
Grand National Consolidated Trades Union.[1] In August 1833 the
Manchester building operatives were locked out, in the famous
dispute about the 'document' (in which employers tried to forbid
trade-union membership, and required that all employees sign a
statement that they did not, and would not, hold allegiance to a
union). In his address to these workers, Robert Owen said:

> 'The turn-out of the building operatives, and the existing differ-
> ences with their masters, will, I doubt not, tend greatly to effect
> a permanent good for both parties. It affords a fair opportunity
> for you, the producing classes (and masters and men are both
> producers), quietly, calmly, but most effectively, to make a stand,
> at once, and put yourselves in your right position, and thereby
> gradually accomplish the great change required : that is, that
> individual competition, the bane of the producing class, shall
> cease among you, that your children shall be well trained and
> instructed in all that is useful from their birth, that they may
> become men and women possessing superior dispositions, habits,
> manners and conduct, and that whatever is injurious or inferior
> may speedily be removed out of society. . . .'

By December, the union men of Derby were 'turned out', and they
went well beyond Owen to declare :

> 'Fellow countrymen, we are going to set the Derby people to
> work—we decline to contest the matter with the masters—we
> remove ourselves totally away from them. Every penny shall be
> applied to a reproductive end. The silk trade and the bobbin-net
> branch shall have warehouses and machinery of their own, and
> every thousand pounds of yours shall not only be maintained

---

[1] Cf. Raymond Postgate, *Revolution from 1789 to 1906* (Harper Torchbooks,
1962), pp. 90 *et seq.*; also Cole and Filson, *British Working Class Movements: Select Documents* (Macmillan, 1951), pp. 241–91.

without diminution but shall be increased by the industry of Derby—

'With this view we call upon the machinists and working engineers of Glasgow and elsewhere to bethink themselves of the propriety of supplying a steam engine or engines to work the power looms. We call upon the men of Nottingham, Leicester, Macclesfield, Manchester, Congleton and Leek, to look out for, and supply, such machines as may be of instant use to the silk-throwsters, the spinners, the weavers and bobbin-net work-people; if each will contribute in this way, the groundwork will be established of a weekly increase. . . .

'Of the unemployed builders in Derby suffering from this persecution, we intend to select as many as the fund will admit of . . . to erect workshops and factories, and, it may be, dwelling houses, for the use of this Grand Union Association.'[2]

But even the most successful attempts of the Owenites, to equip their own Builders' Guild-Hall in Birmingham, came to grief.[3] Repeated experiments in communes, and lower-level attempts to establish producer co-operatives, all tended to failure on the same general ground : as we have intimated in Chapter 5, even if the famine of capital among workpeople could be partly relieved by wealthy donors, the division of labour outside the experimental units was more ruthless and more productive because it was arranged around more concentrated capital investment. So one tended to work harder in communist co-operation for less material reward.[4] The lessons of the failure of the communist colonies, and the weakness of the producer co-operatives were carefully discussed in the International Working Men's Association. In 1868, at its Brussels Congress, the International resolved :

If we are such partisans . . . of trade unions . . . it is not only from regard to the necessities of the present, but also the future social order. To explain, we do not simply consider these as necessary palliatives (note that we do not say remedies), no, our views are much higher. From the bottom of the chaos and misery in which we struggle, we lift our eyes to a more har-monious and happy society. Then we see in these trades unions the embryos of the great workers' companies which will one day

[2] Postgate, op. cit., p. 93.
[3] G. D. H. Cole, *Robert Owen* (Ernest Benn, 1925), pp. 203–7.
[4] Cf. *Workers' Control*, ed. Coates and Topham, pp. xxviii–xxxvii, for a documentation of these experiments.

replace the capitalist companies with their thousands of wage-earners, at least in all industries where collective force is used and there is no middle way between wage-slavery and association. (As has been shown by recent strikes, Union funds may be used for setting up co-operative productive societies.)

Yet it must be noted (and this is an important point) that the productive associations to arise from the trades unions will not be the trifling societies that the present-day associations are. These latter, excellent, we admit, as example and precept, do not seem to us to have in fact any great social future, any part to play in the renovation of society, for, consisting only of a few individuals, they can only end . . . by creating beside the bourgeoisie or *third estate*, a *fourth estate*, having beneath it a *fifth estate* yet more wretched. On the other hand the productive societies arising from the trades unions will embrace whole industries . . . thus forming the new corporation . . . founded on mutuality and justice and open to all.

. . . This transformation of trade unions will take place not in one country alone, but in all, or all at least that are at the head of civilisation. . . .[5]

Within three years, one of the foremost nations 'at the head of civilisation' had given remarkable support to this prophecy. The Commune of Paris, during the short period of its rule, before its bloody suppression, went far towards implementing the principles advanced by the IWMA. On 16th April, 1871, it decreed that those factories abandoned by their directors should be investigated and enumerated by the workers' *trade.councils* 'to present a report on the practical means of exploiting again at once these deserted shops, not by the renegades who have left them but by a co-operative association of the workers once employed therein'.[6]

The Commune itself, elected by universal suffrage throughout Paris, set other rival patterns, recorded by Karl Marx in these words :

The majority of its members were naturally working men, or acknowledged representatives of the working class. The Commune was to be a working, not a Parliamentary body, executive and legislative at the same time. Instead of continuing to be the agent of the central Government, the police was at once stripped

---

[5] International Working Men's Association, Resolution carried 15th September, 1868. Cf. Postgate, op. cit., pp. 393–4.
[6] Postgate, op, cit., p. 297.

of its political attributes, and turned into the responsible and at all times revocable agent of the Commune. So were the officials of all other branches of the Administration. From the members of the Commune downwards, the public service had to be done at *workmen's wages*.[7]

From this time on, the struggle for self-management was linked in workmen's minds with the struggle for the transformation of political institutions, up to and including the State itself. And necessary though this overall political transformation has remained, it has to be recorded that it has frequently been posed over and against the goal of self-management, in a manner which has had grave consequences not only for the development of co-operative democracy in industrial organization, but also for the maintenance of democratic controls of any kind over political processes themselves. The upsurge of the soviets in Russia, first in 1905 and then in 1917, was always linked in the minds of socialists with the example of the Paris Commune. But although the soviets were authentic and spontaneous workers' organs, once their rule had been established in the October Revolution, the dominance of the norms established in Paris in 1871, and cogently reaffirmed in Lenin's tract *The State and Revolution*, was short-lived.[8] However one evaluates the process by which the power of the soviets passed to the Communist Party, and the power of the Communist Party became concentrated in the hands first of its leadership, and ultimately of its leader, two linked facts must be squarely faced. First, the hostile encirclement of the new Soviet Union, and successive armed interventions, created a siege society and a quasi-military style of government: and second, at an early stage in this development, effective democracy in the factories gave place to increasingly centralized management, under diminishingly effective trade-union surveillance. The most baneful effects of these processes, it should be said, were not during the worst days of the Civil War, during which time social disruption was unbelievably

[7] Karl Marx, *The Civil War in France* in *Selected Works*, Vol. 2 (Lawrence & Wishart, 1945), p. 459.
[8] For key documents, see Ernest Mandel, *Controle Ouvrier, Conseils Ouvriers, Autogestion* (Paris: François Maspero, 1970), pp. 85–154; also V. I. Lenin, *On Workers' Control and the Nationalisation of Industry* (anthology) (Moscow: Foreign Language Publishing House, 1970). For a convenient short analysis, see Isaac Deutscher, *Soviet Trade Unions* (Royal Institute of International Affairs, Oxford University Press, 1950).

acute but the socialist culture of the Revolution remained vividly alive and present. It was during the long years of rebuilding and the launching of the industrialization programme that the autocracy of the party leadership crystallized (while the principle of autocratic management in industry became firmly established) and ultimately transformed itself into personal dictatorship over the whole State, in which the only effective means of communication between the Government and the people was through the eyes and ears of the secret police.

Libraries of books have been written about this evolution. For our purposes, it is enough to say here that it powerfully assisted in the demobilization of the Labour movements of the majority of advanced countries during the inter-war years, and in the immediate post-war period—after 1945. Sidney and Beatrice Webb were able to write of a 'New Civilization' in which all nonsense about workers' control, let alone self-management, had been finally refuted. Herbert Morrison was able to take himself to a Labour Party Conference in order to justify the London Passenger Transport Board as the best conceivable model for public enterprise, by genuflecting to the 'Russian experience'.[9]

It was not until 1948 that a major sector of the communist movement began to rediscover the central importance of self-management in the development of a new society. Lucien Goldmann has described this event with characteristic force : 'It will be the glory of the Yugoslav socialists to have been the first to introduce self-management into the real economic policy of a socialist state. Without doubt self-management seeks to correspond with the idea of freedom and human development which has always regulated the thoughts and hopes of socialists.'[10] When the Yugoslav communists were expelled from the Cominform by Stalin in 1948 they were faced with the immediate prospect of diplomatic, political and economic isolation. Since the country was neither economically self-supporting nor technologically developed, it could not remain in that condition without risking serious social and economic crisis. At the same time, there was a clear short-term need to mobilize to the full the internal human resources of the

9 Cf. *Workers' Control*, pp. 285 *et seq.*
10 Speech to the Stockholm Conference of the Russell Foundation on Czechoslovakia, February 1969 : published by the Bertrand Russell Peace Foundation.

country, since no immediate external aid would materialize to fill the gap left by the withdrawal of the country from the Eastern bloc and from access to Russian economic assistance. The system of self-management of enterprises and social institutions was the Yugoslav answer to this problem of mobilization : through this method, the Government and the Communist Party aimed to raise the level of managerial skills in a society still backward and limited in its experience of industrial growth and organization. At the same time, self-management developed enthusiasm and commitment to the country's success and to the political leadership, and was a living demonstration that the Yugoslavs had rejected Stalinism not only at a diplomatic level, but also as a model for socialist theory and practice. Finally, the decentralization of command from the Stalinist ministries in Belgrade to the republics, the local communes and the individual enterprises, although controlled and limited during the 1950s, met a further need of the system; namely, to find a means of tolerating and harmonizing the nationalist and particularist tendencies of the different republics and nationalities within the country, without resorting to a repression and recentralization which the Party had rejected alike on ideological and economic grounds.

Thus, self-management of the factories, combined with a measure of internal decentralization of planning and resource-allocation, represented a brilliant solution to many of the regime's most pressing problems. That this solution—in the absence of a *political* system which would have allowed democratic planning to evolve in place of bureaucratic planning—also led to the growth of market relationships between the self-managing enterprises and institutions, seemed in those early days only to confirm the advantages of the chosen road. For market relations encouraged the emergence of financial incentives : methods of payment, and differentials, which stimulated both individual and collective effort to raise productivity —the overriding need of the stricken and isolated economy. Moreover, a market system enabled the regime to adjust its relations with the still dominant peasant farming sector, collision with which could have produced a permanent social tension at the heart of the society, if it had been subject to the drastic methods of a siege economy. There is no evidence now to suggest that at that time (we are speaking roughly of the decade between 1951 and 1961) the Yugoslavs consciously recognized that the encouragement of

H

market relations also prepared the economy for easier 'harmoniz-
ation' with, and penetration by, the economies of the capitalist
Western world. During that period indeed, the regime—and particularly President Tito personally—strove vigorously to create
a neutral bloc of countries which could establish its economic
and diplomatic independence of both the Western and Eastern
spheres of influence. The combined effects of CIA subversion and
the objectively determined dominance of Western capital in the
Third World, however, undermined the edifice which Tito aimed
to build with Nehru, Nasser, Sukarno and the rest. Meanwhile, the
Titoist heresy of 'separate roads to socialism' remained a recurrent
threat to the internal security and cohesion of the Eastern
European countries, thus ensuring that Yugoslavia could not adjust
to an international division of labour by reharmonizing its economy
with those of the Comecon members. This combination of circumstances determined the country's eventual orientation towards the
Western world economy, and in particular towards the countries
of the Common Market. Lacking the self-sufficiency of a Russia
or a China, and not being able—because of internal differences
of nationality and culture—to impose the stern controls which had
been developed in, say, Cuba, the Yugoslavs were drawn inexorably
towards the West. Their 'separate road to socialism' became diverted
by external as much as by internal forces.

This experience should lead socialists in the West to a number
of conclusions. First, that the self-management system of the
Yugoslav workers' councils was always incomplete and vulnerable
whilst set in a market economy. Secondly, that the obligation of
socialists and trade unionists in a Western capitalist society, towards
the Yugoslav working class, is a dual one. Trade unionists should
not only appraise and defend its great positive contribution towards
the global, historical experience of socialist theory and practice,
but should also recognize that they, too, are involved in the negative evolution of that experience; whilst capitalism thrives and
dominates the world economy, neither the Yugoslavs nor any other
small nation can embark with impunity upon an unambiguous
attempt to emancipate human beings from alienated, market,
relationships. Thus, the deterioration of self-management in Yugoslavia is not only the concern, but also in a sense the responsibility, of
workpeople in the West. Finally, we should acknowledge that despite
the serious inroads made into the system, which have now reached

the stage of invasion of the basic socialization of the means of production (Yugoslav enterprises now issue interest-bearing bonds for sale to individuals and institutions), the Yugoslav working class is the heir to an ideology which is anti-bureaucratic and which stresses the principle of self-management, and is therefore uniquely equipped, amongst the countries which have undergone a social revolution, to stage an aggressive defence of the values it has been taught.

There is no necessity for us here to enter into a detailed description of the formal structures of Yugoslav workers' self-management. They have been amply documented elsewhere.[11] Suffice it to remind readers that all economic and social organizations are managed by elected workers' councils, with which the ultimate legal authority for the whole range of decisions normally associated with boards of directors and boards of governors in a capitalist society is vested. Elaborate internal devolution of decision-making within each enterprise has been developed; there are workers' councils for separate departments, and collective decision-making on a number of matters has been handed down to the work group itself. As business methods have developed, so has the process of mergers between enterprises, so that multi-plant, cross-industry combines are increasingly common; for them yet another level of self-managing councils is necessary. It is not, we believe, the increasing scale and complexity of self-management institutions which threaten the reality of their power, but their subjection to market forces. To 'manage' the market, a new breed of businessman, the salaried executive, has come into being, who often has considerable scope to increase his income through commission, expenses, personal savings and 'speculation'. He may be formally accountable to the workers' council, but is able to place before it the necessities of the market, which become commercial restraints on the exercise of socially based decisions. Indeed, the social nature of economic decisions becomes itself obscure: the market assumes the same

[11] For example in Fred Singleton and Tony Topham, *Workers' Control in Yugoslavia*, Fabian Research Series 233 (1963); Roy Moore, *Self-Management in Yugoslavia*, Fabian Research Series 281 (1970); *Workers' Management in Yugoslavia* (ILO, Geneva, 1962); Jiri Kolaja, *Workers' Councils: The Yugoslav Experience* (Tavistock, 1965); Paul Blumberg, *Industrial Democracy: The Sociology of Participation* (Constable, 1968), Chaps 8 and 9; and *Yugoslav Workers' Self-Management*, ed. M. J. Broeckmeyer (Dordrecht, Holland: Reidel, 1970).

blind but imperative power as it has in a capitalist economy, and consequently the workers' council (where it does not abdicate its authority to a board of 'experts', a step which the law now tolerates) becomes alienated from its constituency; status and class differentiation reappears, and the working class withdraws from its commitment to the aims of the system.

Reinforcing these tendencies, which have gathered full momentum over the past eight years or so, the banks have emerged as dominant influences over the decisions taken by productive enterprises. The availability of loans and credit is crucial for expansion and prosperity of the enterprises; the criteria of the banks are increasingly commercial rather than social. In line with the consistent purpose of the regime in these later years (to insert the Yugoslav economy fully into the international divisions of labour), the State's management of external economic relations has been more and more 'liberalized', which has meant that the infant industries of the country feel the weight of competition from advanced economies, and that the currency has been subject to frequent devaluations. Pursuing the logic of this evolution further, the Yugoslav Government has amended the laws on self-management on several occasions to allow more and more foreign, mainly West German and Italian capital, to invest in Yugoslav enterprises.[12] Where this occurs, the law on the supremacy of the workers' council may be suspended, whilst the foreign investor is permitted greater and greater leniency over the repatriation of his profits.[13]

A critical phenomenon which has now assumed serious proportions is the level of urban unemployment and rural underemployment.[14] Indeed this would be twice as serious were it not for another equally negative feature; the mass exodus of Yugoslav workers, involving both skilled workers and professional grades, to work in the factories and institutions of Western Europe, notably in West Germany. Yet further tensions are created for the hardpressed leadership and for President Tito himself by the reappearance in strength of nationalism, which has thrived on the divisive influence of market-oriented and uneven development in

[12] See Tony Topham, 'Yugoslavia's Peaceful Road to Capitalism?', Institute for Workers' Control *Bulletin*, Vol. 2, No. 5.
[13] See Fred Singleton, 'Workers' Self-Management and the Role of the Trade Unions in Yugoslavia', *Trade Union Register* 1970.
[14] 311,000 were unemployed, out of 3½ million normally employed in the social sector, in 1968. Figures in Singleton, op. cit., p. 236.

the different regions of the country. This may take the form of revanchist neo-fascism, in the case of the Croat organization of the Ustaša, which is now active in the émigré Croat working-class communities in Western Europe. It had an appalling record of genocidal attacks on Serbian and other minorities in Croatia during the Second World War. In another form, nationalism threatens the cohesion and purpose of the Yugoslav League of Communists itself, as Tito has made clear in recent speeches attacking these tendencies. This is a critical factor as the long years of Tito's dominance over the Party and the State near their end. Clearly a collective leadership must succeed to power on his death or retirement, and clearly collective leadership requires a minimum of common commitment amongst the leaders to the interests of the Federal economy.

In all this gathering crisis, the victim at present is the working class and its instruments of self-management. Yet a strange phenomenon is occurring. The Yugoslav trade unions, which in the past have been the transmission-belt for State and Communist League priorities, have begun to assume an independent role. They have, in recent years, frequently expressed support for unofficial strikes, which have often been directed against the formal authority of the workers' council and the elite managerial class; and they have instituted post-strike inquiries in which 'heads have rolled'— figuratively speaking, of course. Last year the miners' union took a further step by actually declaring official a stoppage in that industry.[15] In 1971, the central body of the Federal Trade Union hierarchy itself was in direct controversy with the Government over the injustices of an incomes policy imposed to curb inflation. The divisions between new business-bureaucracy and old political-bureaucracy, between nationalists and federalists, between North and South, town and country, middle class and working class, are reflected in the political leadership and in the trade unions.

The outcome is impossible to assess, but we may be sure that it will not take the form of a simple reversion to capitalist relations, with the trade unions becoming the only and purely defensive expression of workers' interests. A new synthesis between socialist politics, trade-union practice, and self-management aspirations could emerge to challenge and halt the drift towards the re-Balkanization

[15] See Fred Singleton, 'Socialist Yugoslavia's First Official Strike', *The Spokesman*, No. 8 (December 1970).

of Yugoslavia. Hopefully, the Yugoslav experience of self-management has still much to contribute to our understanding of the
transition to socialism. Certainly we learn from the struggles of
that country and its working class, that self-management does not
easily detach itself from the concrete historical, political and
economic circumstances in which it appears. The Western working
classes do not inhabit economically handicapped Balkan countries in
which most of the economic and technological cards would be
stacked against them.

The salvation of the Yugoslav experiment could have been
achieved by its extension to neighbouring countries, and the creation
of an expanded economic base powerful enough to inspire the
Labour movements of the Western capitalist countries, as well as
the workers of the Soviet Union itself.

An abortive but brave attempt to follow the Yugoslav example,
also inspired by the Paris Commune, was made in Algeria
after the victory of the National Liberation Front over the French
forces. In 1963 the abandoned properties of French settlers were
seized by the new government of Ben Bella and placed under
self-managed administration.[16] A 'bureau for the animation of the
socialist sector' was established and manned by dedicated and
intelligent socialists, and a serious effort was made to extend the
principles established in Yugoslavia to the Algerian economy. But
with the fall of Ben Bella, his protégés were exiled from the country
or imprisoned, and the young self-managed firms and enterprises
entered into a swift decline.[17] If the Yugoslavs suffered from this
blow, it was nothing compared to what came after, in 1968.

The centralized and heavily bureaucratic political and economic
machines that had been established in the early post-war years in
Eastern Europe on the Russian model, had been accelerating towards open crisis throughout the 1960s. Czechoslovakia, the most
industrially advanced country in the socialist bloc, suffered particularly under a remarkably sclerotic political hierarchy, headed
by Antonin Novotny, which maintained a ludicrously rigid and top-
heavy planning system and a command economy. The early post-

[16] Cf. Michael Raptis, 'Le Dossier de L'Autogestion en Algérie', *Autogestion*,
No. 3; also *International Studies in Industrial Democracy: The Algerian
Experience* (Institute for Workers' Control, 1971).
[17] Cf. Arslan Humbarici, *Algeria – A Revolution That Failed* (Pall Mall
Press, 1966), pp. 114–27. Also Clegg, *Workers' Self-Management in Algeria*
(Allen Lane, Penguin Press, 1971).

war successes of this economy having exhausted themselves, it lapsed into an irremediable stagnation. Developing theories already tentatively advanced in the Soviet Union by 'liberal' economists, the Czech theoretician Ota Šik began to argue the case for a renewed role for the market in the Czechoslovak economy.[18] Having developed his ideas on this theme, he began to canvass them not only in the Communist Party, but also in the factories, where they became linked with the demand for autonomy by managers, and self-management by workers. The political movement of the Prague Spring gathered rapid momentum, and every aspect of social life experienced a radical democratization. For the first time in many years a socialist country found itself engaged in profound debate, openly conducted, about its goals and direction. Not a voice was raised for the return of capitalist forms. But keen concern was revealed, everywhere, for the achievement of the long-withheld democratic promise of socialism, in both industry and society. Workers' councils were formed in the factories and laws were drafted giving them substantial administrative powers. These were never implemented. In August 1968, the armies of five Warsaw Pact nations, headed by the Soviet Union, occupied Czechoslovakia, arrested the leaders of the Czech Government, and began a prolonged process of 'normalization', or, to be more precise, of restoration of the same abnormalities which have become the established institutions of the Soviet Union and its Eastern European allies.

But in Eastern Europe, and in the Soviet Union itself, socialism with a human face remains a potential challenge to those who inhabit the morally empty corridors of present power. We do not doubt that the challenge will find new expression in practice, throughout those territories in the future.

Meanwhile, in France in May 1968,[19] and in the subsequent Italian hot autumn,[20] Western Europe began to see the pattern of a

[18] Cf. *Czechoslovakia and Socialism*, ed. Ken Coates (Bertrand Russell Peace Foundation, 1969), especially the essays by Mandel, Guerin and Bodington, and the lectures by Sik; also Ludek Rychetnik, *Two Models of an Enterprise in Market Socialism* (Institute for Workers' Control, 1971).

[19] Cf. Andrée Hoyles, article in *Trade Union Register* 1969 (see Chap. 4 n. 17 above).

[20] Cf. Stephen Bodington, 'Struggles of the Workers' Movement in Italy', *The Spokesman*, No. 11 (April 1971).

new kind of political awareness, directly challenging the old order. Workers' control, self-management, are ceasing to be the dreams of a mere coterie of idealists and are possessing the imagination of whole sectors of the European work-force. Even in England, things are moving.

The extraordinary struggle of the workers of the Upper Clyde shipyards, who, in their struggle to safeguard their employment, have raised the whole question of workers' control to a new level, has already triggered off a series of quite unparalleled actions, in which, from Plessey's at Dumbarton down to the River Don Steel Plant in Sheffield, and in enterprises from Bristol to Essex and from South Wales to London, workers' rights to control their jobs and to affect or set aside the investment decisions which determine them have been dramatically asserted. The main obstacles that prevents the incorporation of such episodes into an overall challenge to the whole social order is the domination under which the political councils of the Labour Movement suffer : domination by generations of men intellectually impoverished by the Cold War and its debilitating ideologies.

During the 1950s British Labour leaders converged on the discovery that socialism was all about equality. True, they tended to measure this in cash, and, true again, they were prone grossly to exaggerate their successes in realizing it, since they were misled by the official statistics of the day, provided in the main by the Inland Revenue.[21] England, they thought, was going through an egalitarian revolution, because the taxman showed that the range between the top and bottom levels of taxable income had been somewhat diminished. Indeed, incomes subject to tax *were* to some extent equalized : because a highly trained school of accountants were dedicating a developed (and expensive) expertise to the purpose of 'reducing' the size of units of income, precisely in order to shed as much as possible of the burden of taxation. But all this was very largely irrelevant to the facts of the distribution of *wealth* in Britain : and totally unrelated to the distribution of effective social power. Since, however, they believed themselves to be architects of the best of all possible social worlds, members of the Labour Establishment studiously abstained from discussing questions that might disrupt this comfortable assumption, and,

[21] For a summary of the evidence on this matter, see Coates and Silburn, *Poverty: The Forgotten Englishmen.*

instead, prescribed a simple solution to all such problems as they deigned to acknowledge. Poverty recurs? Frustration rules work? Even when they were forced to recognize such questions, the same mixture as before, only less of it, was all these pundits could ever bring themselves to recommend. In this way Labour leaders not only discredited themselves but also, to a certain extent, some valid ideals. Equality is a good goal, but not for reasons of dogma. The reason to move towards an equal society of free men and women is that the potential of individual people cannot be realized outside one. Inequalities invariably engender, just as they rise out of, the exploitation and manipulation of one man by another. When one person can subordinate another to his will, he diminishes both the other and himself in the act. When, together, men form common aspirations and find ways to move towards them, their development is mutually extended. For these reasons, the trite cry of 'equality of opportunity' is usually not only ill-thought out, but self-defeating. Normally, it is a call for an equal start in the rat-race.

The real question is how to take people out of the rat-race and put them into the human race. Equality of opportunity can mean something valuable and real if it is interpreted as requiring that all men and women should have the optimal chance to develop their capacities to their fullest potential. There is no good reason not to assume that potential to be infinite : although how far it can be realized will depend on the human evolution of society as a whole. What is clear today, is that the finest achievements of humanity remain, to the vast masses of human beings, a virtually closed book : and, even to the fortunate elites for whom they have some reality, they are refracted through a haze of misery and deprivation. Men in advanced civilizations commonly do not develop even a fractional part of their present capacities. Indeed, they are actively *prevented* from developing, because they could never accommodate to the routines of present industrial life if their abilities were ever even partially awoken. Production in our society has nothing to do with the development of human personalities and talents : it has everything to do with the subordination of those personalities and talents to the mechanical needs of the manufacturing processes.

The enemy, in this case, is the division of labour itself : that very social arrangement which stimulated an unprecedented growth in human powers, has become, increasingly, a fetter on those powers. At the beginning of modern political economy, Adam Smith pointed out that the difference between a porter and a philosopher depended primarily upon the use which society had made of their talents, rather than upon the 'original' state of those talents themselves. Nothing in modern psychology in any way effectively undermines this cry of faith. But industry creates the actual psychology of today's men, and, as Adam Smith again saw, the scope actually afforded to men to become either porters or philosophers is determined in the market available for those respective talents.

What stops human beings from making war on the division of labour? Modern communications media could make us all linguists, mathematicians, musicians at will. Electronics could reduce the hours of compulsory social labour to hitherto unimaginable minima. Every factory could become a school, and a true school at that, not an educational prison for preparing wage-slaves to accept their lot. Why don't we move in this direction? The main reason for social inertia, for failure to attack the crucial problem of human under-development, is that the division of labour has solidified into a class structure, which, crystallized around institutions of property and manipulative indoctrination, has become self-perpetuating. Industry would be better run, even in the improvement of its levels of productivity, if it were based on the growing awareness and increasing initiative of all those at work within it. But such aware-ness and initiative are incompatible with the irrationalities of the power structure which industry serves, and so they cannot safely be allowed to grow.

Socialists, confronting this situation, face two linked but separable problems : they must move to overcome the division of labour, so that 'every cook may learn to govern the State' (and every labourer can control his enterprise's investment); but simultaneously they must seek to overcome the power of the market, by extending the principle of free distribution of goods to ever-wider limits. True equality can never be quantified, because all men are truly different from each other. Appetites, needs and interests differ, and will differ the more as opportunities for social, which is to say spiritual, fulfilment, widen. Equal rations are merely equally applied constraints of unequal demands, so we may be sure that the market will not finally succumb to a *higher* order by the imposition of policies artificially restricting appetites. Openly or covertly, legally or illegally, the market will continue, albeit with restricted scope, until society can cope equally with all the multiform needs which it is increasingly engendering. But if we can see that men have unequal needs for wooden legs, yet still have equal need of access to medical treatment, cost what it may, we should also see the need to apply welfare norms of distribution to housing, public transport, fuel, food and to any new services an advanced civilization can create. Welfare or free distribution requires social planning, which can only be effective in the long run when it involves not merely the consent, but also the active involvement, of every citizen.

Self-management as a model will necessarily require the solution of the difficulties involved in this progess. Today, all this is still the music of the future. But it *will* be heard : it *must* be heard, if humanity is not to relapse into a new and unthinkable barbarism. We know enough to comprehend that we must live better. We do not yet know how to begin doing so. But unless we strive forward, there is no doubt that the technologies we have already unleashed *can* destroy us all, and probably will. The quest for self-management is the quest for humane, socially conscious control over technological development. Only in a self-managed society may we begin to see rational approaches to the solution of some of the world's most pressing problems—pollution, environmental development, unemployment, poverty, alienation in work, and so on. The more prolonged the reign of the market system and its concomitant divisions of labour and authority, the more threatening will those problems become.

Bibliography

Selected Works for Further Reading

Ashwell, J., *Four Steps to Progress,* IWC, 1969

Alexander, K. J. W., *Fairfields: A Study of Industrial Change,* Allen Lane, 1970.

Barratt Brown, M., 'Yugoslavia Revisited', *New Left Review,* No. 1 (1960).

——, 'Workers' Control in a Planned Economy', *New Left Review,* No. 2 (1960).

——, *Labour and Sterling,* IWC, 1968.

——, *Opening the Books,* IWC, 1968.

——, *UCS: The Social Audit,* IWC, 1970.

——, *What Economics Is About,* Weidenfeld & Nicolson, 1970.

——, *Public Enterprise Defended,* IWC, 1971.

——, *What Really Happened to the Coal Industry,* IWC, 1972.

Barratt Brown, M., and Coates, K., *The 'Big Flame' and What Is the IWC?,* IWC, 1969.

Barratt Brown, M., Coates, K., and Topham, T., *The Trade Union Register* 1969, Merlin Press, 1969.

——, *The Trade Union Register* 1970, Merlin Press, 1970.

Blauner, R., *Alienation and Freedom,* University of Chicago Press, 1964.

Blum, F. H., *Work and Community: The Scott Bader Commonwealth and the Quest for a New Social Order,* Routledge & Kegan Paul, 1968.

Blumberg, P., *Industrial Democracy: The Sociology of Participation,* Constable, 1968.

Broeckmeyer, M. J. (ed.), *Yugoslav Workers' Self-Management,* Dordrecht, Holland: Reidel, 1970.

Clegg, H. A., *A New Approach to Industrial Democracy,* Blackwell, 1960.

Clegg, I., *Industrial Democracy,* Sheed & Ward, 1968.

——, *Workers' Self-Management in Algeria*, Allen Lane, Penguin Press, 1971.

Coates, K. (ed.), *Can the Workers Run Industry?*, Sphere Books, 1968.

——, *Democracy in the Motor Industry*, IWC, 1969.

——, *A Trade Union Strategy in the Common Market: The Programme of the Belgian Trade Unions*, 1971.

Coates, K., *Essays on Industrial Democracy*, Spokesman Books, 1971.

Coates, K., Daly, L., Jones, B., and Smillie, B., *Bertrand Russell and Industrial Democracy*, IWC, 1970.

Coates, K., and Topham, T., *The Labour Party's Plans for Industrial Democracy*, IWC, 1968.

——, *The Law Versus the Unions*, IWC, 1969.

——, *Workers' Control: A Book of Readings and Witnesses for Workers' Control*, Panther Books, 1970.

Coates, K., and Williams, W., *How and Why Industry Must Be Democratised*, IWC, 1969.

Cole, G. D. H., *The Case for Industrial Partnership*, Macmillan, 1967.

Cole, M., *The Story of Fabian Socialism*, Heinemann, 1961.

Collins, R., *Job Evaluation and Workers' Control*, IWC, 1969.

Derrick, P., and Phipps, J. F. (eds), *Co-Ownership, Co-operation and Control*, Longmans, 1969.

Eaton, J., *The New Society: Planning and Workers' Control*, IWC, 1972.

Eaton, J., Hughes, J., and Coates, K., *UCS: Workers' Control*, IWC, 1971.

Fabian Group, *The Future of Public Ownership*, Fabian Tract No. 344, Fabian Society, 1963.

Flanders, A., *et al*, *Experiment in Industrial Democracy: A Study of the John Lewis Partnership*, Faber & Faber, 1967.

Fleet, K., *Whatever Happened at UCS?*, IWC, 1971.

Fletcher, R., *Problems of Trade Union Democracy*, IWC, 1970.

Fraser, R. (ed.), *Work*, Vols 1-2, Pelican Books, 1968-9.

Glass, S. T., *The Responsible Society: The Ideas of the English Guild Socialists*, Longmans, 1966.

Hanson, A. H. (ed.), *Nationalisation—a Book of Readings*, Allen & Unwin, 1963.

Harrison, B., and Kendall, W., *Workers' Control and the Motor Industry*, IWC, 1968.

Institute of Personnel Management, *Workers' Participation in Western Europe*, IPM Information Report No. 10, London Institute of Personnel Management, 1971.

Institute for Workers' Control, *Industrial Democracy and the National Fuel Policy*, IWC, 1968.

——, *GEC-EE Workers' Takeover*, IWC, 1969.

——, *Trade Unions and Rising Prices*, IWC, 1970.

——, *Archives in Trade Union History*, Series I-II, IWC, 1968/71.

——, *International Studies in Industrial Democracy*, IWC, 1971.

Kolaja, J., *Workers' Councils: The Yugoslav Experience*, Tavistock, 1965.

Labour Party, *Industrial Democracy: Working Party Report*, 1967.

Leonard, J., *Co-operative Co-Partnership Productive Societies*, Co-operative Productive Federation, 1965.

McCarthy, W. E. J. (ed.), *Trade Unions*, Penguin Books, 1972.

Mandel, E., *A Socialist Strategy in Western Europe*, IWC, 1969.

Moore, R., *Self-Management in Yugoslavia*, Fabian Research Series Pamphlet No. 281, Fabian Society, 1970.

Murray, R., *UCS: The Anatomy of Bankruptcy*, Spokesman Books, 1972.

Nicholson, B., *UCS: An Open Letter*, IWC, 1971.

Nicholson, B., and Greendale, W., *Docks III: A National Strategy*, IWC, 1972.

Pateman, C., *Participation and Democratic Theory*, Cambridge University Press, 1970.

Pribicevic, B., *The Shop Stewards' Movement and Workers' Control*, Blackwell, 1961.

Ramelson, B., et al., *The Debate on Workers' Control. A Symposium from Marxism Today*, IWC, 1970.

Reid, G. L., and Allen, K., *Nationalised Industries*, Penguin Books, 1970.

Riddell, D., 'Social Self-Government: The Background of Theory and Practice in Yugoslav Socialism', *British Journal of Sociology*, Vol. 19 (1968).

Roberts, E., *The Fight against Unemployment: The Best Defence Is Attack*, IWC, 1972.

Royal Commission on Trade Unions and Employers' Associations, *Report*, Cmnd 3623, HMSO, 1968.

Scanlon, H., *The Way Forward for Workers' Control*, IWC, 1968.

——, *Workers' Control and the Transnational Company*, IWC, 1970.

Select Committee on Nationalised Industries, *Ministerial Control of the Nationalised Industries*, 3 vols, HMSO, 1968.

Sheffield Steel Workers Group, *The Steel Workers Next Step*, IWC, 1968.

Singleton, F., and Topham, T., 'Yugoslav Workers' Control: The Latest Phase', *New Left Review*, No. 18 (1963).

——, *Workers' Control in Yugoslavia*, Fabian Research Series Pamphlet No. 233, Fabian Society, 1968.

Sturmthal, A., *Workers Councils. A Study of Workplace Organisation on Both Sides of the Iron Curtain*, Harvard University Press, 1964.

Tivey, L., *Nationalisation in British Industry*, Jonathan Cape, 1966.

Topham, T., 'Shop Stewards and Workers' Control', *New Left Review*, No. 25 (1964).

——, 'The Campaign for Workers' Control in Britain', *International Socialist Journal*, Vol. 2 (1965).

——, *Productivity Bargaining and Workers' Control*, IWC, 1968.

——, *Democracy on the Docks*, IWC, 1970.

Touraine, A., et al., *Workers' Attitudes to Technical Change: An Integrated Survey of Research* (Industrial Relations Aspects of Manpower Policy), Paris: OECD, 1965.

Trades Union Congress, *Trade Unionism in Yugoslavia*, TUC, 1965.

——, *Trade Unionism* (Evidence to Donovan Commission), TUC, 1966.

Walker, K. F., *Industrial Democracy: Fantasy, Fiction or Fact*, The Times Newspapers, 1970.

Index

absenteeism, 33–6, 98
accidents, *see* industrial safety
Acton Society Trust, 193
ACTS (Association of Clerical,
Technical and Supervisory Staffs),
175
ACTT (Association of Cinemato-
graph, Television and Allied Tech-
nicians), 153
Adamson, Campbell, 197
AEF (Amalgamated Engineering
Foundry Section—of AUEW), 176
AEU (Amalgamated Engineering
Union), 32, 91
air freight, 164
aircraft industry workers, 122–7
Airlie, James, 136
airport workers, 165
Alexander, Ken, 8–9
Algeria, self-management in, 230
alienation of workers, 33–8, 235
Allis Chalmers (Mold), 'sit-in' at, 6
Altvater, Elmer, 209
American Federation of Labor, 89
'Americanization' of unions, 102, 107
Anderson, Perry, 185
Area Boards (NSC), 52–3
Artists for Peace, 181
ASLEF (Associated Society of Loco-
motive Engineers and Firemen),
165
Associated Container Transport
(ACT), 159, 160
ASTMS (Association of Scientific,
Technical and Managerial Staffs),
32, 33, 37
Attlee government (1945–50), sup-
port for joint consultation by, 47,
49; Trade Dispute Act (1927)
repealed by, 65; nationalization of
mining by, 111; and plans to
nationalize docks, 117–18; defeat
of, 182; *see also* Labour Party;
Wilson government
AUEW (Amalgamated Union of
Engineering Workers), 51, 91, 97,
151, 171; support for workers'

control, 73; membership, 167;
merger with EETPTU proposed,
168; co-operation with TGWU,
176, 177; democratic reform,
177–8
Auto Workers' Union (USA), 92–3

Bailey, W. Milne, *Towards a Postal
Guild*, 120
Barber, Anthony, 125
Barratt Brown, Michael, 12, 99,
138n.
Basnett, Andrew, 171
Basnett, David, 171
Beeching, Dr, 110
Belgium, 88, 92, 166; FGTB's con-
cept of workers' control, 209–13
Ben Bella, 230
Besant, Mrs, 19
Bevin, Ernest, 28
BISAKTA (British Iron, Steel
and Kindred Trades' Association),
165
Black, John, 162, 163
Black Power, 38, 217
blacklegging, 90
Blake, William, 15
Blastfurnacemen's Union (NUB), 165
Boilermakers' Union, 28, 130, 172
Booth, Charles, *Labour and Life of
the People*, 27
Bridlington Agreement, 175 &n.
Bristol Evening Post, 153
Bristol Siddeley, 123
British Aircraft Corporation, 87, 123
British Association of Colliery Man-
agers, 155
British Communist Party, 48, 173,
180, 181; *see also* communism
British Leyland Motor Company,
78–9, 86, 87, 124, 125, 126
British Peace Committee, 181
British Productivity Council, confer-
ence on Foulness, 162–5
British Rail, 117, 119, 143, 144,
158, 159, 162, 164; *see also* rail-
waymen

British Road Services, 119; *see also* road hauliers

British Socialist Party (formerly: Social Democratic Federation), 180

BSC (British Steel Corporation), 8, 86, 114–15, 175; in Teesside, 103; ancillary activities, 143; Special Steels division of, 144; greenfield project, 160, 161; Heath government's discrimination against, 159, 160–1; Foulness project, 161–2, 166; *see also* steel industry

Bühning, Meino, 206

building industry workers, 84, 220–1

Burns, John, 19, 20

Canada, closure of Toronto Dunlop plant, 94–5, 98

Cannon, Sir Leslie, 168, 177

Carr, Robert, 92, 139

Carron, Lord, 177, 178

Castle, Barbara, 172

CAWU (Clerical and Administrative Workers' Union), 175

cement industry, 86

CGT (Confédération générale du travail), 91

Chapple, Frank, 149n.

cheap labour (West Germany), 203, 228

chemicals industry, 86, 158, 159; *see also* ACTS

Chevron Oil Company, 160

Child Poverty Action Group, 134

Chrysler, 87, 88

CIA (Central Intelligence Agency), 90, 226

Citrine, Sir Walter, 64–5

civil conspiracy, *see* Conspiracy and Protection of Property Act

Clegg, H. A. (Prof. Hugh), 21, 49, 50, 139, 171, 194; opposition theory of, 40–6, 47, 63–4; on employee-directors, 52–3

closed-shop (or union-shop), 71, 169

Clyde Port Authority, 160

co-determination, *see* Mitbestimmung

Cole, Lord, 125–6

Cole, G. D. H., 185, 193

Collard, G., 162

Colliery Overmen and Deputies, *see* NACODS

Collison, Lord, 196

'Combine Committees', 72–3, 89

Comecon, 226

Cominform, 224

Comintern, 184

Common Market (EEC), 114, 162, 203, 210, 226

Commonwealth Party, 180

communism, 46, 90, 91, 181, 184, 221–2; Soviet, 223–4; Yugoslav, 224–30; Czech, 230–1; *see also* British Communist Party

companies, *see* multi-national companies

Companies Act, 53, 100

company finances, *see* social audit

'company unionism', 48

computer information, 106

Concorde project, 123

Confederation of British Industry (CBI), 40, 195, 197, 202, 208

Congress of Industrial Organizations (USA), 89

Connell, Charles, shipyard (now: Scotstoun DUN), 127, 129, 131

Conservative Election Manifesto (1970), 138

Conservative Party, 40; *see also* Heath government

Conspiracy and Protection of Property Act (1875), 64, 65

containerization, 117, 118, 119, 158, 159

'contradiction of gestation', 126 &n.

'control bargains', 77

Cook, Thomas, 144

Cooper, Lord, 9, 28, 168, 170, 171, 172, 175

co-operative factories, 69–70

Cowley Body Plant (Austin-Morris), 78

craft unions, 21, 22, 27, 28, 52, 89, 90, 116, 172

Craig, Thomas, 160

criminal conspiracy, *see* Conspiracy and Protection of Property Act

Crosland, Anthony, 40, 44, 45n., 49

Crossman, R. H. S., 182

Cuba, 181, 226

Cunningham, Alderman Andrew, 172–4
Cunninghame-Graham, R. B., 26
Czechoslovakia, self-management movement in, 46, 230–1

DATA (Draughtsmen's and Allied Technicians' Association), 32, 37
Davies, John, 128, 132, 162
Deakin, Arthur, 28, 176
death duties, introduction of, 39n.
Debunne, Georges, 210–11
deep-sea fishing industry, 84
demarcation of jobs, 74, 75
Department of Employment and Productivity, 202; survey on absenteeism by, 33–6
Director, The, on worker-directors, 53
dismissals, 55, 68, 81, 118; *see also* redundancies
dispute procedures, 79, 80–1
district committee (TGWU), 176
division of labour, 233–4
Dock Labour Boards, 117
Dock Labour Scheme, 117
Dock, Wharf and Riverside Labourers' Union, 20
dockers/docks, 27, 38, 56, 109, 117–20, 126; Foulness seaport project and, 165, 166; *see also* Great Dock Strike; NASDU; transport industry
Donovan Royal Commission on Trade Unions and Employers' Associations, 45n., 54, 78, 194–7, 203
Dubček, Alexander, 198
Dukes, Charles (later: Lord Dukeston), 171
Dunlop International Ltd, 88; closure of Toronto plant, 94–5, 98

East Germany, 203
Eccles, Fleming, 171
Eccles, Jack, 171
Eccles, Tom, 171
education, 33, 68, 69, 82, 102, 183, 218–19
EETPTU (Electrical, Electronic, Telecommunications Union/ Plumbing Trades Union), 167, 168

EETU (Electrical, Electronic and Telecommunications Union), 73
eight-hour working day, *see* shorter working week
electricians/electricity industry, 113, 138, 141, 144
Electricity Generating Boards, 7, 12, 143
Employed Persons Health and Safety Bill (1970), 84
'employment faculties', 200, 201
Engels, Friedrich, 23, 26–7
Engineering Employers' Federation, 81
engineering industry, workers, 6, 9, 28, 48, 72, 81, 115, 175–6; *see also* AEU; AUEW
Engineering National Council, 48
equal pay, 68, 69
equality, 232–5
Esso Refinery, *see* Fawley
European Limited Company, 210, 213
Europoort (Rotterdam), 158, 163
Evening Standard, 153

Fabian Society, 26, 179, 180, 185
Factories Act (1961), 84
factory occupations, 5–6, 9, 57, 137
Fairfields (Govan) shipyard, 127, 129, 130–1, 132, 174
Fawley Oil Refinery, 72, 74, 113
feasibility studies, 94, 95, 98
FGTB (General Federation of Belgian Workers), 210–13
Fiat, 87
Field, Frank, 134–5
Field Aircraft Services, 162
Financial Times, on absenteeism, 36; profile of Andrew Cunningham, 172–4; on West German banks, 205
First International, *see* International Working Men's Association
Fisher-Bendix (Liverpool), 'sit-in' at, 6
Flanders, Allan, 72
food preparation, 119, 158
Ford, Henry, 92–3
Ford's, 87, 88, 91; multi-national work-force, 91–3; parity strike (1971), 107; *Echo's* ballot of

strikers, 153–4; 1969 dispute, 168, 169, 175

Foulness, development plan for third airport, 9, 158, 161; and seaport project, 161–7

France, 124, 125; May 1968 revolt, 51, 231; car industry, 88; international co-operation, 91, 166; development schemes, 163; communists, 181; Paris Commune, 222–3

Free Communications Group, 152–3

Free Labour World, on Belgian trade unions, 210–11

Freemasons, 101

freight, *see* air freight; port transport

Frost, David, 152

fuel policy, call for workers', 113

Gaitskell, Hugh, 170, 180

Garner, P. F., 192

gas industry workers, 112, 113, 141, 143

Gas-Workers and General Labourers' Union, 19, 20, 21, 23–4, 27

Gaulle, General Charles de, 51

GEC-EE (General Electric-Associated Electrical Industries-English Electric), 86, 88

GEC Shop Stewards' Action Committee, 98

Geddes Report, 130

Gefeller, Herr, 208

General Elections, 1945: 180; 1966: 148; 1970: 84, 118, 197

General Motors (USA), 87–8, 200

General Railway Workers' Union, 21

General Strike (1926), 28, 29, 48

General Unions, 28, 167–75

Goldmann, Lucien, 224

Goodyear, 88

Gormley, Joe, 7

gradualism, 182–3, 185

Grand National Consolidated Trades Union, 220

Great Dock Strike (1889), 18, 19–21, 22, 23

Greenwood, Anthony, 183

Grenville, D., 162, 163–4

Guild Socialism, 28, 120, 180n.

Hall, Lord, 120

Harcourt, Sir William, 39, 40

Harlands, 126

Hawker Siddeley, 87, 123

Hayday, Arthur, 172

Hayday, Fred, 171–2

health and hospitals, 109

Heath, Edward, 92, 139, 197

Heath government, 5, 31, 84; Industrial Relations legislation, 7, 63–4, 67; attitude to social audit, 100, 101; steel policy, 114–15, 159, 160–1; Rolls-Royce affair, 124; shipbuilding policy, 127, 128; and public sector workers, 138–47

Hepper, Anthony, 127, 130, 131

Hobsbawm, Eric, 27–8

Holt Committee (House of Commons), 120

Hoogovens-Hoesch steelworks merger, 9, 161

Horner, Arthur, 146, 147

Howard, Anthony, 162, 163

Hughes, John, 31, 107, 138n., 185

human underdevelopment, 233, 234

Hungarian revolution, 46

ICFTU (International Confederation of Free Trade Unions), 90

ICI, Works Councils, 48, 202; in Teesside, 103–7

IG Chemie (West Germany), 208

IG Metall (West Germany), 208

In Place of Strife (Labour White Paper 1969), 63, 172, 196–7, 198

incentive schemes, 72, 73

Independent Labour Party, 179, 180

industrial democracy, definitions of, 40–59; opposition theory, 40–6; joint consultation, 47–51; participation, 51–5; workers' control, 55–7; self-management, 58–9; Scanlon's view, 93–4

Industrial Democracy Act, Labour proposal for, 8

Industrial Democracy: A Labour Party Report (1969), 96, 98–9

industrial espionage, 67

Industrial Relations Act (1971), 7–8, 9, 54, 63–4, 66–7, 83, 133, 146, 151–2, 153, 183, 197, 202; Code of Practice, 54

Industrial Relations Court, 66

industrial safety and health, 68, 83–5, 98, 105, 116; benefits, 21–2
Industrial Tribunals, 66
Industrial Welfare Society, 194
industry, structural crisis in, 30–8; workers' control at level of, 109–37; mining, 111–14; steel, 114–16; port transport, 117–20; post office, 120–2; aircraft, 122–7; shipbuilding, 127–37
Industry Week, 197
inflation, 127, 128, 138, 139
information, *see* social audit
Institute of Directors, 53
Institute for Workers' Control, 12, 40
intelligence, myth of, 218–19
International Chemical Workers, 95
International Marxists, 185
International Socialists, 185
International Transport Workers' Federation, 91
International Working Men's Association (IWMA: First International), 90, 221–2
Iron and Steel Trades Confederation, 175
iron-ore processing, 119, 158, 159, 160, 161, 163–4
Italy, 91, 125, 181, 228, 231

Jackson, Tom, 145–6
Jaguar strike fighter (Anglo-French), 125
Jak, 153
Japan, 30, 94, 114
Jenkins, Clive, 37–8, 175
job evaluation, 54, 74, 75, 76, 78, 79, 116
John Brown's shipyard (Clydebank Dvn), 127, 129, 131
Johnson, J. J., 162
joint consultation, 47–51, 52, 191–4
Joint Industrial Councils, 47
Joint Production Committees, 48–9
joint productivity committees, 54
Joint Works Councils, 48, 49
Jones, Jack, 67, 84–5, 97, 175, 177; *The Right to Participate: Key to Industrial Progress* by, 198–202

Kahn-Freund, Professor, 196
Krelle, Professor, 207–8

Labour Party, 5, 28, 50, 77, 174; Industrial Relations Bill rejected by, 7–8; origins and development, 24, 27; *Industrial Democracy* report, 96, 98–9; power and steel group, 162; unilateralist debate, 170; Clause IV, 180; leadership's attitude to socialism, 179–87; *see also* Attlee government; Wilson government
Labour Representation Committee, 179
Lane, A. D., 36–7
Lane, Tony, 170
Laski, Harold, 185
leisure, demand for, 201
Lenin, V. I., 180, 223
Ley's Malleable Castings (Lincoln), 192
Listener, The, 153
Lloyd, Selwyn, 138
Lloyd George, David, 39
local council government workers, 139, 144, 145
Lockheed Aircraft Company (USA), 124
London Passenger Transport Board, 224
London Trades Council, 26
lorry-drivers, 7, 119; *see also* transport industry
Lucas, 124

McCarthy, Eugene, 90
MacDonald, Ramsay, 180, 182
McGarvey, Dan, 130
McKinnes, William, 136
Malcolm X, 217
management, unions' independence from, 41, 43, 44; and joint consultation, 47, 48–9; 'Management in the Seventies', 53; workers' participation exploited by, 54–5; authority of, 55–6; York Agreement, 81, 176; in mining industry, 111–12, 113; in steel industry, 116; in UCS, 129–34; NUGMW leaders' relations with, 170, 173–4; Soviet autocracy in, 223–4; in Yugoslavia, 227, 229; in Czechoslovakia, 231; *see also* shop-floor controls; social audit

Mann, Tom, 18, 19, 20, 24–6, 27, 28–9, 111
manning of jobs/manpower, 67, 71, 74, 75, 78, 79, 81, 98–9, 104
Manpower Utilization and Payments System, 104
manual workers, decrease in number of, 32–3; female absenteeism, 34–5
Marsh, Richard, 52
Marx, Karl, 25, 40, 201, 222–3
mass media, see newspapers; television
match-girls' strike (1888), 18, 19
measured day-work (m.d.w.), 74, 78
merchant seamen, 119, 166
mergers, of companies, 30–1, 86–7, 148; of unions, 168–9; see also UCS
Mersey Docks and Harbour Board, 159–60
MIDAS (Maritime Industrial Development Area Scheme), 158, 159, 160, 161, 162
Miliband, Ralph, 185
miners, 89, 142n., 173; strikes, 7, 138, 139, 141, 148; Derbyshire campaign, 50, 113; workers' control, 111–14; union structure, 155–6; see also MFGB; NACODS; NCS; NUM
Miners' Federation of Great Britain (MFGB), 111, 112
minimum wage, 68, 69, 183
Mitbestimmung (co-determination), 203–9, 210
Mond, Sir Alfred, 48
Monopolies Commission, 31
Morris, William, 217
Morrison, Herbert, 224
Morrow, Ian, 126
motor-car industry, 87–8, 115, 122–3; see also Ford's; Rolls-Royce
Motoren-und-Turbinen Union (MTU), 125
MRCA (multi-role combat aircraft), 125
multi-national companies, 9, 31, 87–95, 164, 185
multi-plant companies, 31, 86–7, 89, 102
munition factories, 48
Murray, Robin, 126

mutuality/mutual agreement, 74, 75–6, 78, 116

NACODS (National Association of Colliery Overmen, Deputies and Shotfirers), 155
NASDU (National Amalgamated Stevedore and Dockers Union), 165
National Amalgamated Union of Labour, 21
National Coal Board (NCB), 7, 112, 113, 115, 117, 141, 142, 156, 193
National Conference on Workers' Control (Sheffield, 1969), 91–4
National Freight Corporation, 143
National Graphical Association, 157
National Guilds League, 120
national incomes policy, 44, 45n., 63, 73, 96, 149–50
National Joint Craftsmen's Co-ordinating Committee, 52
National Liberation Front (Algeria), 230
National Ports Council, 158
National Steel Corporation, 52
National Union for Energy Workers, proposal for, 156
National Union of Agricultural Labourers, 21
National Union of General and Municipal Workers (NUGMW), 151, 178; new militancy in, 9–10, 91; membership, 167, 169, 174; Pilkington glass-workers' strike and, 169–70; oligarchic bureaucracy, 168–74; transfer to TGWU of members from, 175
nationalization, joint consultation and, 47, 49, 50; and workers' control, 69, 109–11; of docks, 117–18; of transport, 119; of aircraft industry, 123–6; of shipbuilding, 5, 135–6; need for union co-ordinated strategy, 138–47; profitability of ancillary activities, 142–4
Nationalized Industries Committee (TUC), 145, 146–7
NATO, 124, 185
NATSOPA (National Society of Operative Printers and Assistants), 154
NCB, see National Coal Board

NCB Labour Staff Association, 155
Netherlands, 9, 158, 163; Foulness project and, 161–2, 166
New Democratic Party (Canada), 95
newspapers, 22–3, 38, 67, 157; misrepresentation of union activity by, 148–54
Northcliffe, Lord, 38
Novotny, Antonin, 230
NUB, see Blastfurnacemen's Union
NUGMW, see National Union of General and Municipal Workers
NUM, see National Union of Mineworkers), 112n., 142n., 155, 156; see also miners
NUR (National Union of Railwaymen), 165; see also railwaymen

oil industry workers, 110, 112, 113, 119, 120, 158, 159, 160; Foulness project and, 162, 163
Open Secret, The, 152–3
Orwell, George, 163
Overseas Containers Ltd (OCL), 159, 160
overtime, 68, 71, 72, 74, 75
Owen, Robert/Owenites, 220–1

Paris Commune (1871), 222–3, 230
Parliament, false analogy between industry and, 41–2
Pateman, Carole, 192n.
Paynter, Will, 156n.
Peace Factories, 69
Peyton, Rt Hon. John, 164
picketing, 7, 22, 65
Pickford's, 143, 144
piece-work/piece-rates, 71, 72, 73, 74, 75, 78, 79, 112
Pilkington glass-workers' dispute (1970), 169–70
Pirelli, 88, 94
plant bargaining, 54, 73–85, 88, 96, 103, 108, 191
Plessey's (Dunbarton), 'work-in' at, 5, 232
Plowden Report, 123
plumbers, see EETPTU; PTU
'poaching', 175 &n.
POEU (Post Office Engineering Union), 144
Poland, industrial revolt in, 46
pollution, 105, 106, 163, 235

Port, The, 164–5
Port of London Authority, 162, 164
port transport industry, 117–20, 158–60; Foulness project, 162–7
'positive employment programme' (for ICI), 104–5
Post Office Corporation, 120, 121
post office and telephone services, workers, 109, 120–2, 138, 139, 140–1, 144, 145–6; see also POEU; UPW
power élite, 32, 46, 68, 201
Power Loading Agreement (miners), 112, 113
Prices and Incomes Board, 45, 74, 101, 150
printing industry, 156–7; see also NATSOPA
procedural agreements, 81, 82
productivity bargaining, 74–80, 103, 104, 106–7, 108, 116, 130
property (ownership), 55, 56; private v. social, 41, 44, 45–6; British law based on, 64; myth of, 219
proscription, 180–1, 185, 186
protective (or 'restrictive') practices, 71
PTU (Plumbers' Trade Union), 73
public ownership, see nationalization
Pusey, H. H., 162, 164–5

QE2 (Queen Elizabeth II), 132

railways/railwaymen, 7, 89, 109, 110–11, 119, 140, 141, 144, 165; Taff Vale judgment against, 26, 179; see also ASLEF; British Rail; NUR; TSSA; transport industry
rationalization, 68, 86, 110; Wilson government's policy of, 30; of steel industry, 104, 114–15; of port transport industry, 117; of aircraft industry, 124; in UCS, 132–3, 134; Foulness project and, 166; of General Unions, 175
RB-211 project, 124, 125, 219
Record, The, 177
recruitment, 68, 71, 104, 175
redundancy, 68, 81, 82, 96; in steel industry, 6, 114–15; GEC, 98; ICI, 104; of dockers, 118–19; in Rolls-Royce companies, 125; UCS, 130–1, 133, 135

representation, workers' right of, 68, 81, 94, 116, 117
'responsibility without power', 53, 54
retirement, early voluntary, 200–1
Reynolds Newspaper, 22–3
'right to work', workers' defence of, 6–7
Rio Tinto Zinc Corporation, 162, 165
River Don Steel Plant (Sheffield), 'work-in' at, 5–6, 232
road haulage/hauliers, 118, 120, 141, 148, 165
Robens, Lord, 142
Roberts, Ernie, 51–2
Roberts, Kenneth, 170
Rolls-Royce, collapse of, 5, 122, 124–6, 127
Rookes *v.* Barnard case, 65
Rowntree, B. Seebohm, 27
Royal Arsenal Co-operative Society, 180
Russell, Bertrand, 181
Rylands, William, 121–2

Sankey Commission (1919), 111
Satchwell, P. A., 162, 164
Scamp Inquiry (1970), 139
Scanlon, Hugh, 177, 202; on 1969 Ford strike, 91–2; on industrial democracy, 93–4; on information, 97–8; democratic leadership of, 177–8
Schumacher, Erhard, 207
Scott-Bader Commonwealth, 69–70
Scottish TUC, 6; *see also* TUC
Scottish Typographical Association, 157
Scunthorpe steelworkers, 114, 115
Seamen's Union, 21; *see also* merchant seamen
self-employment, decline in, 32
self-management, 6, 46, 55, 58–9, 212, 217–35; co-operative factories, 69–70; in Yugoslavia, 224–30; in Algeria, 230; movement in Czechoslovakia for, 231
severance payments, 94, 104
Shaw, George Bernard, 23
shipbuilding industry, 5, 86, 115, 127–37, 172, 173
Shipbuilding Industry Board, 127, 130, 131

shipping companies, 118, 120, 159, 162
Shonfield, Andrew, 196
shop-floor controls, 69, 71–85
shop stewards, role in joint consultation, 48–9, 50; and participation, 52, 54–5, 201; authority of, 155; and training, 69; Combine Committees, 72–3, 89, 98; UCS, 136; TGWU, 177; AUEW, 177; 1950s and 1960s style of, 198–9; *see also* shop-floor control
Shopworkers' Union, 56, 167
shorter working week, campaign for, 18, 19, 24–6, 38, 201
sickness (and nervous debility), absenteeism through, 35, 36, 98; *see also* industrial safety and health
Sik, Ota, 231
Silvertown Lighterage Services, 162
'sit-ins', *see* factory occupations
skilled labour, decline of, 27–8
SLADE (Society of Lithographic Artists, Designers, Engravers and Process Workers), 157
Smith, Adam, 234
Snecma (French state-owned company), 125
social audit, 6–7, 68, 81, 82, 88, 94–5, 96–108, 116, 123–4
Social Democratic Federation, 179, 180
socialism, capitalist interpretation of, 39–40; use of resources by, 105–6; Labour Party's attitude to, 179–81; 184–7
Socialist Labour League, 185
Socialist Outlook, 181
SOGAT (Society of Graphical and Allied Trades), 157
South Africa, 163, 165
South America, 163
Southend Evening Echo, 153–4
Soviet Union, 181; state monopoly in, 46; evolution of communism in, 223–4; Yugoslavia expelled from Cominform by, 224–5; Czechoslovakia occupied by, 231
speeds-ups/speed (of work), 55, 68, 71–2, 75, 80, 81
Stalin, Josef/Stalinism, 46, 224
Star, 23, 38

State Register (of trade unions), 66
status quo provision, demand for, 81,
116, 176
steel industry, workers, 109, 126,
136, 144, 158, 159; 'work-ins', 5–6;
worker-director scheme, 8–9, 52–3,
116; mergers, 86; in Teesside,
103–4; workers' control, 114–16;
Foulness project, 161–2, 165; *see
also* BISAKTA; BSC
Stephen, Alexander, shipyard, 127,
132
Stewart, Sir Iain, 127, 129–34
Stokes, Lord, 125
Stonehouse, John, 121
strikes, 65, 83, 180; miners', 7, 138,
139, 141; penalties under new
legislation for, 66, 67; at Ford's,
91–2; one-day strike of dockers,
118; of postal workers, 120,
121–2, 138, 140–1; of council
workers, 139; of railwaymen, 140;
press misrepresentation of, 149,
151–2; Foulness project and,
165–6; of Pilkington glass-workers,
169–70; in Yugoslavia, 229
students, 32, 33
Sun, 148
super-tankers, 158–9
supervision, workers' power to
establish, 68, 74, 81, 82, 94

Taff Vale judgment, 26, 179
take-overs, 86–7
Tea-workers and General Labourers'
Union, 20
Teesside industrial community, 103–
7, 115
television and radio, 38, 67, 109,
151, 152, 154; *see also* ACTT
TGWU, *see* Transport and General
Workers' Union
Thames Aeroport Group, 162
Thames Estuary Development Com-
pany, 162
Thompson, E. P., 185
Thorne, William, 19, 21, 27
Thornton, David, 162, 164, 165
Tillett, Benjamin, 19, 20
Times, The, on UCS, 129–33, 136
Tito, President Josip Broz, 226, 228,
229
Townsend, Peter, 185

Trade Disputes Acts, 1906: 64, 65;
1927: 65
trade unions, reform of structure,
16–17, 89–90, 155–78; 1889 new
union movement, 18–29; independent opposition of, 40–6, 63–4;
1871 definition, 64–5; aims and
methods, 67–70; political representation, 68–9, 108, 167, 177,
179–87; need for accountancy
service, 82, 102; international co-
operation, 90–5, 165–7; in West
Germany, 203–9; Belgian, 209–13;
Yugoslav, 229
Trade Union Acts (1871–1940), 64–5
Transport and General Workers'
Union (TGWU), 33, 67, 97, 171;
Clerical and Supervisory Group
of, 32; joint consultation policy,
50; and workers' control, 73;
plant-level bargaining, 77–81, 83;
Biennial Delegate Conference
(1969), 85; internationalism, 91;
social audit claims, 104, 107;
in dock industry, 118, 119; Foulness project, 165, 166; membership, 167; structural reform of,
175–7; proscription of communists
by, 181
transport industry, 108, 119, 165,
166; *see also* lorry drivers; port
transport; railways
Tribune, Frank Field on UCS in,
134–5; Tom Jackson in, 145–6
Trotskyist Revolutionary Communist
Party, 180
TSSA (Transport Salaried Staffs'
Association), 165
TUC, 81, 83, 98, 165; UCS and, 5;
rejection of Industrial Relations
Bill by, 7, 151–2; Steel Unions'
Committee of, 8, 52, 116; joint
consultation policy, 50; attitude
to postal strike, 145; recommendations to Donovan Commission,
194–7
Tyneside and National Labour
Union, 20

UCS (Upper Clyde Shipbuilders),
5, 6, 9, 127–37, 232
unemployment, 82, 83, 105, 111,
115, 134–5, 183, 228, 235

'unfair industrial practices', 66
unilateral nuclear disarmament, 170, 181
United Automobile Workers' Union (USA), 78, 79, 91
United States, 30, 38, 39, 48, 87–8, 89, 90, 91, 94, 217
UPW (Union of Postal Workers), 120–1, 145; see also postal workers
URTU (United Road Transport Union), 165
Urwin, Harry, 177; *Plant and Productivity Bargaining* by, 78–9

veto, workers' power of, 68, 81, 82, 94, 116, 117, 118, 119–20, 193
VFW 614 airliner, 125
Volkswagen, 87

wage-restraint, 45 &n., 73, 108, 122, 138
Walker, Professor Kenneth F., 207
wallpaper workers' union, 157
Walpole, G. S., 191–2 &n.
Warren, Kenneth, 162, 164
Webb, Sidney and Beatrice, 18, 19–21, 22, 23, 26, 28, 29, 182, 185, 224
Wedgwood Benn, Anthony, 124, 136, 183
West Germany, 39, 124, 125; workers' participation (*Mitbestimmung*) in, 9, 203–9; car industry, 87–8, 92; participation in Foulness project, 161–2, 166; 'economic miracle', 199, 203; cheap labour in, 203, 228; capital investment in Yugoslavia by, 228
WFTU (World Federation of Trade Unions), 90
white-collar workers, 32, 37, 144, 175
Whitley Committee/'Whitley Councils', 47
Wigham, Eric, 196
Wilberforce Inquiry, 138n., 139, 149n.

Williams, Francis, 23
Williams, Raymond, 185
Williamson, Lord, 28, 172
Williamson, T., 172
Wilson government, 45n., 63, 65, 117, 121, 184; 'rationalization' policy, 30; productivity bargaining by, 74; industrial safety and health bill of, 84; promised reform of company law, 101; aircraft industry policy, 124; and shipbuilding, 128; failure of, 182–3, 185; see also Labour Party
Women's Liberation, 217
Woodcock, George, 16, 196
Woodcock, Leonard, 92
'work-ins', see factory occupations
work study schemes, 75, 78, 79, 116
work-to-rule, 6, 138
worker-directors scheme, 8–9, 52–3, 116, 195–7
workers' control, defined, 55–7; Belgian FGTB's concept of, 210–13
workers' councils, 57; in post-war Germany, 203; in Yugoslavia, 227–8, 229
workers' participation, 79, 121, 132–3, 191-213; defined, 51–5; Donovan Commission's consideration of, 194–7; Jack Jones's view of, 198–202; in West Germany, 203–9
Works Constitution Law (West Germany), 204, 205, 206
Works Councils, see ICI
Wright, Dr Beric, 36
WSA (Weekly Staff Agreement, ICI), 104, 105
Wynn, Bert, 113

Yarrow, 127
York Memorandum (1922), 81, 176
Yugoslavia, workers' self-management in, 46, 58, 224–30